D0110060

Also by Carole Golder

The Seductive Art of Astrology
Love Lives
Moon Signs for Lovers
Carole Golder's Star Signs
Success Through the Stars

YOUR STARS
AT WORK

YOUR STARS
AT WORK

☆ ☆ ☆

Using the Power of Astrology
to Get Along and Get Ahead on the Job

CAROLE GOLDER

AN OWL BOOK
HENRY HOLT AND COMPANY
NEW YORK

Henry Holt and Company, Inc.
Publishers since 1866
15 West 18th Street
New York, New York 10011

Henry Holt® is a registered
trademark of Henry Holt and Company, Inc.

Library of Congress Cataloging-in-Publication Data
Golder, Carole.
Your stars at work : using the power of astrology to get along and
get ahead on the job / Carole Golder. —1st ed.
p.   cm.
"An Owl book."
ISBN 0-8050-5101-5 (pbk. : alk. paper)
1. Astrology.   2. Occupations—Miscellanea.   I. Title.
BF1729.025.G65   1998
133.5—dc21   97-28246

Henry Holt books are available for special
promotions and premiums. For details contact:
Director, Special Markets.

First Edition 1997

Designed by Paula R. Szafranski
Illustrations by Peter Prins

Printed in the United States of America
All first editions are printed on acid-free paper. ∞

1   3   5   7   9   10   8   6   4   2

Contents

Acknowledgments

*This book is dedicated to my wonderful
artist soulmate Peter Prins*

I want to thank my friends and clients all over the world, who inspire me to keep on working in the wonderful world of astrology; Gigi and Elisa for the joy of being able to write most of this book in southern Italy; Air India and the Gracie Inn for making my New York trips so pleasant; and Jayne Cooper of Canon.

Thank you to my agents, Alice and Mike Sharland, to my editors, Theresa Burns and Alessandra Bocco, and everyone else at Henry Holt for making this my sixth book to be published under its imprint.

And in memory of my first radio producer, David Price, and my mentor, Patric Walker, who first encouraged me to become an astrologer.

Introduction

Working toward the Next Millennium

When I wrote my last book, *Success Through the Stars: An Astrological Guide to Defining and Living a Satisfying Life,* I wanted to help you make your life more successful in every possible way. My previous book, *Star Signs: An Astrological Guide to the Inner You,* showed you how to become more in touch with your inner self and to grow spiritually. *The Seductive Art of Astrology, Love Lives,* and *Moon Signs for Lovers* showed you how to relate better in emotional relationships.

Now with *Your Stars at Work,* I would like to help you reach a better understanding of your professional strengths and weaknesses. You possess the ability to become not just another number in the millions of employed or unemployed men and women out there but someone who can achieve his or her very best in the jungle we call the workplace.

It does not seem so very long ago that I wrote my books on a small typewriter, even though admittedly it was an electronic one. I remember saying that I could not imagine learning to use a computer, and that I had no intention of ever doing so. Now I cannot imagine what I would do without my little Compaq laptop, even though I am currently quite happy to use it simply as a word processor. Information technology has been growing at such a fast rate over the past few years that, regardless of your star sign, you simply have to keep up with what is going on. If you don't, you can bet your bottom dollar that there will be someone keen on taking over your job who *does* know all about it.

In *Your Stars at Work* I want to show you why your attitude toward your particular work is so important, and why it will also be different according to your star sign. Naturally, in any book I come up against the same problem of having to generalize somewhat. In order to make a complete in-depth analysis of *you,* it is necessary to prepare a chart for your particular date, time, and place of birth. But I am confident that if you read the following chapters and discover more about your own behavior in the workplace, as well as that of your boss, colleague, or employee, you will be able to develop the perfect career strategies to succeed in the workplace of today *and* tomorrow.

While writing this book, I found it extremely interesting to gauge the reaction of friends and clients to particular situations in their working lives. Their reactions have *always* depended on their basic star sign characteristics. In many instances the situation would have turned out differently and more successfully had they modified their perspective or behavior. A good friend of mine, a prominent psychologist, suggested the theory of people "playing a different sign once in a while." I decided to do some research on this and discovered that it really does work. I have always subscribed to the theory that we have something to learn from our opposite sign in the Zodiac. For example, an impulsive Aries will always benefit from the advice of a Libra, who prefers to weigh things carefully before reaching an important decision. But when I took this further, I realized that we have something important to learn from *all* the signs. In *Your Stars at Work* you will learn how to play a different sign for a day.

Every star sign has its positive and negative qualities, but not all of you are always aware of the effects these qualities have on the people with whom you work. I will show you how and why your personality at work affects your long-term career prospects, and how a great deal depends on your attitude toward your work.

Questions often raised by clients in my astrological consultations include wondering whether they are sufficiently ambitious to reach the pinnacle of their chosen profession and what they would do if passed over for promotion. These are two of the areas I address in *Your Stars at Work*. I am sure most of you who are involved in today's workplace have suffered from overwork, stress, and the fear of not making sufficient money. These are issues that will affect all of you in different ways.

While writing this book, I came across a magazine article that ranked the five hundred richest people in the world according to their astrological sign (where known). Here are the results:

Taurus	50
Libra	34
Pisces	34
Virgo	33
Aries	32
Aquarius	31
Cancer	30
Scorpio	29
Sagittarius	29
Leo	28
Gemini	28
Capricorn	26

Some of these rankings I found quite surprising as I thought certain signs would be higher up the list—others perhaps have good reason to expect a round of applause for their efforts!

Sometimes you may have to work for, or with, someone whose personality appears very difficult to understand. I have therefore included a section that will show you how to improve your work relationships. If you work for or with a highly critical Virgo, it is important to make sure you set your own standards sufficiently high; and even if you are content to be a slow but sure Taurus, you must learn to accept that there will be moments when taking risks will be immensely beneficial. These same ideas will also explain how and why other people are likely to relate to you based on *their* particular star sign.

In *Your Stars at Work* I raise the issue of ambition and your love life. I have come across many clients who have sacrificed a long-term, stable emotional relationship for the sake of their careers, only to regret this down the line. I'll show you that it is perfectly possible to achieve your professional and your emotional goals. At the same time I will discuss how each of you is likely to feel about love relationships within the workplace, which are rarely the easiest emotional ties.

Getting longevity out of your career is always a vital issue. These days it is becoming even more of a primary concern for many men and women. I'll show you that although job security is no longer a given, your own self-confidence and ability to tackle problems can be increased by a greater understanding of yourself, regardless of your age. Throughout the book you will also find various tips and strategies to assist you along the path to greater success.

Your Stars at Work starts with a quiz that will put you in the right frame of mind to get the most out of your sign section. It will show you that going into battle does not necessarily make you a winner, and that appeasing someone can at times be equally wrong. From your answers you will be able to deduce whether a more assertive image, or perhaps a less aggressive one, will help you become more of a star in the workplace.

By reading *Your Stars at Work,* you will learn everything you need to know about your star sign in order to be an integral part of today's ever-changing, continually challenging, fiercely competitive, and forward-thinking workplace. This life guide will help you stay on top of your chosen field, so that you become one of the real stars not just of today but of the new millennium.

YOUR STARS
AT WORK

THE FIRE SIGNS:
ARIES, LEO, SAGITTARIUS

1. *What do you consider to be your most valuable asset in today's competitive workplace?*

   a. Being a trailblazer.
   b. Relying on pragmatism at all times.
   c. Being able to get along with people at all levels.
   d. Feeling at ease in a high-profile role.

2. *If you encounter problems at work are you able to analyze your positive and negative qualities?*

   a. I'm never negative.
   b. My positive qualities overrule my negative ones.
   c. I don't have time even to think about them.
   d. I think they're about equal.

3. *What is your basic attitude toward your work?*

   a. I want to be a real star.
   b. It gives me a constant challenge.
   c. I pursue my goals with enthusiasm.
   d. It's something that has to be done.

4. *When you are aiming for promotion, do you:*

   a. Focus all your attention on the right targets?
   b. Show you can work as a team member and on your own initiative?
   c. Take the boss to lunch?
   d. Aggressively assert your opinions and ideas to everyone who will listen?

5. *How do you cope with being passed over for a promotion? By:*

   a. Assuring myself that it won't happen again!
   b. Challenging the decision with the people at the top.
   c. Proclaiming to my coworkers that it was absolute favoritism toward someone else.
   d. Asking my inner self if perhaps I wasn't quite ready yet.

Make Your Star Sign
Work for You: A Quiz

People tend to deal with their lives in different ways, depending on their star signs. In the following quiz, I want to show you how your behavior in the workplace will differ because of your sign.

Fire signs are more likely to go into battle taking certain risks, while Earth signs are more likely to trade (and tread) cautiously. Air signs are often better at discussing strategies and negotiating, while the Water signs may be more inclined to downplay or even ignore problems when they arise.

Make sure you answer the questions *honestly* before you read the chapter that relates to your star sign. This will help you become even more successful in the workplace and thus achieve maximum career longevity.

Each question for Fire, Earth, Air, and Water has an *a, b, c,* or *d* answer. You must circle only one answer. The number of points you earn will illuminate your current working style and enable you to see how much work you may need to do in order to be more successful.

6. *When you're in a really ambitious mood, do you:*

   a. Work extralong hours?
   b. Make your presence impossible to ignore?
   c. Get into a panic in case you're not far enough ahead?
   d. Create a long-term game plan that you know is feasible?

7. *How do you feel about romantic relationships with coworkers?*

   a. They could add excitement to my life.
   b. I don't want anything to interfere with my goals.
   c. Whatever comes along is fine with me.
   d. They're crazy and not worth the risks.

8. *How do you deal with stress?*

   a. I never think about it.
   b. I use it to keep the adrenaline running.
   c. I listen to what my body is trying to tell me.
   d. I look for some less stressful work.

9. *In your attitude toward making money, do you:*

   a. Aim for quick results?
   b. Create a realistic business plan to double your income?
   c. Invariably spend more than you can earn?
   d. Take certain risks to make a killing?

10. *If you hear that a coworker is gossiping about you behind your back, do you:*

    a. React immediately and aim for a direct confrontation?
    b. Shrug your shoulders and resolve to ignore it?
    c. Make a big deal out of it to everyone but the person responsible?
    d. Resolve to beat the perpetrator at his or her own game, and spread the word that this person can't be trusted?

11. *To get longevity out of your career, do you:*

    a. Always keep up-to-date in your field?
    b. Demonstrate strategic skills in information technology?
    c. Make it your business to develop strong working relationships at the executive level?

    d.   Consider that specialist skills are less important than a high profile and energetic personality?

THE EARTH SIGNS: TAURUS, VIRGO, CAPRICORN

1. *What do you consider to be your most valuable asset in today's competitive workplace?*

    a.   Being a total pragmatist.
    b.   My loyalty and dependability.
    c.   The fact that I don't mind working late.
    d.   My strong sense of purpose.

2. *Do you deal with a problem at work by:*

    a.   Taking risks?
    b.   Proceeding with caution?
    c.   Dealing with it head-on?
    d.   Ignoring it in the hope that it will disappear?

3. *What is your basic attitude toward your work?*

    a.   I feel it's my duty to work hard for my living.
    b.   It gives me a strong sense of purpose and stability.
    c.   I enjoy fulfilling a realizable goal.
    d.   I enjoy giving shape to other people's concepts.

4. *When you are aiming for promotion, do you:*

    a.   Develop a stronger competitive streak?
    b.   Manage to convince the powers that be that you have tenacity *plus* entrepreneurial flair?
    c.   Always feel confident about your response to the fast-changing needs of today's workplace?
    d.   Constantly have the right blend of personal, business, and technical skills?

5. *How do you cope with being passed over for a promotion? By:*

    a.   Resolving to find out why I've been passed over.
    b.   Shrugging my shoulders and keeping quiet.

    c.   Mentally refusing to be defeated for long but being fairly laid-back in my attitude.

    d.   Rising determinedly to the challenge of getting a new promotion soon.

6. *When you're in a really ambitious mood, do you:*

    a.   Become more dynamic in your approach to everyone and everything?

    b.   Make sure that you're always the last one to leave the office, and often the first one in?

    c.   Promote yourself by gaining greater visibility at the corporate level?

    d.   Take more initiatives and get an adrenaline buzz when you do so?

7. *How do you feel about romantic relationships with coworkers?*

    a.   I'd never want to create problems in my working life.

    b.   Sometimes you can't control your passions.

    c.   It wouldn't be a problem for me, although I wouldn't seek out such a relationship.

    d.   I'd rather concentrate on my long-term career goals.

8. *How do you deal with stress?*

    a.   I just accept that I can't avoid it if I'm under lots of pressure.

    b.   I make sure I become more flexible, both mentally and physically.

    c.   I try to have a good massage once a week.

    d.   I relax in front of the TV.

9. *In your attitude toward making money, do you:*

    a.   Rarely feel secure without it?

    b.   Set yourself financial goals and stick to them?

    c.   Always go for a slow but steady gain?

    d.   Sometimes take shortcuts that could be risky?

10. *If you hear that a coworker is gossiping about you behind your back, do you:*

    a.   Start a verbal fight with the perpetrator?

b. Ignore the gossip, knowing it's unlikely to be believed by anyone else?
c. Complain to your boss?
d. Spread some gossip yourself?

11. *To get longevity out of your career, do you:*

a. Make sure you have good working relationships at all levels?
b. Have lofty ideals at all times?
c. Mentally step into the shoes of any adversaries and learn to understand their viewpoints?
d. Combine strategic vision and leadership with a disciplined approach to your skills?

THE AIR SIGNS: GEMINI, LIBRA, AQUARIUS

1. *What do you consider to be your most valuable asset in today's competitive workplace?*

a. My ability to communicate intellectually on all levels.
b. My knowledge of strategies and techniques.
c. My willingness to change with the times.
d. My academic qualifications.

2. *Do you deal with a problem at work by:*

a. Weighing the pros and cons of the situation?
b. Trying to talk your way out of it?
c. Discussing your strategy with the rest of the team?
d. Analyzing your inner feelings before doing anything else?

3. *What is your basic attitude toward your work?*

a. It enables me to meet interesting people and make money too.
b. I enjoy being part of a hardworking team.
c. It motivates me to become more creative.
d. It gives me a regimen in my life.

4. *When you are aiming for promotion, do you:*

a. Always have an eye for the crucial details?
b. Make attitude adjustments if you know they're necessary?

    c.   Look at the long-term consequences of all your actions?

    d.   Make sure you befriend the right people?

5.   *How do you cope with being passed over for a promotion? By:*

    a.   Sending my résumé out to some other companies.

    b.   Endeavoring to find out where I went wrong.

    c.   Challenging the decision by going right to the top.

    d.   Showing a competitive streak and determination to be promoted very soon.

6.   *When you're in a really ambitious mood, do you:*

    a.   Let it be known that you're a great negotiator and wheeler-dealer?

    b.   Improve on your record of practical achievements?

    c.   Network over power breakfasts to make sure you don't miss out on anything?

    d.   Enhance your knowledge of the information highway even if it means working even longer hours?

7.   *How do you feel about romantic relationships with coworkers?*

    a.   I'd never let the possibility enter my mind!

    b.   I'd analyze the pros and cons before getting involved.

    c.   I prefer not to get involved with my coworkers, even when I do feel an attraction.

    d.   A little mental flirting is fine, but sex in the workplace—never!

8.   *How do you deal with stress?*

    a.   I've resolved to start meditating when I'm under pressure.

    b.   I tell myself it doesn't exist and just ignore it.

    c.   I take lots of coffee breaks.

    d.   I try not to have too many late nights.

9.   *In your attitude toward making money, do you:*

    a.   Shoot for the moon?

    b.   Always follow through on your moneymaking ideas?

    c.   Plan ahead logically and rationally?

    d.   Care less about the money than the job?

10. *If you hear that a coworker is gossiping about you behind your back, do you:*

    a. Start a big scene with the perpetrator?
    b. Calmly ignore it and get on with your work?
    c. Discuss what to do about it with people you know you can trust?
    d. Complain to the powers that be?

11. *To get longevity out of your career, do you:*

    a. Form effective cross-functional relationships at all levels?
    b. Show constant evidence of initiative, tenacity, and flair?
    c. Demonstrate specialist skills and a disciplined approach?
    d. Exhibit strategic, analytical thinking combined with commercial acumen?

THE WATER SIGNS: CANCER, PISCES, SCORPIO

1. *What do you consider to be your most valuable asset in today's competitive workplace?*

    a. My ability to navigate the ups and downs of my career.
    b. My strong but subtle style of influencing others.
    c. The knowledge that my instincts and intuition will guide me in the right direction.
    d. My ability to communicate and take responsibility for my decisions.

2. *Do you deal with a problem at work by:*

    a. Facing it head-on without delay?
    b. Making a gut decision based on your instincts?
    c. Always trying to negotiate a compromise?
    d. Asking your boss for some advice?

3. *What is your basic attitude toward your work?*

    a. I need some financial security.
    b. It keeps me from drifting aimlessly through life.

    c.   It enables me to express myself creatively.

    d.   I figure if other people can be successful, so can I.

4. *When you are aiming for promotion, do you:*

    a.   Define a clear goal and work harder than ever?

    b.   Make sure you review the positive, pragmatic effects, as well as the potential losses, of *all* your moves?

    c.   Remember that sometimes you have to zigzag to get to the top?

    d.   Have the inner hunger necessary to achieve your goals?

5. *How do you cope with being passed over for a promotion? By:*

    a.   Taking defeat in stride and getting on with my work.

    b.   Accepting that self-pity is allowed once in a while, but not for too long!

    c.   Taking a dispassionate analysis of my weaknesses and my strengths.

    d.   Blaming the current state of the job market.

6. *When you're in a really ambitious mood, do you:*

    a.   Keep a record of how often your gut decisions have been right?

    b.   Cultivate good relationships with the people at the top?

    c.   Show a deep commitment to your superiors, coworkers, and subordinates?

    d.   Take a crash course in the latest strategies and techniques in your field?

7. *How do you feel about romantic relationships with coworkers?*

    a.   I think that love is always important, no matter *where* it starts.

    b.   I'm aware that I'm highly emotional, and always weigh the pros and cons.

    c.   Once in a while a romantic liaison can even help you get to the top.

    d.   I try never to let my heart rule my head when work is involved.

8. *How do you deal with stress?*

   a. I use medication to calm me down.
   b. I accept that it's a fact of life in today's workplace and try to ignore it.
   c. I try to have a peaceful lifestyle outside of work, and find that being near the water helps to calm my nerves.
   d. I make sure I avoid loud people and stressful situations.

9. *In your attitude toward making money, do you:*

   a. Care desperately about your financial security?
   b. Have a fairly laid-back attitude when times are good?
   c. Make sure you have a realistic plan to provide for the future?
   d. Achieve more satisfaction from being creative than making money?

10. *If you hear that a coworker is gossiping about you behind your back, do you:*

    a. Vow you will never have anything to do with that person again?
    b. Resolve to pay the perpetrator back in kind?
    c. Feel sufficiently self-confident to know that no one will believe the gossip?
    d. Let your emotions get the better of you and show how upset you are?

11. *To get longevity out of your career, do you:*

    a. Take whatever position is offered in order to stay where you are?
    b. Maintain a strongly competitive streak and keep your résumé up-to-date?
    c. Act as friendly with your superiors and coworkers out of the office as you do within?
    d. Constantly prove not only your ability to operate on your own initiative but also your willingness to be a focused team player?

Scoring:

The Fire Signs

	a	b	c	d
1.	4	2	①	3
2.	1	④	2	3
3.	4	②	3	1
4.	3	④	2	1
5.	4	2	1	③
6.	③	2	1	4
7.	1	4	②	3
8.	1	2	④	3
9.	2	④	1	3
10.	4	3	2	①
11.	3	4	2	①

The Earth Signs

	a	b	c	d
1.	3	②	1	4
2.	1	3	④	2
3.	②	3	4	1
4.	1	4	3	②
5.	3	1	2	④
6.	③	1	4	2
7.	3	1	②	4
8.	2	4	3	①
9.	2	4	③	1
10.	3	④	2	1
11.	②	3	1	4

The Air Signs

	a	b	c	d
1.	2	3	4	1
2.	4	2	3	1
3.	2	3	4	1
4.	2	4	3	1
5.	2	3	1	4
6.	3	1	2	4
7.	1	3	4	2
8.	4	1	2	3
9.	1	4	3	2
10.	2	4	3	1
11.	1	2	3	4

The Water Signs

	a	b	c	d
1.	2	1	3	4
2.	3	4	2	1
3.	3	1	4	2
4.	2	3	1	4
5.	3	2	4	1
6.	2	1	3	4
7.	2	4	1	3
8.	1	2	4	3
9.	1	2	3	4
10.	3	1	4	2
11.	2	3	1	4

What's the Score?

Tally up the points that correspond to each of your answers.

16 points or less: You'd better get your act together fast and read up on your sign to prove you have what it takes to be successful in today's increasingly competitive workplace.

17–28 points: Outwardly you may seem to be a good worker, but inwardly you know you're not doing the best that you can. Raise your self-esteem and your work performance too by making the most of your star sign chapter.

29–38 points: No one can deny that you're a smart player, but at times you may still be selling yourself short. Read up on your sign, and you'll become even more motivated.

39 points or above: There is no doubt that you're able to gain visibility at corporate levels. But watch out you're not so busy shooting for the moon that you get careless and forget the crucial details.

ARIES IN THE WORKPLACE

March 21 ☆ April 20

If you were born between March 21 and April 20, you were born under the sign of Aries, first sign of the Zodiac. You are a Masculine, Cardinal, Positive, Fire sign, and your planetary symbol is the Ram. Because Mars, God of War, is your ruler, you often spend your life "going into battle."

Dynamic, enterprising, and pioneering, you are a fiery, impatient leader. An ambitious self-starter, you possess entrepreneurial acumen combined with shrewd negotiating skills that enable you to explore new opportunities. You are able to operate with flair, and you possess no shortage of energy and enthusiasm. A battle gets your adrenaline flowing faster than just about anything else.

But what about those times when a more laid-back approach would be infinitely preferable to everyone around you? It may not be easy, but it *is* possible for you to slow down and revise your strategy; remember, you thrive on a challenge!

One of the easiest ways to revise your work strategy, regardless of how and where you work, is to learn more about your opposite sign, Libra. Libra, sign of balance and harmony, charm and diplomacy, can teach you a great deal. You can learn something from every sign, which is why you might try to play a different sign once in a while.

Take a typical workday in the Aries life. You intend to go into work early, but the subway has a problem and the trains are jammed; someone beats you to the cab as the rain pours down, and when you do arrive you find an important letter has jammed the fax machine.

Playing Yourself: You waste another thirty minutes by relating the dramas of your morning to everyone, lash out at the fax machine, upset your coffee in the process, scatter your energy, and send your blood pressure sky-high!

Playing Taurus: You may be fuming inside, but your calm exterior belies your mood. You silently attend to the fax machine, then you call the sender, asking him to fax through the letter again, enjoy your coffee, and get on with your day.

Playing Gemini: By the time you've unscrambled the faxed letter, called the sender, made three other calls, and checked your lunch appointment, your coffee is cold but you've forgotten all about your terrible journey!

Playing Cancer: After checking the Moon's phases to see why everything seems to be against you, you're more inclined to sulk than throw a tantrum. You silently meditate and tell yourself tomorrow will be a better day.

Playing Leo: Your pride won't let you admit you might have caused some of the problems yourself! You smile brightly, find some lesser mortal to clear the machine, and tell yourself that even star players can have off days.

Playing Virgo: Once you've analyzed *why* the day started so disastrously, you worry about getting on with the work. You are too conscientious to throw a tantrum, and too health-conscious to risk the caffeine in the coffee.

Playing Libra: You know two can often do things better than one, and you charm everyone around into helping you make today a better working day! What you *won't* do is make a big production out of your problems!

Playing Scorpio: You silently congratulate yourself that you're the most invincible of all the signs. If problems are trying, they will soon pass. You won't show that you're fazed by anything or anyone.

Playing Sagittarius: Making your colleagues laugh when you tell them of your morning will lighten things up. Besides, your optimism tells you that the day is going to get better from now on, and you will make sure it does!

Playing Capricorn: You would never try to clear the fax machine yourself. You are far too cautious for that. You hate the fact you've come in late. Because you are so conscientious, it might be you who leaves the office last tonight!

Playing Aquarius: The one thing you *won't* be is true to form, for an unpredictable Aquarian doesn't even know what that means! The temptation to make a big deal out of the situation could still be irresistible, but not quite so apparent as when playing yourself.

Playing Pisces: By the time you've told your story, there may not be a dry eye in the office. Hoping for sympathy is one thing, but don't expect preferential treatment that could make your colleagues jealous!

The Positive and Negative Qualities of an Aries at Work

When it's the right time to battle, it's comforting to know you usually *do* win. Meanwhile, *creating* a battleground won't necessarily take you higher up the ladder of success. Sometimes you have to comply with regulations, rules, and red tape even if you don't necessarily agree with them. Few Ariens need to take a refresher course in assertiveness, but many will benefit from a more moderate approach to their daily problems.

The three *Es*—enterprising, enthusiastic, energetic—are among your most admired qualities. Your lack of patience, a headstrong gung-ho approach to almost everything, and your self-confident assumption that you alone should rule the world can be exhausting. Not only do you exhaust other people, you often end up wearing yourself out too.

You are a born leader but are not necessarily a good follower. By developing greater patience, you will gain perspective and be able to plug into life with greater depth and clarity.

The sign of Aries relates to the first day of spring; it represents birth. You are the child who enters the world with an indefatigable "me first" approach. Your sharp and focused approach to life's problems is often admirable. Your preoccupation with "me, myself, and I" is not. Your tendency to act on impulses can work against you.

The positive Aries thrives on deadlines, challenges, and power struggles, but recognizes that too much stress can be one's undoing, and accordingly seeks to create a balance in life. You also believe that it is not a weakness to ask for help when it's needed or to admit to a mistake.

The negative Aries also thrives on deadlines, challenges, and power struggles. The difference is that when megalomania sets in, you could find yourself being overlooked for the very positions you seek. Being assertive is one thing, but being unduly aggressive will work against you nine times out of ten. Although aggressiveness is accepted in the competitive world of sports, in the corporate world an aggressive person, especially if female, is thought of as hostile, and that is a perception you *don't* want to convey. You cannot win *all* the time, and sulking when you lose is just about the worst thing you can do.

The wise Aries will have lots of drive and vision, be independent minded with a direct and forceful style, and keep up-to-date with the latest information and technology. You will demonstrate that you can work within a strongly established work culture as part of a team— not always as a leader! Your irrepressible desire to succeed will be combined with the maturity and credibility to establish and maintain working relationships at every level.

Careers for Aries

As a self-motivated, high-achieving pioneer, you're one of the best. J. Pierpont Morgan, F. W. Woolworth, Walter Chrysler, and Hugh Hefner were all born under your sign. Great at high-powered selling work and being a spokesperson, you have the ability to come up with journalistic scoops that make the lead story in newspapers or on TV. Public relations and advertising give you scope for your trendsetting ideas, and you also make a terrific agent. The worlds of politics and high finance excite you, while acting, music, and sport provide the challenges you thrive on! The military, fire fighting, exploring the world, and dentistry are also careers associated with your sign. Many Ariens gravitate to self-employed professions since this means you don't have to answer to anyone but yourself!

Famous Ariens include Elton John, Alec Baldwin, David Letterman, Andrew Lloyd Webber, Eric Clapton, Eddie Murphy, Quentin Tarantino, Mariah Carey, Shannen Doherty, Diana Ross, Emma Thompson; models Paulina Porizkova and Elle Macpherson; high-profile writers Gloria Steinem and Maya Angelou; and sports stars Jennifer Capriati and Cale Yarborough. Charlemagne, Casanova, and Houdini were also born under your sign.

Your Attitude toward Work

Naturally, your rising sign, together with all the other factors of your personal horoscope, will also influence your attitude toward your work.

Aries rules the head. While you may not possess a big head in a physical sense, you may easily do so in a metaphorical one! You are convinced you and your fellow Ariens are the leaders of the world— you're not the first sign of the Zodiac for nothing. It is often better to work *for* you than *with* you. You *can* take second and even third place, but only if you have the challenge of getting to the top in the shortest possible time.

Life becomes difficult if you find yourself doing work that's too mundane, with little chance of becoming prominent in your field. Your boredom threshold is horribly low, and you never suffer fools gladly. More of a risk taker than most other signs, you often do well when you follow your first instincts. But you cannot afford to become careless. Consider the consequences of each step you take. Many people are jostling for success in the workplace, including other Ariens!

One great asset of your sign is that when you enjoy your work, you are not a shirker. And you perform extremely well under pressure, demonstrating your high energy, drive, and stamina. Whereas Capricorn is often the last to leave the office, you will frequently be the first in the door. Many of you find your minds are bursting with creative ideas when you first wake up, which is great for your working life but not always in sync with your emotional life.

You enjoy working in your own office, provided that you are not too far away from other people with whom you can bounce off ideas. A little cubicle would make you feel too closed in and would deflate your Aries ego. An open floor plan might be distracting, for your attention would be diverted too easily by conversations you could not help but overhear. You need peace and quiet in which to think, because it's hard enough for you to still your own restless mind, but you can't hide yourself away for too long.

The more action-packed your day becomes, the more you can accomplish with your work. You need to focus on a goal, something that poses a challenge for you. If the challenge changes daily, you like it even more. You seem to thrive on the challenge of meeting a "panic deadline." Working this way might be fine when you're young, but since stress in the workplace is an ever-increasing phenomenon, it's not the best idea to overwork that gray matter too much! In a fiercely competitive job market, you must make sure you're constantly motivated—not just when a deadline is close at hand.

You are a creator and pioneer in the workplace, but not so good at following things up. The latter trait can easily alienate and aggravate your superiors and colleagues. You would benefit from having someone working under you, but unfortunately you tend to think you can do everything faster than anyone else. This may be true with your thinking process, but it doesn't follow you will be as thorough in your actions. Always take time to understand the issues and then apply your influence and leadership skills in order to deliver the results.

TIPS FOR A HEALTHY WORK ATTITUDE

- Keep your mind, body, and soul in harmony.
- Retain your individuality without being an egomaniac!
- Never give in to defeat; always recognize good timing.

Aiming for Promotion

Very few Ariens appear to be content with their lot unless they are aiming for *something*, so it is always worth remembering that you possess the ingredients to be a real star.

You come across as an outgoing, competitive, assertive person, brimming over with initiative, more than able to hone in on your own particular talents and abilities. Sometimes you almost appear *too* over-the-top and conscious of your success rating.

Underneath your often brash exterior, there is a far more vulnerable individual who has far less faith in your talents than others do. You must find a way to walk the line between arrogance and insecurity.

There are moments when you need to let go, although this is very different from admitting defeat. There is a wonderful Rune that tells you to "wait upon the will of heaven." In life there are times when you may have to take second or even third place. This may be hard for an impatient Arien to contemplate, when you're convinced you possess all the natural ingredients to be at the top. But sometimes you try to achieve too much visibility too soon; you become so busy *achieving* that you don't keep an eye on the big picture.

Primarily an idealist, albeit an impatient one, you are happy to work long hours, especially if the carrot being dangled in front of you is a promotion, and if you're working on an exciting project. If sheer enthusiasm and lots of initial hard work were all that was needed to make it in the workaday world, you would score high on the winners' list. Unfortunately, you sometimes give up on projects much too soon because something else has caught your interest. Always prove you're a seasoned business professional, with the flair, tenacity, and ability to successfully drive a company forward and to develop long-term business relationships in your field. Show that you're fit for the race and will never be left at the post!

If promotion eludes you through no known fault of your own, try to ascertain why. Avoid taking an extreme position. Neither self-pity ("Why have you overlooked poor little me?") nor an aggressive stance ("I have to know *now!*") will create the desired results. At this stage, you need to exercise tact and diplomacy!

People are becoming more and more competitive in the workplace, and perhaps you haven't paid enough attention to how others are handling their workload. Sometimes you must devise new and ingenuous methods to outwit opponents. Being completely open to coworkers about your ambitions is not always the best way to succeed, for someone may be determined to undermine you in order to achieve his or her own career goals.

- Try to be high-profile in a nonaggressive way!
- Never try to undermine your boss.
- Prove you have real staying power.

How to Cope with Being Passed Over for Promotion

The mere thought of missing out on a promotion could be enough to create a major panic in your life. Don't lose sight of your long-term ambitions, and continue to channel your energies into achieving them, even if you miss out the first time around.

Don't give in to indecision and doubt. Retain faith in yourself and your abilities without being arrogant in any way. When you believe in yourself, you have an incredible ability to persuade others to believe in you too.

Be thankful that you were born an Aries, for this gives you a great advantage. The ability to overcome disappointments and start over is one of your major attributes.

Always remember that you're a true trailblazer who is brilliant at playing key strategic roles in today's challenging and performance-driven environment, and be confident that something good is sure to come your way.

Ambition—or the Lack of It

Most of you are ambitious, or at least you start off that way. The trouble is that if at first you don't succeed, you don't necessarily "try again." Resolve to rise above rejection if a job, promotion, or business opportunity doesn't materialize when you expect it!

Because you're not terribly good at "losing," you are tempted to move on to something new that enables you to climb higher. If a lateral move comes along, don't dismiss it out of hand. The way to the top isn't always a straight line, but might involve a few zigzag moves along the way.

To sustain your ambition, you need to renounce the fear of rejection, connected with the vulnerable side of your character. Since you came into the world with your inimitable "me first" attitude, it's often hard for you to realize that you're not always going to be the flavor of the month.

Try to recognize your ambitious streak for what it is: a determination to be better than anyone else! Don't make the mistake of thinking that delays, obstructions, and even frustrations with certain ambitions mean you've failed. You can succeed at more than one career in your lifetime. It simply depends on your attitude and your behavior at any given time.

Remember that your energy, initiative, and courage, combined with your ambition, are a powerful force to be reckoned with!

Ambition—and Your Love Life

It's often hard for anyone who is ambitious to devote the right amount of time to finding and keeping a good relationship. As an idealistic and passionate Aries, you're unlikely to let your love life suffer because of your work. You're more likely to become stressed out trying to devote the maximum amount of time and attention to both.

For work *and* love to run smoothly requires considerable negotiation and understanding on all sides. You're more than happy to go it alone in the workplace when you're in an especially hardworking mood, but a good emotional relationship is just as satisfying to you. Always consider a partner's feelings as well as your own. As sentimental and romantic as any Piscean, you're not always the best of company when you feel thwarted in the workplace. It's usually the one who loves you who will suffer for that! Your ability to talk over your deepest feelings with ease is a positive quality. It is decidedly negative to vent your anger on someone whose only fault in the matter is loving you.

If you're in love with a real die-hard workaholic, life may not always be easy, especially if there is a conflict over who is destined to be more successful in the workplace. If you have a high-powered businessman or -woman as your spouse or lover, you may find it extremely difficult to accept that you could be taking second place not to another person, but to his or her work.

- Don't overdo the "power" syndrome at home and at work.
- Leave work problems where they belong: back in your office or workplace.
- Never let your work cause you to forget an important date like a birthday or anniversary in your personal agenda.
- Depending on just *how* ambitious you are, try to have a mate who won't cause conflicts, and who doesn't try to make you feel guilty either.

Romance in the Workplace

It's almost certainly better to direct your strong passions and emotions toward your work rather than toward your boss or one of your peers. How many office affairs do you know of that failed because of various mitigating circumstances?

A romantic liaison in the workplace is never likely to run smoothly, especially for an Aries who finds it hard to keep secrets at the best of times. Since Aries rules the head, *headstrong* and *falling headlong* are words that come to mind with you, especially where love is concerned!

Because you form instant attractions toward people, and are spontaneous rather than standoffish, you may inwardly rebel at the thought that anyone within your working environment is out of bounds. You thrive on the challenge and the chase, but in this case it's often wise to take up the challenge *to remain uninvolved!* You're unlikely to have an affair with someone just because you think that person can advance your career. The chemistry of pure physical attraction is the way to get your adrenaline running, but the place and the time need to be right.

I wouldn't dare to suggest you ignore your normal sexual desires, but I do recommend you don't allow them to interfere with your commitment to your chosen career. If you do get yourself into emotional tangles in the workplace, you must then cope with the consequences. Making a major Aries emotional scene will not enhance your reputation at work.

Make sure your enthusiastically flirtatious ways are not misinterpreted. Remember that sexual harassment can be construed as verbal as well as physical and that you do have a tendency to make impulsive remarks! You can be especially self-assertive when your passions are aroused. Don't let your love of that "chase and challenge" be misconstrued by the object of your desires. If someone tried to sexually harass *you*, I think the whole world would probably hear of it right away. You're definitely not someone to take that kind of situation lightly. All the more reason to control your own emotions when you are attracted to someone at work.

You and Your Stress Factor

Since Aries is the sign that rules the head, it is no wonder that you are prone to raging headaches and migraines, neuralgia, toothache, insomnia, and nervous exhaustion.

In my book *Star Signs* I suggested ways to get in touch with the inner you so that you could align your mind, body, and spirit for a healthy lifestyle. Anyone who is trying to get *anywhere* in the workplace today knows you must find time to recharge your batteries and replenish your energy. If you're a typical Aries, you cannot afford to succumb to stress because it really will take its toll upon your head.

Stress is the body's natural reaction to situations or circumstances that you feel are threatening and that perhaps you cannot cope with. A small amount will put you on your toes, but too much is damaging, both mentally and physically. Stress can creep up on you in many different ways. It may come from your trying to do too much—simply to prove how intensely motivated you are. It may arise from your anger that someone else has been assigned some of your tasks without your being asked. (You don't realize this may have been done for your own benefit.) It is important to accept that even an Aries sometimes needs to delegate to others! Try not to panic about getting certain tasks finished in time—when you know you will! Guard against your tendencies to create false deadlines and to overtax your strength. Driving yourself too hard is exhausting for everyone!

Basically, you are a healthy sign and tend to be extremely fortunate at remaining young at heart, even when you have pushed yourself too hard. But remember: it's usually your mind that needs a break. So listen more frequently to your inner voice and try to spend more time out in the fresh air to breathe in some oxygen. Make sure you're eating a healthy diet; sandwiches gulped between tasks are not the answer. And do remember to take in some early nights once in a while.

If overexhaustion makes it hard for you to get to sleep early because your mind is whirling around in a dozen directions, why not take a good book to bed with you or watch a movie on TV or a video. Focus on something other than your work.

Just as you're prepared to work hard at something you enjoy, many of you are quite prepared to play hard too! You often enjoy sports, especially those activities in which you can excel. You hate to miss out on an opening of anything—be it a new club or an art exhibition. You love going on vacation, preferably to somewhere hot, sunny, and exotic (although of course there are Ariens who like to ski in Aspen too!) where there is also plenty of entertainment.

Always make sure there *is* a life outside your work. It's too easy for you to keep going, faster and faster, running yourself into the ground, without allowing your Aries batteries to recharge. A hardworking Aries woman of my acquaintance loves to take long walks in the country or along the beach every spare moment she has. She wasn't always like that! She's much happier now—and more successful in her job too.

Your Attitude toward Making Money

Ariens' attitude toward money tends to be the following: "If it's there, fine; if not, it's time to panic!"

You're often too concerned with the present. You need to formulate a long-term plan (preferably with the aid of a good business adviser and accountant). Try not to listen to any get-rich-quick schemes no matter how tempting they appear. Take the time and trouble to make sure you have the right kind of bank account. Start to save your small change each day—you'd be surprised how quickly it can start to add up.

You sometimes forget to make sure you're protected financially. You are definitely an entrepreneur, taking risks where other more pragmatic signs would resist. And if there is something in which you truly believe, you will put in long hours night and day, without expecting an enormous reward for your efforts. But you simply cannot afford to work just for love!

Many of you have fantastically brilliant ideas and executive ability that could almost turn you into millionaires overnight! Frequently you lack the patience to refine some of the all-important details that are the name of the game. Always analyze the positives and negatives of your tactics and maneuvers—and try to ensure you have a good adviser around too! You possess all the energy and enthusiasm in the world, combined with a shining aura of self-confidence that is more than sufficient to convince others that you have millionaire potential. When you *do* want to make money, you are capable of doing so in a big, big way.

How to Improve Your Work Relationships

As an Aries, you pride yourself on getting on brilliantly with most people, but then you would, wouldn't you? Since you are such a positive firebrand of energy, however, you don't always appreciate that other people can't, or don't want to, keep up with your pace. Never forget the importance of teamwork and team spirit in today's workplace. The way you fit in with other people also counts a great deal when you're being considered for promotion.

The following guide will show you the best way to relate to all the signs, whether they are those of your boss, your peer, or an employee:

Aries with Aries Boss: Sometimes you have to take second place in life, even to another Ram, so try to do it gracefully. Show respect to your boss, and don't constantly challenge! Life is not always a battleground!

Aries with Aries Colleague: Don't let your sense of competition prevent you from keeping up a good working relationship. You will recognize *your own* strengths and weaknesses in an Aries colleague!

Aries with Aries Employee: Remember when *you* were aiming for the top, and don't be unnerved by that Arien ambitious streak. It will help to keep you on your toes.

Aries with Taurus Boss: Learn to respect the Bull's tried-and-true methodical approach to everything. But remember Taurus can be stubborn, so don't overstep your mark.

Aries with Taurus Colleague: It's no using being too pushy, because Taureans will always dig in their heels and refuse to budge. Perseverance can work better than impatience!

Aries with Taurus Employee: Be thankful that each task will be completed satisfactorily with the maximum of efficiency. Give praise where it's due, and you will have a loyal and hardworking employee.

Aries with Gemini Boss: Always keep your mind alert, and try to continually come up with innovative ideas. Don't be frustrated if you can't elicit quick answers from this boss.

Aries with Gemini Colleague: You make a good pair with your quick-witted approach to life. But make a pact to avoid gossip in the office so you'll both learn to concentrate more.

Aries with Gemini Employee: Start to practice what you expect others to do! If you give up on things halfway through because you're bored, don't be surprised if Gemini follows suit and leaves tasks unfinished.

Aries with Cancer Boss: Never scream and shout, rant or rave in the presence of a Cancerian boss. Cancerians need to feel the right vibes in their office ambience and dislike noisy or aggressive people!

Aries with Cancer Colleague: Always use your head before you say anything that could be misconstrued. Cancerians are notoriously sensitive. Don't spoil a good working relationship almost before it starts.

Aries with Cancer Employee: You tackle everything head-on, but Cancer is used to taking the sideways approach. Too much Aries fire will result in sulkiness all around, so play this relationship with care.

Aries with Leo Boss: Flattery is often a good tactic with a Leo boss, as long as it's genuine. Never let on that you might be after Leo's job one day, even if you are!

Aries with Leo Colleague: Two determined Fire signs competing for promotion could create a problem. Remember that if you're loyal, Leo will be equally loyal.

Aries with Leo Employee: Accept that Leo, like you, finds it hard to take orders. Always make sure you're worthy of respect. It works wonders with this kind and generous sign.

Aries with Virgo Boss: Be prepared for plenty of criticism when you have a boss of this sign. Learn to be more self-disciplined in your working techniques. Don't expect to leave the office early very often.

Aries with Virgo Colleague: Virgo's dedication to the task at hand fills you with envy. Don't leave all the dirty work to this colleague while you have all the fun. Virgo will teach you patience!

Aries with Virgo Employee: For a fast-moving Aries who lacks the patience to follow things through, a Virgo employee is a dream come true. You won't have to worry, but don't make Virgo worry too much instead!

Aries with Libra Boss: Learn tact, diplomacy, charm, good taste, and the art of harmony from your Libran boss. You can fire up Libra with your enthusiasm, while she will exert a calming influence on you.

Aries with Libra Colleague: Librans work better in partnership, often because they hate to make decisions on their own. Of all the signs, Libra is the most accommodating teammate, so don't be too aggressive.

Aries with Libra Employee: Since it will be such a pleasure to have a friendly and helpful Libran working for you, enjoy it! Just don't let your "new best friend" forget that you do have to be the boss too.

Aries with Scorpio Boss: It could be dangerous to get involved in a power struggle with this sign. Scorpio won't relinquish a top position unless it's his own decision.

Aries with Scorpio Colleague: Don't expect confidential chats on everything that's going on. Scorpios keep things to themselves. Scorpio's quiet intensity also hides a powerhouse of emotions.

Aries with Scorpio Employee: Always respect your Scorpio employee. This employee will give you an abundance of loyalty as long as he feels he's in the right place.

Aries with Sagittarius Boss: Don't consider you're equals just because of this boss's free-and-easy approach. The Archer may sometimes appear careless and sloppy but expects you to toe the line.

Aries with Sagittarius Colleague: Life could easily appear to be all fun and games with the optimistic attitude of Sagittarius to inspire you. But don't overlook important tasks.

Aries with Sagittarius Employee: This employee is ready, willing, and able to help. Don't develop a "good buddies" relationship, though, or you'll feel guilty giving orders.

Aries with Capricorn Boss: Your enthusiasm and vitality might impress this boss. But prove you have the staying power to finish what you start (even if you do arrive early), or you could be out!

Aries with Capricorn Colleague: Don't allow Capricorn's willingness to work hard make you lazy. Watch the Goat climbing surefootedly up the ladder to success—and don't be left behind.

Aries with Capricorn Employee: Sitting back to let this employee run your life in a brilliantly organized way could be almost irresistible. But watch out. If you're careless, Capricorn could be your boss one day!

Aries with Aquarius Boss: An Aquarian boss is an interesting livewire, brimming with imaginative ideas but fairly unpredictable too. Don't risk thinking *being pals* means not having to follow rules.

Aries with Aquarius Colleague: Your days will never be boring, and you'll soon learn the latest technology from this sign. Make sure you can keep pace with the agile mental and inspirational skills of Aquarius.

Aries with Aquarius Employee: Allow this employee the opportunity to be inventive with the day's tasks. Don't pin her down too hard on getting in right on time; she will make up the hours anyway!

Aries with Pisces Boss: Don't be fooled into thinking you could take over just because Pisces seems all sweetness and light. Underneath that soft and sentimental exterior is someone shrewd and calculating too.

Aries with Pisces Colleague: Remember that Pisceans get bored nearly as quickly as you! A sensitive Pisces colleague will be sympathetic to romantic problems but ineffective with economic ones.

Aries with Pisces Employee: Be tough (but not *too* tough) with dreamy-eyed Pisces. Most Pisceans have wonderfully imaginative and creative ideas, but practicality is not usually their strong point.

Getting Longevity out of Your Career

In today's fiercely competitive workplace, getting fired takes place more frequently even if it now has different names, such as downsizing and staff cutbacks. Job security is no longer a given, no matter how good you may be at your work. As an entrepreneurial Aries, you often thrive on being your own boss. However, if you're *not* working for yourself, you can improve the odds of getting longevity out of your career by making sure you are always a key player within a multi-disciplined team—not someone who is simply out for himself. Your trailblazing and leadership skills can rarely be disputed, but you must also demonstrate an ability to form effective cross-functional relationships at all levels.

The thought of being dismissed from a company is an affront both to your pride and to everything else you believe in. You cannot imagine why anyone would want to get rid of someone as enterprising and eager as you. You may try to convince yourself it's because someone higher up the ladder has a grudge against you. You may even dissolve into self-pity, although this is unlikely to last long. But if you know deep down that your work hasn't been up to scratch for some time, be big enough to accept the blame for your own mistakes. As a natural and fearless fighter, your fighting spirit will soon return.

Deciding to take action against the people who fired you isn't necessarily the best approach. Remember how impulsive and argumentative you can be, and realize that you cannot afford to take risks unless you are 100 percent sure you have a strong case for unfair dismissal. Legal action can take a long time and cost a great deal of money. If justice is not on your side, it might only be the lawyers who become rich.

Getting fired doesn't have to end all your aims and aspirations. You're quite capable of taking defeat in stride because you know full well that you will win again in some other way. These days, there are many reasons beyond your control for firing staff, with companies cutting back because of economic problems and computers doing more and more of the work. Begin to look on your situation as a question of "timing," although not necessarily "bad" timing. Convince yourself instead that you have reached the ideal moment to do something new.

Naturally it's difficult to think about this if the rent has to be paid, you need new clothes, and you are not entitled to much severance pay. But the more positive you can be about advancing your career by finding a new job, the more your assertive and self-confident attitude will inspire the people who interview you. Be grateful that you were born under the sign of the Ram, for you possess an amazing ability to forget the bad things in your life much faster than most other signs. Never let the thought of aging get you down. You remain young at heart throughout your life. With your inimitable initiative, there will *always* be work for you in one workplace or another!

I read recently that most people change their careers at least three times during the course of their working lives. And they are likely to change *jobs* even more frequently. Getting older doesn't mean you cannot work, but rather that you might be better off changing to a new field. Many people work beyond the age of sixty-five these days, even taking courses they had no time for earlier in their lives. If you're a typical Aries, your entrepreneurial skills will soon enable you to come up with something else you can do. I'm sure this work will be exciting, stimulating, and probably bring in good money too.

Always keep your sights set on the top. Resolve that you will consider it a challenge to achieve something even more worthwhile in the workplace. If your old employers then hear just how successful you are, well, so much the better!

ARIES CAREER STRATEGIES—A CHECKLIST FOR EVERY AGE

- Always stay alert and assertive—but be adaptable too.
- Remember that with Mars as your ruling planet, your inner strength will be a weapon as powerful as any display of outward aggression.
- There's no time for slacking off in today's world, so always do high-quality work. Someone could be moving behind you up the ladder very fast.
- Never be too needy for praise and recognition. You'll know soon enough if something is not done well. Busy people often don't have time to pay compliments these days.
- Remember that rules, red tape, and regulations have always existed. They weren't invented just for you!
- Don't get involved in office affairs—your own or anyone else's. It's safer that way.
- Have a long-range plan. A successful one will last forever, especially if you will finally accept *patience* as one of your guiding principles.

TAURUS IN THE WORKPLACE

April 21 ☆ May 20

If you were born between April 21 and May 20, you were born under the sign of Taurus, second sign of the Zodiac. You are a Feminine, Fixed, Negative, Earth sign. Your planetary symbol is the Bull.

Ruled by Venus, the Goddess of Love, you are less gung ho and self-assertive than Aries, the sign that precedes yours, but you are more determined and disciplined in your working life. Venus brings you a calmer and more contented approach to life, together with an eye for beauty in all its forms.

You are sometimes too laid-back and low-key in your approach. You don't have to be as impulsive and headstrong as Aries, but learn to develop more of a competitive streak and focus with greater self-confidence on what you have to offer.

No one can fault your social vision and practical realism. You're a determined professional, who can be a key player in today's workplace, performing well under pressure. You have the ability to make gut decisions calmly and confidently, based not only on your deepest instincts but also on your experience.

However, many of you appear too content to take second place, even to someone whose skills and abilities do not match up to your own. If you feel insecure about certain aspects of your personality, remember that each star sign has something to learn from its opposite sign in the Zodiac.

Scorpio, sign of big business, inheritance, death, and regeneration, is *your* opposite sign. Since most Scorpios are convinced they are unconquerable, why not take some Scorpio invincibility for yourself? You can learn something from every sign, which is why you might try to wear a different astrological hat at times.

Take a typical workday in the Taurus life. Your schedule for this day has been arranged for weeks but then you arrive at your workplace to find that you must work on something totally different.

Playing Aries: A momentary panic is soon overcome. You relish the challenge of devising the best solution to any given problem in the fastest possible time! You simply rearrange your schedule and get to work.

Playing Yourself: It takes a few minutes for the news to sink in, and you're obviously not happy. Stubbornly you might insist it's impossible to change your schedule. But think about those contenders lurking in the background, ready to take over your job!

Playing Gemini: Your mind immediately goes into overdrive. It doesn't take you long to invent a brilliant way to overcome the problem. You soon alter your day's appointments without upsetting anyone or anything.

Playing Cancer: Your sensitivity to situations enables you to decide whether the current one is worth arguing over. You might feel moody about the whole thing, but you would never go against your superiors' wishes.

Playing Leo: You think of this day as the perfect opportunity to prove what a star you are. You know you can rise above any problems, just as long as you are sufficiently praised for your efforts!

Playing Virgo: Because you are so disciplined, you'll probably enjoy resolving this difficult situation, even if you *are* concerned. You figure out the best way to change the old appointments with a minimum of fuss.

Playing Libra: Your diplomatic and tactful manner enables you to deal with everything in the best possible way. You'll probably enlist the help of your coworkers, knowing you work best in a team.

Playing Scorpio: If you decide to argue, you must be sure that you'll win. You also understand that there must have been a good reason to change everything—you know you can take any difficulty in stride.

Playing Sagittarius: An aura of self-confidence permeates your attitude in dealing with the situation at hand. You quickly bluff your way out of the prearranged appointments and cheerfully greet the new arrivals.

Playing Capricorn: Your ambitions and your professional life come before *almost* everything else. There is no way you'd fall short of anything demanded of you. But you might almost be too ruthless in the way you handle things.

Playing Aquarius: There's almost no exact way to predict Aquarius's behavior! Hard-and-fast rules simply do not apply. But you'll be sure to deal with things benevolently.

Playing Pisces: You are able to deal with the practical matter of rescheduling the original appointments in a sympathetic way. You won't hold a grudge against your superiors for landing you in a difficult situation.

The Positive and Negative Qualities of a Taurus at Work

You're somewhat like the Rock of Gibraltar, steady and enduring regardless of what is taking place around you. You are the true builder of the Zodiac, bequeathed with amazing patience and persistence to achieve your ambitions.

As the first of the Earth signs, your feet are planted firmly on the ground! Sometimes you don't just set down your feet, you dig them in so deeply that you cannot even move. This can hold you back in today's fast-moving world. The whole labor market is becoming more flexible, and job security is no longer automatic. Don't assume complacently that because your work is good you will be safe. *Good* is not necessarily enough. Continually strive to prove that you're irreplaceable!

Some Taureans allow their ambitions to take second place to their talents, contentedly plodding along and remaining perfectly happy. Others end up frustrated, having always assumed that they would *get there in the end*. If *getting there in the end* means achieving your ambitions in the workplace, things cannot be left to chance. You are concerned about your prestige and standing in the world, and don't like feeling inferior in any way, so you have even more reason to make sure you keep ahead of the game.

Make your presence known by being sufficiently assertive both in words and positive actions. This will enable you to become more decisive and to express yourself clearly and distinctly. Keep the field in perspective, but set your sights on the top. Be more independent minded, creating your own direct and forceful style of work, and make sure that your task-orientated approach is recognized as being uniquely yours. Don't allow anyone else to take the credit and praise for your efforts.

The positive Taurus is highly organized and disciplined, brilliant at dealing with structure, and usually unflappable when faced with problems. Kind and nurturing toward your colleagues, you're a dependable worker. You will never take unnecessary risks—a highly important quality in these times, when fortunes can be made and lost in a single day.

The negative Taurus is noticeable when you become too much of a megalomaniac by being too aggressive. Adolf Hitler, Saddam Hussein, and Eva Perón were all born under this sign, and all of them have definitely exhibited aggressive behavior.

We all reach a point where we can take only so much—and no more—but always try to deal with problems calmly and confidently in an understated way. If you place too much emphasis on status and material rewards, you become shallow and superficial along the way. Fortunately, your positive characteristics usually outweigh the negative ones.

The wise Taurus not only will have the ability to generate ideas but will also see them through to fulfillment. You will be capable of adapting to changes in your field, and you will make your contribution both visible and influential.

Careers for Taurus

Taurus men and women are often drawn to the fields of real estate, banking (anything in the banking field is good for you!), economics, architecture, and building and construction. The influence of your ruling planet Venus also leads many of you into working in the arts, and you make great interior decorators, craftspeople, gardeners, and florists. Music, painting, and acting are all Taurean careers. Some of you make brilliant restaurant owners or chefs. With your inborn managerial skills, you can front a company, large or small.

Hotel management is something at which many Taureans excel. While writing this book in Italy, I made a wonderful new friend, Signora Nina Aielli, owner of the beautiful Hotel Cappuccini Convento in Amalfi. Early on in her life, she made the decision to be a business manager. At that time it was not easy for an Italian girl to be a businesswoman in an extremely macho man's world! Nevertheless, she has been extremely successful in her career. When Taureans truly want to do something, they will never give up.

Famous Taureans include Leonardo da Vinci, Rudolph Valentino, Willem De Kooning, William Shakespeare, Sigmund Freud, Orson Welles, Zubin Mehta, photographer Richard Avedon, Aaron Spelling, George Lucas, Jack Nicholson, Uma Thurman, Jay Leno, Billy Joel, Ella Fitzgerald, Carol Burnett, Barbra Streisand, Jessica Lange, Michelle Pfeiffer, Nora Ephron, Linda Evangelista, Andre Agassi, Dennis Rodman, Pope John Paul II, Yogi Berra, and best-selling novelist Barbara Taylor Bradford.

Your Attitude toward Work

Naturally, your rising sign, together with all the other factors of your own particular horoscope, will also influence your attitude toward work.

If you are a fairly typical Taurus, you will possess the necessary stamina to do extremely well in your chosen profession. You will achieve even greater success if you become more of a self-starter. Don't sit back and wait for someone else to give the orders. And don't be so scared of taking risks. Have faith in the power of your own particular talents and abilities.

You become extraordinarily obstinate when faced with someone whose working methods conflict with yours, or when forced to deal with something with which you do not agree. Greater flexibility is often the way to achieve success in today's demanding environment. Remember, you have a great sense of humor; sometimes you may even need to use it against yourself!

You are perfectly capable of tackling repeatedly the most mundane tasks without a complaint. Occasionally you become too set in your routines and too slow or old-fashioned in your methods. It's great to have a "never-give-up" attitude, but do take advantage of the modern technology that is around now. Be aware that you may have many contenders in your field, who are prepared to be completely up-to-date.

Although your feet are so firmly on the ground, and although deep down you are a born survivor, you also suffer deeply if you worry about material security and creature comforts for yourself and your family. You possess the necessary patience to put in long hours at work, plus the ability to make yourself indispensable in today's global marketplace. This can bring good results, provided you are prepared to be a little less uncompromising.

A smart attitude toward work must include the ability to take the initiative, to gain the right visibility at the corporate level, and to be plugged into your company's requirements. Because these requirements do not always stay the same, *flexibility* should become your new watchword. Although staying grounded is a commendable quality—especially when so many other people are living with their heads in the clouds—you must also have the vision to understand and accept the impact of change.

TIPS FOR A HEALTHY WORK ATTITUDE

- Try to be more versatile in your attitude and your actions.
- Praise yourself for your determination and dependability, but be more of a self-starter too.
- Always fall back on your Taurean sense of humor if things get tough out there.

Aiming for Promotion

Unfortunately, you're not always quick enough off the mark to get something done. You have the capacity to achieve what you truly want, but if you work in a competitive field you cannot afford to leave *anything* to chance, nor to take too long climbing the ladder to greater success.

You hate feeling inferior to anyone. You may even bear grudges almost as strongly as your opposite sign, Scorpio, and you possess a tendency as strong as any Capricorn to place status and material rewards over almost everything else.

Many of you possess talent and ambition in unequal parts—with the former often outweighing the latter. Make sure your skills are always highly visible, so that you are up there with any other serious contenders.

You are the only person who is truly in charge of your own career. If you are determined to get a promotion, you must manage your career in the same brilliantly organized and structured way that you manage everything else in your life.

You will almost certainly have paid your dues by starting off on the lower steps of the ladder. When pursuing a promotion, remember everything you learned from the beginning—then be prepared to learn some more. Don't be left behind by other determined promotion seekers, whose style of working is perhaps more flexible and less restrained than yours. Keep an eye on the other players. Outwit them with your ability to communicate, implement, and take responsibility for your decisions with strategic insight. Prove that *you're* the best. Remind yourself that you can be as invincible as any Scorpio when it comes to campaigning for a promotion. Believe in what you tell yourself (without becoming too power crazy), and you will be halfway there!

In today's world, it is rarely enough to be responsible, loyal, and steadfast. You must also demonstrate that you have what it takes to be a real star. Aiming at a special promotion means pulling out all the stops to ensure you are not overlooked. If promotion eludes you, through no known fault of your own, your ability to hang in there, for what you truly want, will stand you in good stead. Nothing prevents you from trying again, and next time you'll do your homework even better so that the other contenders don't get a foot in the door. I have rarely met a Taurean who is willing to give up—certainly not without a fight!

TIPS FOR PROMOTION SEEKERS

- Remember that we're in the Information Age. Always keep up-to-date with the latest information and technology.
- Sit back when you're home at the end of the day—but never relax when you're aiming higher up the ladder of success.
- Be more fiery, flexible, and work faster too.

How to Cope with Being Passed Over for Promotion

Never shrug your shoulders and say that you'll wait for the next opportunity for promotion. Although getting into a panic is often self-defeating, being too easygoing and dismissive about the situation can be equally detrimental.

Make every possible endeavor to find out why you've been overlooked. Have you kept up-to-date with innovations in your field? Do you have credibility at the highest levels? Are you able to fulfill a high-profile role—whether working as a team member or on your own initiative? Are you perceived as an upwardly mobile individual who is more than capable of taking ownership of your career? If you answer "yes" to all these questions, you may have been passed over for promotion through no apparent fault of your own.

Life isn't always fair—especially in the workplace. Never lose sight of your objectives, for you possess the ability to make sure that you won't be overlooked again!

Ambition—or the Lack of It

It would be unfair to say that Taureans are unambitious. Some of my Taurean friends and clients are *exceedingly* ambitious. But sometimes you do display a laissez-faire attitude.

A truly ambitious Taurean will leave no stone unturned to achieve greater status. You share with the other Earth signs, Virgo and Capricorn, a disposition toward hard work, but you may need to move faster and to display stronger entrepreneurial flair in order to be recognized as one of the main players in the workplace.

Interestingly enough, for someone who can be very concerned with power and material status, and who is good at building empires (publishing magnate William Randolph Hearst was born under your sign), you seem to prefer to keep your ambitions hidden away. Sometimes you appear to be more of a *non*achiever than a *high* achiever. Do you figure that it is better to underplay your ambitions so that your competitors do not realize they are up against you? Don't play this particular game too brilliantly or it will backfire, with the bosses at the top thinking you're not sufficiently interested in advancement.

To sustain your ambition, you must learn to be less rigid. Sometimes you cling far too long to the past—both good and bad. Your patience and persistence are legendary, but be more assertive and more independent too. Don't sit back and let other people take over the positions that could have been yours. I'm tired of telling Taureans that they're too content to take second place, when they should be out there in the number one spot!

Ambition—and Your Love Life

You *can* combine the two. I know many Taureans who have done so for years! Even if you are highly ambitious, your love life should not suffer. You are one of the most sensual signs in the Zodiac, with strong physical desires. Ruled by Venus, Goddess of Love, you will rarely want to miss out on the tender, loving care of a good relationship by being totally consumed with your work. Naturally, things will work out best if you have a partner who understands there are sure to be days when you will not give up in the middle of a task. You're a Taurus, and you don't leave *anything* half-done. Don't become unnecessarily obstinate about finishing something unimportant in order to prove this point—especially if you're supposed to be at a more important event with the love of your life.

If you're involved with another Taurean, or a partner who is equally hardworking and committed to his or her particular profession, you will understand this person's behavior. In these circumstances, you will need to control your own stubbornness and be more unselfish too. At these times, it's fine for you to take second place!

- Always be understanding of other people's needs in their relationships, at home and at work.
- Make sure a relationship doesn't suffer irrevocably because of your long working hours. I've known too many divorced Taureans.
- Try to forget workplace conflicts when you're home in bed.
- Never be too reticent in lovingly showing your partner how much you *do* care—even if your workload has gone into overdrive.

Romance in the Workplace

You are one of the most highly sexed signs of the Zodiac, but you are also exceedingly practical on all counts. You're unlikely to risk creating problems by getting unnecessarily involved in a sexual relationship with someone in your workplace.

Because your ruling planet Venus *is* the Goddess of Love, you're strongly attracted to beauty in every shape and form. Love is extremely important to you, and sexual fulfillment is too. Even if uncontrollable passion burns intensely inside you, remember that sexual harassment cases reach the courts more frequently now. You're not usually likely to throw yourself impulsively at someone you fancy, but you *are* someone who is sensitive about being rebuffed.

The sensuous side of your personality goes hand in hand with a strongly developed romantic idealism. If you fall hook, line, and sinker for someone in the workplace, you will usually restrain yourself from rushing headlong into a sexual relationship. The *romantic* you prefers things to build slowly. You also want security and stability in your life, a cozy domestic scene with someone who is a permanent partner, and not in a committed relationship with somebody else.

Naturally, there *will* be relationships that start in the workplace. The wise Taurean will allow them to begin as friendships, developing step by step, and preferably not with someone who is your boss—and a married boss at that. No matter how determined you are to reach the top of your profession, sleeping with the boss is rarely the best way to achieve your long-term professional goals.

Without trying to underestimate your sexual wiles, I've always noticed that most of you are far too busy dealing with the day's workload to embark on a love affair which could create more problems than it may be worth.

You and Your Stress Factor

Because the neck is ruled by Taurus, when you are under stress, your neck will be particularly affected. Sometimes you may also find yourself prone to throat problems, especially if you have a job that involves a great deal of talking.

Taurus rules the neck and throat. Many of you suffer from stiffness and tight muscles in your necks and upper shoulders, perhaps because you are not sufficiently flexible. One negative by-product of modern technology is that people must sit stationary for hours in front of a computer.

Stress in the workplace is not uncommon. People work under more and more pressure, fearful of losing their jobs. Long hours and heavy workloads, perhaps combined with conflicting demands from superiors and worries about promotion, all combine to create anxiety in your life. You have the ability to survive a great deal of pressure, but even you will have your own breaking point when things appear to be out of control—perhaps because you have stubbornly insisted on taking on more and more work.

You tend to be extremely unbending in your attitude. When you extend this rigidity into your physical body, invariably you will end up with problems! Try not to become a couch potato in front of the television at the end of a hard workday. Move around more, and get your circulation going and your muscles loosened up.

Don't stubbornly refuse to admit when you're overtired. You fail to realize that a respite from your tasks will give you a perfect opportunity to recharge your batteries. You sometimes think that admitting to difficulty makes you appear weak. If you don't relax in order to reduce feelings of stress, then you *will* be weak. Learn how to reap the benefits of deep breathing, and of meditation, as discussed in my earlier book *Star Signs*. Remember that unwinding is not only good for your mind but also essential for the health of your body.

As a Taurus, you are likely to be interested in the arts—whether it be music, painting, or the theater. Not usually the most energetic or sports-loving sign, you may get all your physical exercise at a health club. You love to be pampered with saunas, steam rooms, and massages. A good aromatherapist will help you relax your tensed-up body and mind.

Taureans are reputed to have "green fingers," with great prowess at gardening. Even if you have very little space outside, you will enjoy growing plants and herbs around your house or apartment. Many of you also love food and are often great gourmet cooks. Creating haute cuisine menus could be a wonderfully therapeutic way for you to relax and release some of that stress!

With Venus, Goddess of Love, as your ruling planet, you're a true romantic at heart. You adore spending romantic evenings with a partner. An overworked Taurean friend was given a wonderful surprise by her husband, who took her to Paris on a long weekend, having arranged for her parents to look after the children while they were away. Even if you don't have someone to give you such delightful surprises, you can always give some to yourself. I'm sure that you deserve them!

Your Attitude toward Making Money

Your attitude toward money is, in many ways, determined by your attitude toward life itself. You enjoy watching things grow, sprouting up like seeds in the earth. You take your time to make things happen and are brilliant at planning your strategies. There is often an extremely materialistic side to your nature. Or perhaps it's simply that you become insecure if you feel you have not achieved enough.

Taurus is known as the builder of the Zodiac, and building up your financial security enables you to face the future with greater confidence. You would hate the thought of becoming older with insufficient funds to cover your needs. You would also dread the idea of becoming dependent on other people, even your closest family.

For you, money is power. It is also the lifeblood of business. Taurus is astrologically linked to the second house of your horoscope, which relates to your personal finances and to your earning potential. But watch out that money doesn't dominate your thoughts to the extent that nothing else is important. Sometimes there is a conflict between your material needs and your spiritual ones. Don't allow inner fears about your security to prevent you from feeling confident about your material prospects. Even if you're out of work unexpectedly, you will rise to the challenge of creating a new income for yourself.

You understand money more than most of us. You know the whole terminology of finances and budgeting, gross and net profits, tax returns, the right rates for the job, and ways to achieve greater financial freedom. If there is anything you *don't* understand, you are prepared to put in sufficient hours to make sure you do.

How to Improve Your Work Relationships

As a steadfast and unflappable Taurean with somewhat inflexible ways, it is always important to cultivate the ability to get on even better with your coworkers.

The following guide will show you the best way to relate to all the signs, whether they are those of your boss, your peer, or an employee:

Taurus with Aries Boss: Being both efficient and perfectly willing to take second place isn't necessarily enough for this go-getter boss! Try to be quicker off the mark with your thoughts and your actions.

Taurus with Aries Colleague: Your practical methods combined with the Ram's entrepreneurial skills can move mountains. You cannot afford to be a slow starter if you're both aiming for promotion; otherwise you will be left at the starting gate.

Taurus with Aries Employee: The enthusiasm and motivation of this employee will delight you. But you may have to ask him politely to do things a little less quickly in order to avoid mistakes.

Taurus with Taurus Boss: When you become the boss, you're entitled to be unyielding at times, but meanwhile always remember who is working for whom. Be more flexible and less stubborn!

Taurus with Taurus Colleague: You are both loyal, dependable, and amazingly patient. However, you will each need to be less rigid and set in your own particular routines if you want to be more successful.

Taurus with Taurus Employee: Don't give yourself a power complex just because you're in the boss's seat. Remember that this employee is happy to take orders but is as determined as you to make it to the top.

Taurus with Gemini Boss: Stay continually alert to keep up with this boss's razor-sharp mind and inventive thoughts and ideas. Being too inflexible and set in your routine will go against you.

Taurus with Gemini Colleague: Remember that this colleague's mind can work much more quickly than yours but isn't necessarily as thorough! You'll get on better if prepared to adapt more to each other's ways.

Taurus with Gemini Employee: This employee's live-wire methods may sometimes infuriate you. At times you may need to ask her tactfully to talk a whole lot less and concentrate a whole lot more.

Taurus with Cancer Boss: Don't let your obstinacy create problems with this boss. Cancer's moods fluctuate depending on the phases of the Moon, but remember that this sign is highly workmanlike too.

Taurus with Cancer Colleague: Both of you are pretty sensitive to atmosphere. Make sure you're not treading on each other's toes jobwise, or the air will become very frosty.

Taurus with Cancer Employee: This employee will be as loyal and dependable as you are—provided you treat him well. But a Moon Child's emotions are fragile. Never shout and rave even if you are in a justifiably bad mood!

Taurus with Leo Boss: Never become too power crazy and try to steal the limelight from your Leo boss. Carry out your duties diligently. Remember you also have the ability to be in charge one day.

Taurus with Leo Colleague: Here are two loyal and generous Fixed signs, set in their own ideas. Watch out you're not carrying some of Leo's responsibilities when your colleague is in a lazy mood.

Taurus with Leo Employee: This relationship will not run smoothly if you expect Leo to be as grounded and pragmatic as you. Organize your Leo employee well, explaining that she can't always be the star of the show!

Taurus with Virgo Boss: These two Earth signs share dedication, determination, and brilliant organizing skills. But your Virgo boss will still be highly critical if you don't achieve perfection in everything you do.

Taurus with Virgo Colleague: A superb working combination. You are both extremely disciplined, leaving nothing to chance. When you're coworkers on a project, success is guaranteed, but remember you could be equally hardworking competitors too.

Taurus with Virgo Employee: Be grateful that Virgo will always spot any mistakes you might make—not that a typical hardworking Taurus normally makes any errors! Virgo is always a discreet and disciplined employee.

Taurus with Libra Boss: Some Libran bosses may be indecisive at times, but you will benefit by watching how they get on well with almost everyone. You will learn plenty about tact and diplomacy at work too.

Taurus with Libra Colleague: Both signs are ruled by Venus, Goddess of Love, which means peace and harmony should prevail. However, you may both be slightly too laid-back for your own good, so take more initiatives.

Taurus with Libra Employee: It's just as well that you're extremely disciplined, because Libra isn't necessarily so. You may have to lay down a few orders from the start, but please try to do so diplomatically.

Taurus with Scorpio Boss: Don't ever create problems with *this* boss, or you'll soon be out the door. Remember that your opposite sign considers himself unconquerable—and intends to remain the boss!

Taurus with Scorpio Colleague: Both of you could be sufficiently manipulative to try to ease the other out! Never let your attention flag, or Scorpio might take credit for some of your work!

Taurus with Scorpio Employee: This employee won't enjoy life as an employee for very long. Don't try to pry out her inner secrets—Scorpio needs her private space. And keep your secrets to yourself if you can.

Taurus with Sagittarius Boss: The friendly Sagittarian approach may make you forget this is your boss. Sparks will soon fly if you try to undermine his authority by assuming *you* know best. Sagittarians are convinced *they* do.

Taurus with Sagittarius Colleague: It's great to have a Sagittarius on the same team. You'll be highly motivated by her self-confidence and positive approach, and can forge a good friendship too.

Taurus with Sagittarius Employee: Don't try to pin down this sign to a long-term contract. Understand that the Archer needs to feel inwardly free to give his best but will never intentionally let you down.

Taurus with Capricorn Boss: Now you've met someone even more hardworking, materialistic, and unyielding than you! This boss won't permit shirking on the job, so respect her views and defer to them too!

Taurus with Capricorn Colleague: Immovable force meets immovable force—this is a heavy combination! Working together makes for an unbeatable team, but when both parties are seeking promotion it will be tough competition.

Taurus with Capricorn Employee: You'll respect each other's working methods. A Capricorn employee is a workaholic who will never leave tasks unfinished, so always acknowledge and respect this.

Taurus with Aquarius Boss: This boss may be fairly unpredictable. Try to be more flexible and more amenable toward doing things in a slightly different way than you've been used to in the past.

Taurus with Aquarius Colleague: Learn to appreciate the Water Bearer's unique approach to each and every task, and allow Aquarius to recognize the practicality of *your* methods.

Taurus with Aquarius Employee: If the work you delegate is done professionally, don't be overly critical of this employee's working style. Accept that Aquarius is unconventional in almost *everything*.

Taurus with Pisces Boss: Pisces may not always appear to be the most business-oriented boss, but remember that the newspaper and media magnate Rupert Murdoch is a Piscean! Learn to accept the Piscean instinct and intuition.

Taurus with Pisces Colleague: You're the more practical one here. But Pisces has a lot to teach you about inspiration and idealism, so don't be too critical or uncaring about his feelings.

Taurus with Pisces Employee: It's fine to be firm and unyielding in your approach to work methods, but don't be too hard on this highly sensitive employee, who isn't always as structured as you.

Getting Longevity out of Your Career

Although you rarely panic when faced with a problem, the thought of being laid off may fill you with a paralyzing horror. It's not necessarily a case of injured pride or fears that perhaps your work was not up to standard. It's often difficult for you even to think of *quitting* a job, because your first thoughts would be your financial security—for today, tomorrow, and forevermore.

As one of the most down-to-earth and resourceful signs of the Zodiac, you recognize and accept that life in the global workplace has been changing very fast over the past years. Job security is no longer a given, and things are sure to continue in the same way as we approach the next millennium. Technology is the name of the game now, so if you haven't kept up with everything taking place, you may have reason to blame yourself for being out of a job in the future. Meanwhile, there is nothing to stop you—and everything to gain—from staying up-to-date with the latest advances.

Getting longevity out of one's career does not necessarily correlate with job performance. More and more companies are forced to cut back in staff—even staff as dependable and conscientious as you. This has become a crisis of our times. Being fired is not something to be ashamed of, but I have heard people describe it as somewhat like having to cope with a bereavement or being told they have a terminal disease.

Remember that you are one of the most resilient signs of the Zodiac, even in adversity! Keep your Taurean feet firmly on the ground, and refuse to lose sleep worrying about tomorrow! Always make sure that you sort out details related to any severance pay, health benefits, and pensions. If you come up against difficulties that even *your* skills can't unravel, it might be wise to consult a lawyer.

If you are laid off, never discount your considerable talents and abilities. Don't rush into taking the very first offer that comes your way. Learn as much as you can about anyone who offers you new employment. You don't want to find yourself in a new workplace that is going through a lot of cutbacks.

Don't forget the benefits of networking. You never know when someone might pass you some useful information related to a job that requires your qualifications. Don't bear grudges against your ex-employers—unless you truly have a good reason!

You're a hard worker, and your dedication to work will always pay off, regardless of your age. Remember the Rock of Gibraltar, still standing proudly after all these years. Why should *you* worry about getting older? Your resilience is unlikely to diminish, your resourcefulness likewise. Maybe you'll have a few more white hairs, but who cares about that! Your ability to work conscientiously and diligently, with or without supervision, will always be a part of your personality. Even if you don't build yourself an empire or aren't running your own business, you will always organize your affairs in such a way that you will be able to provide for your old age.

People continually change their careers these days, and some companies even prefer employees who have moved around. Try to be less resistant to the idea of changes in your life. Remember that your business and management skills will ensure that you get longevity out of your career for as long as you want, and no matter what your age.

TAURUS CAREER STRATEGIES—A CHECKLIST FOR EVERY AGE

- Always be conscientious and professional, but never become too complacent or too fixed in your attitude and ideas.
- Don't be backward about moving *forward* in this high-tech age!
- Take slow and sure steps up the business ladder without giving way to inner fears.
- Never become too materialistic especially if it means giving up a chosen goal.
- Integrate your creative talents and abilities with your organizational skills.
- Keep your Venusian sex appeal and sensuality under wraps at work.
- Remember that you truly are the builder of the Zodiac, and that your capabilities do not diminish as the years go by!

GEMINI IN THE WORKPLACE

May 21 ☆ June 20

If you were born between May 21 and June 20, you were born under the sign of Gemini, third sign of the Zodiac. You are a Masculine, Mutable, Positive, Air sign. Your planetary symbol is the Twins.

Ruled by Mercury, Winged Messenger of the Gods, and planet of communication, you are highly observant, intelligent, and often extremely intellectual. You are "the storyteller" of the Zodiac, able to communicate fluently on a wide variety of subjects.

Your restless mind sometimes leads you in too many directions at almost the same moment in time. Brilliant at creative ideas, you are not always as brilliant at following them through. Your strong communication skills are a major bonus but remember that organizational skills combined with the ability to bring projects to their successful completion are equally essential.

At times you give up on something too soon, perhaps fearing it might fail, even if deep down you know it will not. Learn to be as optimistic as your opposite sign, Sagittarius. Sagittarians always seem to realize their ambitions. To learn from *each* of the Zodiac signs, try wearing a different astrological hat for a day.

Take a typical workday in the Gemini life. You already have a heavy agenda, with two projects that need your full attention. A phone call comes through which involves a third project, but the time frame conflicts with your current involvements.

Playing Aries: You always love a challenge—it's like going into battle. But knowing how your enthusiasm for something can also disappear halfway through, you will have learned sometimes to say no!

Playing Taurus: Having to deal with three projects simultaneously would weigh heavily upon you. Stubbornly, you may still want to take on the new one but are too practical and responsible to do so.

Playing Yourself: The more the merrier is your motto. You seem to forget there are only twenty-four hours in a day—even for you! Immediately you risk problems by refusing to admit there is insufficient time for each project.

Playing Cancer: Your instinct combined with logic and practicality soon enables you to see trouble ahead! Besides, while you're prepared to work as hard as anyone else, you want some kind of domestic life too!

Playing Leo: Since Leo is never afraid to delegate, you listen to the details of what the third project involves, then put someone suitable in charge. However, you will probably want some of the praise at the end!

Playing Virgo: You are willing to work extremely long hours, requiring perfection at all stages of a task. If doing three things at once is unfeasible, you'd never take them on, for you'd be worrying too much.

Playing Libra: You're happy to work as a team on two or three projects, but rarely alone! This is one decision you'd make fairly quickly. Your diplomatic and tactful refusal would win you brownie points too.

Playing Scorpio: Even an invincible Scorpio would recognize that spreading one's talents too thinly could create an impossible situation. You'll never do anything against your intuition—no matter how hard you're pushed.

Playing Sagittarius: Optimistically, you might initially feel that you could tackle anything. But you know that you're not always great at coping with the nitty-gritty side of turning ideas into actions!

Playing Capricorn: You are far too professional to contemplate taking on something that could divert time away from current projects. Fixed in your ideas, you'd have no compunction about saying no—and meaning it.

Playing Aquarius: You automatically rebel at the very *idea* of being tied down by not two, but three projects! You hastily decline and detach yourself fast.

Playing Pisces: You worry that if you don't work on the third project, you'll let someone down. So you accept the assignment but soon realize you've taken on too much. (Pisces is rarely the most practical of souls.)

The Positive and Negative Qualities of a Gemini at Work

You're amazingly perceptive and receptive to what is going on in the global marketplace, and you are undeniably one of the most mentally active signs around. Your quality of Air enables you to communicate with skill; but since Gemini is also a Mutable sign, you are sometimes too inconstant with your thoughts and ideas.

Many of you can be pragmatic and methodical, but others are the "social butterflies of the Zodiac," unable to concentrate on anything for more than five minutes at a time. If you lack the spirit and fortitude to carry something through to the end, there may be a competitor nearby who is ready and willing to take over. Cultivate the ability and willingness to perform detailed tasks, even if it means following through on *someone else's* ideas.

Your go-with-the-flow flexibility is often admirable, but over-scheduling yourself because of disorganized planning will produce negative results. Keep a pocket diary or organizer up-to-date so you have a record of everything that is in your desk diary or your computer.

The positive Gemini appreciates the opportunity to achieve the benefits of increased productivity, not only through daily planning but also by prioritizing daily tasks. Applying the three *P*s—perception, preparation, and proficiency—to every single task you undertake will invest you with greater power in today's competitive workplace.

The negative Gemini assumes that being savvy and plugged in to what is happening around you is all you need to succeed. You forget that you're only one little player in a vast workplace, and that it's tough out there. A more down-to-earth and responsible approach to life is essential.

Because you are a dual sign, ruled by the Twins, it's almost as though your personality has two sides, constantly in conflict with each other. Are you truly surprised that people sometimes accuse you of having a split mind, of being Jekyll and Hyde?

Fitting in with other people is usually easy for you. You're a charismatic talker with as much charm as any Libran. But your positive qualities must include the ability to listen and concentrate when other people are talking to *you*. You thrive in a mentally stimulating atmosphere, but this is not always easily achieved. Be realistic and understand that sometimes you must *make* your work stimulate you. Don't alienate your superiors or coworkers by being detached. Stay totally in tune with your job duties and resolve to do them well.

No one is better at selling yourself than you, but the wise Gemini will refrain from having too many schemes in the pipeline at the same time. You need to be committed to doing high-caliber work carried out with a disciplined approach. You should be prepared to enhance your knowledge and your reputation while developing your career. Always make sure that you never become a jack-of-all-trades—who is a master of none!

Careers for Gemini

Gemini men and women are excellent salespeople; they are great in the public relations world and as glossy-magazine journalists. The fields of television, the movies, radio, advertising, and copywriting give you lots of scope for your Gemini skills. Anything in the political arena fascinates you, while working in the travel business lets you broaden your horizons—and perhaps see more of the world by becoming a flight attendant! Dealing with stocks and bonds may also be your forte, provided you keep your mind constantly alert! You often enjoy being a freelancer; it gives you the chance to move around.

Gemini is the sign of variety, and a wide variety of Gemini talents were born under your sign, including Walt Whitman, Marilyn Mon-

roe, Anne Frank, Frank Lloyd Wright, Henry Kissinger, Clint East-
wood, Morgan Freeman, Marvin Hamlisch, Steffi Graf, George Bush,
Johnny Depp, Bob Dylan, Joan Rivers, Prince, Dr. Ruth Westheimer,
Isabella Rossellini, Joan Collins, and Naomi Campbell.

Your Attitude toward Work

Naturally, your rising sign, together with all the other factors of your
personal horoscope, will also influence your attitude toward work.

You need to be involved in work that stimulates your mind, but
you don't always possess the necessary stamina to climb high enough
up the success ladder. In most cases, when you *are* determined to
achieve something, nothing will deter you from achieving your goal.

Unfortunately, your attitude toward work often includes the tendency to talk too much about your intentions, rather than getting
down to the work itself.

Your boredom threshold is possibly the lowest in the Zodiac, with
Aries and Sagittarius following close behind you. You will appreciate
the flexibility of choosing your own working hours, but not every
Gemini has the privilege of working for themselves, nor the opportunity to be a successful freelancer. You excel at networking, which
enables you to meet new people and to exchange information and
ideas. If you become as good at note taking as you are at networking,
you will be extremely efficient. Unfortunately, your lack of concentration often means that you miss out on important issues.

Keep up with the latest technology, and use your innate curiosity to
learn how it works, not simply to debate its usefulness! Always try to
combine technical expertise with sound strategic ability and understanding of *all* the business functions that relate to your field.

A smart attitude toward work must include taking responsibility
with ease, dealing with challenging objectives, and making a measur-
able contribution to the success of your particular company or business. In return you will gain job satisfaction and the opportunity to
become more successful. It's important for you to recognize and accept
your own particular strengths and weaknesses. You can't afford to
depend on daily excitement to keep your adrenaline flowing.

Most of you enjoy a busy workplace, so an open floor plan will
probably delight you. This is not always the best environment for

someone who communicates and interacts with others almost too easily. You will work more conscientiously if you are alone at times.

Your communication skills are of prime importance in your attitude toward work, as is your ability to be an enthusiastic team player. Leadership, planning, and organizational skills are also essential, plus an analytical mind and the determination to focus on the right targets.

Many times you busy yourself with trivial and time-wasting activities. This means that important tasks may be left waiting for your attention. Don't risk losing your job by being careless and inconsistent with your work.

Cultivate a more positive attitude, and always give your best. It's not enough to brilliantly *talk* your way into a job; you must be equally committed to carrying out the tasks your work demands. When you're truly involved in your chosen profession, no one will have reasons to accuse you of devoting insufficient time to the tasks at hand.

TIPS FOR A HEALTHY WORK ATTITUDE

- Always be organized, efficient, and a good timekeeper.
- Keep up-to-date in your field, but don't overload yourself with trivia.
- Perfect your skills through determined and conscientious practice.

Aiming for Promotion

First, identify your goals; second, promise not to shortchange yourself by giving up halfway. Although the workplace is more competitive than ever, it never was necessarily easy to achieve one's ultimate objective. What *has* changed is that increasing numbers of people are all running after the same job. Many of them are casualties of corporate downsizing. Concentrate not only on keeping your particular talents and abilities up to scratch, but also on doing whatever it takes to be better than anyone else. Make yourself visible to those at the highest levels by maintaining a high standard of work. Learn to play a key strategic role by combining your strong interpersonal and communication skills with the drive to see projects through.

Promoting yourself is easy if you're a typical Gemini. You are renowned not only as "the master of the fast line" but also as a salesperson extraordinaire. On the surface, you never seem to lack self-confidence, although inwardly you may go into total panic at the very thought of being overlooked for a prized job advancement.

Establishing a compatible work relationship with the powers that be comes easily to you, provided you respect their intellectual qualities! It's more difficult for you to relate to anyone whose intellectual capacities you feel are less than yours, even if that person is your boss. Sometimes there is no way around this situation, other than becoming even more determined to be a boss yourself!

When aiming for promotion, your networking skills are a great bonus. One additional way to increase your prestige is to become a member of societies and associations related to your particular profession. The information you will gain from hearing other people talk about their work could be invaluable. Be careful not to give away too many insider tips yourself—especially not to contenders for the same promotion! Never allow your networking skills to take over to such an extent that you begin to neglect your job, for this would become self-defeating.

Many of you appear to find it difficult to stick to a job once it becomes routine. Remember that most jobs become repetitious in one way or another, so keep in mind it will always be mentally stimulating to focus on a long-range goal.

When aiming for a specific promotion, always make sure you possess the necessary intellectual qualifications for the job, including an excellent understanding of what the market needs today. You will have no difficulty in convincing a future boss that you can be a team player, nor that you have an abundance of credibility and drive, plus mental toughness and savvy negotiating skills.

Always make sure that the promotion you're aiming for is what you really want—something that will give you immense job satisfaction while constantly stimulating your agile Gemini mind.

TIPS FOR PROMOTION SEEKERS

- Make sure you're always target-oriented, structured in your work approach, and disciplined.

- Combine your intellectual skills and strategic abilities with a good knowledge of the latest information technology.
- Display your leadership potential along with your ability and willingness to perform detailed tasks.

How to Cope with Being Passed Over for Promotion

You're unlikely to collapse in a heap if you do fail to be promoted—once in a while, that is! Your alert and idealistic mind will always point you in the direction of interesting new possibilities.

However, sometimes your mind too easily glosses over the nitty-gritty side of life. You don't want to get too close to your feelings, preferring to stay with your thoughts. If, deep down, you feel devastated because you lost out to a coworker on a desired promotion, learn to be honest about it.

Make sure that you possess the maturity and credibility to maintain work relationships at all levels and that your commercial acumen is balanced with an absolute commitment to providing the best possible service in your field. If your lack of concentration has previously created problems, start to focus more sharply on one endeavor at a time. Promotion time will come along again, and you don't want to be left out of the race.

Ambition—or the Lack of It

You like to feel as free as your element of Air. Born under the sign of the Twins, you possess a duality in your persona, and because Gemini is a Mutable sign, there is an inconstancy within your makeup, making it difficult for you to be pinned down.

When you *are* ambitious, you will be as focused on your goal as any other star sign. But ambition isn't necessarily a major issue for you. You're delighted to prove that intellectually you are more than capable of reaching the top of your chosen profession. If this involves a long and circuitous route, some of you may prefer to stop by the wayside and take a different path—and a different profession too!

Remember that Gemini is the sign of communication and that it rules the mind. *Everything* begins in your mind, so that where you direct your thoughts is extremely important. You are able to intellectualize the consequence of turning your thoughts into actions. You must also carry out the necessary actions. If you set your sights on the top, you must also become more centered in your thoughts and more decisive in your actions.

Your chosen direction will come from your own particular needs and desires. You may be perfectly happy working in your own way without a major ambition. But more than a few of my Gemini clients, upon reaching a certain stage in their lives, have confessed that they wished they had been more focused on their career potential earlier on.

To sustain an ambition, it's not always possible to retain your "free as air" persona. Sometimes you will have to deal with tasks that fail to stimulate your mind. Always remember, *you* are in charge of your career—and therefore must make the final decision on just how ambitious you intend to be.

Ambition—and Your Love Life

Flirtatious, fickle, and fun loving you may be, but rarely will you allow any ambitions in the workplace to conflict with your love life, or vice versa! While hardly one of the most structured and organized of star signs at most times, you are usually highly adept at compartmentalizing these two sides of your life.

From my association with Gemini friends and clients, I've learned never to try and pin you down to a social arrangement when you're totally involved in a creative project that requires lots of work. This is an admirable trait. Anyone with whom you are involved emotionally will need to understand that because you were born under the sign of the Twins, it is rather like having *two* people for the price of one! What you desire is a partner who is compatible both mentally and physically; someone who will not complain if you decide you're in a working mood or if you're *not* the most ambitious of folk. Such a partner will need also to accept that you can be as unpredictable as any Aquarius, and that sometimes you are as much of a workaholic as any Capricorn.

If you're involved with another Gemini, it will be easier for you to understand each other. If you are with another sign, try to make sure that your brilliant powers of communication enable you to explain *why* you are the way you are! Always be mindful of your partner's needs too.

TIPS FOR COMBINING WORK AND LOVE

- Try to make your work schedules compatible with your love life!
- Try to discuss your ambitions with your partner. It will be good to get his or her feedback.
- Never accuse your partner or coworkers of being too flirtatious—when you're the master of this game!
- Always try to balance your working life with your private life.

Romance in the Workplace

Inveterate flirts, most Gemini men and women excel at producing the perfect compliment at the perfect time. You are bright, witty, and magnetically captivating, but be warned that even *word-of-mouth* affection can sometimes be misconstrued as sexual harassment today. The pitfalls that surround a romance in the workplace are usually greater than expected.

It's rarely sex alone that would propel you into a love affair with someone at work. First and foremost, you thrive on the stimulation of being with a like-minded person. Mind and body must go hand in hand for you. Not outwardly the most romantic of star signs, you can be highly disciplined at hiding your deepest feelings.

Naturally, when you are working closely with someone whom you find immensely interesting and sexually attractive, it may be hard to ignore your feelings. But you're unlikely to "sleep your way" to the top, even if you have extremely high career goals and a superior who implies with subtle undertones that he or she could help you! You would also fearlessly report a boss or coworker who continually propositioned you with sexual advances.

One additional problem related to a romantic liaison in the work-place is "what do you do when it ends?" You are not the most "commitment oriented" of signs, and while a flirtatious dalliance with a coworker may seem lighthearted to you, it may appear differently to the other person involved. Never play around with anyone's feelings, for this is unlikely to work out well for either party in the end. You may be a brilliant strategist at talking your way out of most potentially compromising situations, but a sexual harassment case is another matter entirely.

Naturally, there will be relationships that not only start in the workplace but also continue successfully as well. It would not necessarily be difficult for you to work in the same environment as a lover. You have the ability not only to intellectualize the consequence of any of your actions but also to be totally controlled. However, there is always the issue of being under the scrutiny of the rest of the workforce. Gossip is rife in working environments; it's one way for everyone to relax over a coffee break or lunch. Gossip can be especially dangerous if you are aiming for a raise or promotion in a company that decries the merest hint of a romance between employees.

You and Your Stress Factor

The areas of the body that relate to Gemini are the hands, the nervous system (including the brain) and the power of speech. I've rarely met a Gemini who doesn't wave his or her hands about to emphasize an issue, nor have I met one with an inactive mind or the inability to converse on a wide variety of subjects.

Your agile mind thrives on mental activity, but at times you suffer from the inability to rest and relax sufficiently. Learn to give yourself more "quality time." It will enable you to recharge your mental abilities, making you even more successful. You will also benefit from meditation and from getting in touch with the inner you, as described in one of my earlier books, *Star Signs*.

A small amount of stress is perfectly normal, for it can put you on your toes when dealing with urgent and important work issues. Stress is also the normal way in which everyone reacts to occurrences that seem in some way threatening, perhaps the fear of being unable to handle certain aspects of one's job, or of failing to obtain a hoped-for raise or promotion. But too much stress will wreak havoc not only with your emotional well-being, but also with your physical body.

When you are under stress, your inability to relax will increase. Your concentration will slip lower than normal, and you may have problems with insomnia. You might suffer with allergies, headaches, and skin conditions.

Examine and analyze your work situation. Remember that Gemini rules the mind, and that your mind is the most powerful tool in your possession. Try to focus it on the benefits of proper relaxation. When you are under stress, remember to breathe deeply and to allow your body to relax by becoming limp. Always try to take sufficient breaks during your workday. Calling in for a club sandwich at lunchtime, when surrounded by a pile of papers on your desk, is *not* the correct way to take a break! Breathing in your fill of sufficient fresh air *is!*

It is virtually impossible to achieve a stress-free working atmosphere. Sometimes you will have to cope with a boss who expects too much of you, or a coworker who lets you down. Sometimes stress will be brought on by your own Gemini tendency to chat too much, or to allow your train of thought to be interrupted far too easily. Try to retain enthusiasm for your job, for lethargy and boredom can also lead to stress.

Since variety is the spice of life to Gemini, I'm sure that your life outside work is interesting. You certainly make every attempt to ensure you're never ever bored!

You're a brilliant host or hostess, a delightful dinner companion, and many times an inveterate movie buff. Almost every Gemini I know books tickets for a new play almost as soon as it has opened. You appreciate a good supply of intellectually interesting reading material, together with the latest gossipy magazines and keeping up-to-date with what is on the Internet.

Because you are an incorrigible flirt, the single Gemini may enjoy frequenting singles' bars and clubs. Your love of communication could also inspire you to join a book club. Travel is often one of your greatest enjoyments, whether you take short trips or long. You may even strive to find the time to learn a foreign language.

Your personality can be like Peter Pan's—you don't always want to grow up. This means that games of every kind delight you. You're not always excessively energetic, although participating in sports, especially in the open air, would also help you to throw off any work-induced stress more easily.

Your Attitude toward Making Money

Even when you're totally focused on the idea of making money, you don't always have the right attitude! Sure, you are brilliant at creating plans and projects—often the more the merrier! But you don't necessarily have the patience and determination to invest enough time to make them successful.

Many Gemini people appear less concerned with making lots of money than in achieving their goals in a more idealistic way. If you enjoy *spending* (more than you can realistically afford), you are being less than honest if you say that the money is not important! You seem to worry when you don't have it, so why not devote more time and attention toward making sure you don't run short!

You are unlikely to take a job on a purely moneymaking basis, unless you're in a situation where it is imperative to do so. Sometimes you find it much easier to make money by working for yourself or on a freelance basis. This will give you more of a challenge and less of an office routine. I have a Gemini freelance friend who likes to commence her paperwork at 6 A.M., when the phones are not ringing off the hook. This early start enables her to take a break later in the day. It also means she is not committed to working set office hours.

Your attitude is generally more lackadaisical than hardheaded. This is fine if you are financially secure through avenues other than your work. If you're battling against the harsh realities of today's workplace, you cannot afford to assume that money doesn't matter. Never take too superficial a view of material issues, especially when they personally affect you.

You are alert, intelligent, clever, and, when you want to be, calculating too! Make sure your moneymaking attitude allows you to have the means to enjoy a life as varied as possible, for then it will be the *right* attitude for you!

How to Improve Your Work Relationships

Your Gemini personality is brimming over with vitality and versatility. You are one of the most gregarious signs of the Zodiac, and you have little difficulty in communicating with your coworkers. Sometimes you're more likely to communicate too much!

The following guide will show you the best way to relate to all the signs, whether they are those of your boss, your peer, or an employee:

Gemini with Aries Boss: This boss does not appreciate someone who fritters away the time. Prove that you can carry out tasks speedily and efficiently if you want to continue working for Aries.

Gemini with Aries Colleague: You communicate extremely well with each other on most levels. If the two of you are competing for a promotion, plan your strategy carefully. Aries loves a battle and always plays to win!

Gemini with Aries Employee: Don't let your concentration and devotion to duty slip for a second. This employee is impatient to get to the top and will always be ready, willing, *and* able to step into your shoes.

Gemini with Taurus Boss: Since Taurus is always working hard in a highly organized way, carry out your tasks diligently and with the minimum of chat. Never let your social life get in the way of work!

Gemini with Taurus Colleague: Try to emulate some of this colleague's disciplined working habits. You make a good team—your innovative ideas combined with Taurus's down-to-earth approach.

Gemini with Taurus Employee: Don't hand over *all* your responsibilities simply because you know everything will be done well. Appreciate the pleasure of having someone to establish order in your life!

Gemini with Gemini Boss: Life will never be dull with your Gemini boss. But although it may seem like you're best friends, always remember that your boss *is* still your boss. Prove you can concentrate and take orders.

Gemini with Gemini Colleague: Talk, talk, talk. It's great discussing all those wonderful ideas, but when does the work get done? The team spirit is fine, but dealing with the nitty-gritty tasks could take forever.

Gemini with Gemini Employee: Even if you don't particularly like giving orders, you can't escape this if you're the boss! Always be prepared to double-check things if your employee is sometimes as scatterbrained as you!

Gemini with Cancer Boss: Remember that Cancerians can be moody, especially if they feel let down in any way. Resolve to show that *even* a restless Gemini can carry out orders in a disciplined manner.

Gemini with Cancer Colleague: You use your mind to rationalize issues, while Cancer prefers to rely on instinct and intuition. This will be a good combination provided you respect each other's work ethics.

Gemini with Cancer Employee: With such a sensitive employee, make sure you're not too flippant with any of your remarks! Be happy that your work will invariably be ready on time, for Cancer can be quite a workaholic too.

Gemini with Leo Boss: Remember that Leo thrives on being the boss but will be high-handed and domineering only if your work is not up to standard. Leo will always give praise when it's due.

Gemini with Leo Colleague: Leo considers that being at the top is the only place to be. You may find you are bossed around—especially if you fritter away too many hours on unimportant chitchat.

Gemini with Leo Employee: Leo doesn't really like to be a mere employee but will faithfully carry out your orders if you've earned his respect. So always try to give the right impression.

Gemini with Virgo Boss: You're working for the critic and analyst of the Zodiac. Don't make too many careless mistakes, or you may be out of a job. "The sign of service" expects good service from you too.

Gemini with Virgo Colleague: Both of you are ruled by Mercury, so mental communication will be easy. Wise up to Virgo's disciplined approach to everything, and try to be more businesslike yourself.

Gemini with Virgo Employee: You've lucked out here! This employee will carry out every task in the most perfect way. Don't spoil the relationship by overloading him, for even a dutiful Virgo could get fed up.

Gemini with Libra Boss: The Libran boss may not be a fast decision maker but will skillfully appraise your talents to make sure you can work well together. Don't take advantage of Libra's good humor; there is a calculating side too!

Gemini with Libra Colleague: Libra is the sign of partnership, so there should be lots of team spirit here. Because you are both ruled by Air, you can communicate brilliantly. Libra helps to rationalize your more unrealistic ideas.

Gemini with Libra Employee: Each of you may sometimes be too slaphappy in your working methods. No matter how much you enjoy chatting and discussing each other's lives, always remember that you are the boss here!

Gemini with Scorpio Boss: A Scorpio boss finds it hard to forgive or forget mistakes. This is all the more reason for you to become a better timekeeper and to be more conscientious in your approach to work.

Gemini with Scorpio Colleague: Never trespass in Scorpio's space! This colleague is probably one of the most private people you've ever known. If you're rivals for a promotion, watch out; Scorpio is a powerful competitor!

Gemini with Scorpio Employee: You won't have any secrets left if a Scorpio works for you. This employee needs to admire your working methods, for then your work will be carried out in an insightful and orderly way.

Gemini with Sagittarius Boss: Sagittarius bosses invariably think they know all the answers—even if they don't! You need to be tactful if you want this arrangement to run smoothly.

Gemini with Sagittarius Colleague: Two opposite signs of the Zodiac, each ready to discuss a zillion and one ideas you're convinced will make you rich. But talk is cheap! Organize yourselves better.

Gemini with Sagittarius Employee: If you're a *truly* disciplined boss, you'll be capable of giving orders to this employee. If the two of you end up chatting like friends for hours, nothing will get done.

Gemini with Capricorn Boss: Unless you're prepared to show that you can work long hours with few breaks, this won't be a good combination! Capricorn demands total devotion to tasks, so your social life may need to take a backseat.

Gemini with Capricorn Colleague: You're the ideas person, while Capricorn is the pragmatist with feet set firmly on the ground. You will make a great team if you're also prepared to work as hard as the Mountain Goat.

Gemini with Capricorn Employee: This employee will be totally focused on the long-term goal, so watch out! If you're not behaving as a boss *should*, someone else could be taking your job before long.

Gemini with Aquarius Boss: This is sure to be an unconventional and unorthodox boss, but a fairly stubborn one too. Don't try to get away with half-finished tasks by coming up with a lame excuse. It won't work!

Gemini with Aquarius Colleague: You should have much in common with this Air-ruled colleague. Communication will flow easily between you, but be sure to stop talking long enough to get the work done!

Gemini with Aquarius Employee: Neither of you are great at following a routine. It is important to remember that you need to be firm with an unpredictable Aquarian, especially when there are deadlines to meet.

Gemini with Pisces Boss: Remember those two fish swimming in opposite directions, and be prepared for a boss whose moods can fluctuate in a similar way! Pisces may appear to be soft and pliable, but never dare to turn in shoddy work!

Gemini with Pisces Colleague: Pisces is the romantic idealist of the Zodiac and tends to see the world through rose-tinted glasses. In any work relationship, remember that Pisces is less practical than you.

Gemini with Pisces Employee: A Pisces employee always tries to do his best but sometimes seems to drift along too slowly. Both of you need to streamline your working methods.

Getting Longevity out of Your Career

Some leading head hunters have said that a long service record with one employer could become a handicap to top executives who are trying to make a career move, and that a diverse résumé is more important these days. If you're a typical Gemini, this statement must sound like music to your ears! However, it doesn't imply that you should be moving on every few months, but rather that after perhaps five years in the same job, your motivation may have waned and your performance may decline.

In today's highly competitive workplace you cannot afford to show either a loss of motivation or a decline in performance, or you will be run out of your job before you've even had time to settle in.

I recently read that the most popular phrase used by companies for terminating an employee is *downsizing*. It's a convenient way for a boss to explain that there is no longer room for you. Whatever it's called, getting laid off is no joke.

Sometimes your active Gemini mind finds it hard to comprehend that you're out of a job. Once the initial shock has worn off, you will usually start immediately to network among friends and contacts, putting out feelers for something new. Since you are brilliant at networking, it is sure to pay off before long.

Being laid off today doesn't have to be seen as a disgrace; it's simply a fact of life. However, if problems with your work performance have been a major factor in your loss of one job after another, you must analyze the situation carefully. It's pretty obvious that you must be doing *something* wrong, and wise to do some soul-searching as to why your performance has been consistently bad.

Your restless Gemini mind is always searching for new pastures, but getting axed is rarely the best way to achieve this. No matter what some of the head hunters say, or how you phrase your terminology, holding too many jobs over a very short period of time could raise a few eyebrows and prompt some unwelcome questions.

Because technology has advanced to such an extent that human skills and abilities are not required as much as they used to be, it's always wise to ensure that your technical know-how is up to scratch and that the information highway holds no hidden roadblocks for you.

You possess an amazing ability to bounce back to life after any setbacks, and to move on to bigger and better things, but always make sure you have sufficient funds put aside to get you through till the next interesting job comes along.

If you've been dismissed unfairly from a job, it is best to discuss the situation with an employment lawyer. It's imperative to know your rights, and to make sure that you exercise them! Don't neglect letters of reference, and fighting for a fair amount of severance pay.

You will never lose your flair for exploiting your talents when it comes down to job-hunting techniques, so don't panic if suddenly your future does seem unsure. I've known more freelance men and women born under Gemini than under any other sign.

Since you're the original Peter Pan of the Zodiac, you never seem to get old! Your brilliantly active and original Gemini mind keeps you youthful in thoughts *and* actions throughout your life. You're someone who will enjoy going back to school to take up new interests that could even lead you into new careers!

Capitalize on your unique talents and abilities. You will always have the power within you to create a working arrangement that is just right for you.

GEMINI CAREER STRATEGIES—A CHECKLIST FOR EVERY AGE

- Resolve to become more structured and organized in everything you undertake.
- Try not to leave projects unfinished just because something more interesting comes your way!
- Always keep thoroughly up-to-date with the latest information technology.
- You have a great gift for talking, but listening is beneficial too!
- Be idealistic by all means, but make sure you are also down-to-earth.
- Remember that your restless mind seeks constant stimulation, and that you will thrive on a busy working life.
- Don't scatter your energies in too many directions. You will benefit from the challenge of a long-term professional goal.

CANCER IN THE WORKPLACE

June 21 ☆ July 21

If you were born between June 21 and July 21, you were born under the sign of Cancer, fourth sign of the Zodiac. You are a Feminine, Cardinal, Negative, Water sign. Your planetary symbol is the Crab.

Ruled by the Moon, you experience mood swings that relate to the actual phases of the Moon. It's not surprising that, considering the Moon's effect on the ocean tides, it also greatly influences *you* in your emotions, instincts, and habits.

Sensitive, sympathetic, and self-protective, when you are unhappy you prefer to avoid reality by escaping into your own little world. But unlike the crab, who can retreat into its shell, you don't have the luxury of giving in to your moods because of today's continually restructuring job market.

Navigating the ups and downs of your career means plugging in to a whole lot more than the phases of the Moon.

You can learn something from your opposite sign, Capricorn, sign of prestige and professional standing in the world, as well as from every other sign in the Zodiac. So you might like to wear a different astrological hat once in a while.

Take a busy day in the Cancer life. You're supposed to be at work early but have had an emotionally draining lovers' tiff the night before. You'd much rather pull the sheets over your head and go back to sleep than deal with work problems.

Playing Aries: Life is too short for you to dwell on your personal problems. Besides, there is work to be done! Even though you're tired, you probably panic more about getting in on time than on letting last night's argument play upon your mind.

Playing Taurus: You'd never let anyone down at work by giving free rein to your emotions, even if badly hurt by a loved one's attitude. You stubbornly refuse to take any personal calls during the day— even if your lover calls to apologize!

Playing Gemini: You have no time for any instant replays in your mind, no matter how you may feel deep down. Inevitably you will have a wide variety of tasks on which to focus your undivided attention.

Playing Yourself: When you arrive at work, it will be obvious to *everyone* that you are in one of your Cancerian moods. Remember that today's workplace is a jungle, and there could be a less moody person after your job!

Playing Leo: You have far too much pride to allow any emotional dramas to influence your day at work. But you might relay last night's events to a few of your coworkers, so they could admire you for the way you're coping now!

Playing Virgo: Because Virgo is so conscientious, you feel your first duty is to your employers and coworkers. That doesn't mean it will be easy for you to refrain from worrying about your relationship with your lover.

Playing Libra: Being with other people helps you put a lovers' tiff at the back of your mind. Since Libra knows how to attain "peace and harmony," you probably sorted out last night's problem even before you went to sleep!

Playing Scorpio: You face the day with renewed vigor and vitality, even if you *didn't* sleep well! Because you're such a private person, you'd never discuss any personal emotional upsets with anyone at work.

Playing Sagittarius: Your natural optimism and sense of humor enable you to rise above the problems of the night before, and even to laugh about them. This also helps you enjoy whatever the day has in store.

Playing Capricorn: Your prestige and standing in the workplace are too important to risk by wallowing in emotional misery, no matter how you feel. You dedicate yourself to the tasks in front of you.

Playing Aquarius: You are able to detach yourself from your emotional feelings with ease and apply yourself to whatever else the new day brings. There is no way you'd let anyone know you felt miserable inside.

Playing Pisces: It's an effort for you not to dissolve into tears of sorrow throughout the day. Since you are brilliant at empathizing with others, why not emulate your superiors and coworkers and get on with your work!

The Positive and Negative Qualities of a Cancer at Work

At times, you are as ambitious and determined as your opposite sign, Capricorn, especially when you're working toward providing greater domestic security for yourself and your loved ones. As a Water sign, you are empowered to listen to and follow your instincts and intuitions, which will heighten your creative abilities.

Never allow yourself to become weakened by your emotions, nor to become too melancholy when things get you down. In today's "downsized" workplace, you cannot afford to give way to feelings of anxiety and depression, confusion, consternation, or panic; nor can you keep creeping into your Cancerian shell to avoid facing someone or something that is problematic. Try to become less closed off and more trusting of your ability to overcome difficulties. Learn to control your fluctuating moods.

The positive Cancerian is extremely work centered. You know your job duties, and you always perform them well. You also possess the determination to perfect your skills with a great deal of conscientious practice. You become conversant with your strengths and your weaknesses. If you are convinced that the New Moon makes you feel more energized, whereas a Full Moon seems to make you more depressed, try to plan your work schedule accordingly. This will, of course, be easier if you're the boss rather than an employee!

The positive Cancerian develops a clear understanding of new technologies in addition to perfecting sound business acumen, together with first-class communication skills. You have a sturdy work ethic and the necessary temperament to recognize and respond to the fast-changing needs of the modern workplace.

The negative Cancerian refuses to learn *how* to handle any negative feelings. When you feel depressed, inadequate, or frustrated in any way, you back away or run in ever-widening circles around whatever is bothering you. Because you are such an instinctive and intuitive sign, it *is* hard for you to ignore your feelings. But don't allow them to create situations whereby you become unproductive in your work.

The wise Cancerian will try always to be outgoing, positive, enthusiastic, and wholly professional, with the personal qualities and drive necessary to rise to any challenge. You will maintain a strong record of practical achievements, and excellent interpersonal and leadership skills.

Today's workforce thrives on people who can carry out high-profile roles and perform assertively and energetically in words and actions—all of which you can do with ease. It has little time for those who carry too much emotional baggage, so make sure you keep yours lightweight!

Careers for Cancer

Cancerians are often drawn to caretaking and service occupations. Medicine (as doctors and nurses), hotel management, teaching, social and community work, personnel, catering, childcare, museum curating, writing cookbooks, and real estate brokering are all good fields for you. Your sensitivity and powerful emotions also lead you to the world of the arts, such as painting, acting, and music. I have also known Cancerians who are brilliant at banking and dealing with antiques.

Since Cancer *is* such a caring sign, it's almost no surprise that the Dalai Lama and Elisabeth Kübler-Ross are Cancerians, and so was Princess Diana. Other famous Cancerians include Hermann Hesse, Marcel Proust, Amedeo Modigliani, Ernest Hemingway, Estée Lauder, Carly Simon, Bill Cosby, Tom Cruise, Harrison Ford, Tom Hanks, Robin Williams, Anjelica Huston, Ringo Starr, Carl Lewis, and Arthur Ashe.

Your Attitude toward Work

Naturally, your rising sign, together with all the other factors of your own particular horoscope, will also influence your attitude toward work.

You will always possess the necessary imagination and creativity to succeed in your chosen profession. You will also do your best work when you have found your perfect comfort zone, because you are extremely sensitive to your environment. However, this sometimes means you linger too long in a certain job, having grown so accustomed to the space that you fear the idea of what might await you elsewhere.

Your attitude toward work is highly influenced by your attitude toward your life as a whole. As the most domesticated sign of the Zodiac, and one who thrives on a contented family life, you are also among the most ambitious when it comes to your work.

One of my close Cancerian friends is a brilliant television anchorman, and I've worked with him several times on his programs. Cancer is one of the most caring signs in the Zodiac, and Clive Pearse really cares about his guests. Most Cancerians have a solicitous and protective attitude toward their work. It's your baby, and you can be fairly jealous and possessive about it too!

Losing yourself completely in your job is fine, perhaps even at times a necessity, but don't create a self-imposed prison by cutting off everything else. Don't let your work become your surrogate family. Whether you're married, have a live-in partner, or reside on your own, you need to enjoy yourself in your domestic surroundings too.

Your instinct and intuition are a great advantage in your attitude toward work, for they allow you to survey the scene and to plot your moves accordingly. Even if you feel ultrasensitive or insecure about your particular work in these unstable times, it is important for you to negotiate with confidence and to be your own public relations firm. Believe in the value of your product—which is YOU—otherwise it will be difficult for other people to believe sufficiently in you. Your value lies not only in your particular talents and abilities but also in your attitude toward yourself and your work.

The late David Price, who was the producer of my very first radio program, rose to the heights of the British Broadcasting Corporation in an extremely important corporate role. *His* Cancerian attitude toward work always included having time for anyone who needed a word of advice, which was appreciated by everyone.

The importance of feeling "at home" in your particular ambience is what counts in the end for many of you. I read that Cancerian actress Meryl Streep prefers to live far away from her working environment with her husband and children. For Streep, her domestic life is just as important as her commitment to her work.

You need to be flexible to survive in the workplace of today. You must be as adept at being a self-starter as fitting into a team, but teamwork *is* becoming increasingly more important. Sometimes you may not particularly like the members of your team, but in today's tough business world, you'd be wise to make every effort to relate to them with good grace.

TIPS FOR A HEALTHY WORK ATTITUDE

- Try to be more flexible to innovation and change.
- Take a positive approach to everything, leaving any "negative" moods behind!
- Always leave a stellar track record, and be a strategic leader with long-term credibility.

Aiming for Promotion

Your Cancerian personality doesn't always make you appear very ambitious to others. When you're emotionally happy in a position, you fear the prospect of finding yourself in a different and less comfortable ambience.

Don't become so involved with your emotions that you lose sight of your long-term goals, especially if they can bring you greater security and stability. I have known Cancerian clients who failed to pluck up sufficient courage to ask for a well-deserved promotion or raise; but then they became bitter because they considered they had been unfairly overlooked.

Today's global workplace is highly competitive. If you don't aim decisively at what you want, there will be many people coming up behind you who will! Don't become so self-protective that the fear of a turndown takes precedence over your aims. Outwit your opponents by being more skillful than they could ever be. You can become a real star if you combine your instincts and intuition with your excellent memory and positive approach toward work.

Be assertive in your behavior, stand up for your rights, and express your feelings in a direct way. Become more of a self-starter—it's well within your power! Promotions don't necessarily just *happen,* not these days anyway. Don't remain too low on the ladder of success when you're ready to set your sights on one of the top rungs.

When you are aiming for promotion, avoid any signs of overly emotional, vulnerable, or moody behavior, and don't demonstrate your Cancerian inclination to self-pity if you find you've been overlooked for a chosen position.

Remember that there are many facets to your performance review. Your professionalism and your accomplishments, together with *all* your strengths and weaknesses, will be considered, as will your ability to empathize with others and successfully form part of a team. More and more often in today's workplace, your performance will be judged not only on your individual success but also on your success and ability to collaborate within the framework of a particular team.

As a Cardinal sign, you have the ability to be extremely enterprising and determined. Because your element is Water, you tend to let things flow by without sufficient direction. When aiming for promotion, you cannot succeed *without* direction; that direction must take you onward and upward. With the Moon as your ruler, you have more honed instincts than the rest of us; make sure you use them fully so you can achieve your chosen goals. The sentimental side of your personality makes it difficult for you to let go of the old ways of doing things. But never be too reticent in learning everything you possibly can about all the new technology that is flooding the marketplace.

TIPS FOR PROMOTION SEEKERS

- Resolve to develop more of a high-profile image—and *never* scuttle sideways into your shell!
- Develop your interpersonal skills and judgment, but make sure you have a proven track record in your job performance too.

- Be a master of strategy, through your instincts and intuition, and you will acquire an even stronger entrepreneurial flair.

How to Cope with Being Passed Over for Promotion

You're not very good at taking defeat in stride, but everyone has to deal with failure at one time or another. It's far better to analyze *why* you failed than to bury your head and expect the bad news to go away.

Never let being turned *down* mean that you are turned *off* by your chosen career. Resolve instead to devise your own personal techniques to deal with the situation. First, come to grips with your emotions. You simply cannot afford to become moody, hypersensitive, and self-pitying. Don't try to escape from reality, and don't let rejection get you down. Next, focus your activity on making your contributions to the workplace more highly visible and influential, and show that you can be as much of a leader as anyone else, with practical, strategic, and analytical skills.

Even in a fiercely competitive job market, there is always room for someone who is as dedicated and task-oriented as you.

Ambition—or the Lack of It

On the surface, you don't appear to be especially ambitious. However, one Cancerian friend of mine made the switch from successful comedy writer to leading literary agent, and now encourages other people to fulfill *their* ambitions. Another Cancerian friend won two promotions in the same year.

There is often a conflict within your personality between your domestic goals and your career goals. If you're a woman, this can be especially difficult, because you possess a natural urge to have children, perhaps more so than any other star sign. Most Cancerian men and women have highly developed paternal and maternal instincts. Some of you have found it difficult to keep the right balance between your work and your family. But it is possible!

To sustain your ambition, you need to become a little more thick-skinned at times. You may be too easily thrown by criticism of your work, and occasionally too easily flattered! When you *are* truly ambitious, you become a hands-on natural leader who will do everything in your power to prevent anyone or anything from thwarting your attempts to achieve greater success.

Sometimes you may feel as though you have been stopped dead in your tracks and blocked from moving higher up in your particular company. Don't sit back and accept such a situation without giving it sufficient thought even if you do fear the idea of any kind of change. If you are really ambitious, look at other possibilities for advancement, perhaps in a different company.

To succeed in today's workplace, you can't afford to sit back, even if you do feel settled in a cozy nest.

Ambition—and Your Love Life

For an emotional and home-loving Cancerian, at times it may be difficult to combine fulfilling a professional goal and enjoying an equally fulfilling love life; difficult, but not impossible. I have Cancerian friends and clients who have managed to do so, including a successful Cancerian man whose equally successful working partner happens to be his wife!

When you *are* tenaciously goal-oriented, it occasionally means that your love life must take second place, which doesn't necessarily go down too well with your partner. Happily, your talent for empathy usually enables you to put yourself in the other person's place. You become as solicitous and protective of your emotional life as you are of your career.

Make sure that you never become so preoccupied with your own emotional moods (especially around Full Moon time!) that you create unnecessary problems in your work life *and* your love life. Try to compartmentalize these areas. Resolve not to be quite as powerless over your emotions. You are a highly sensitive Water sign, but remember that you have hidden emotional resources to tap as well.

And remember, even the most sympathetic-sounding superior or coworker prepared to listen to your woes could use them against you in the future. Keep your own counsel—it's usually the wisest one in the end!

TIPS FOR COMBINING WORK AND LOVE

- Try to create workable schedules for your job and your love life.
- Vow not to let upsets in a love affair intrude into your working day.
- Don't let your job become a self-imposed prison. You need the emotional security of a good love relationship too.
- Try not to indulge in a real downer too often—even if you do blame it on a Full Moon.

Romance in the Workplace

If you're a typical Cancerian, love in the workplace is rarely a good idea. When you love someone, you tend to subjugate yourself within the love relationship, which is not a healthy situation, especially if one of you is the boss at work. Given your sensitive and emotional nature, it is extremely difficult for you to be tough about your professional goals when you're emotionally involved with the person who has the power to grant you greater success, whether that person is married or not. You are not someone who is prepared to sleep your way to the top. Sex without love is seldom something you enjoy since your emotions are so highly attuned to the deeper meanings of love.

It can be equally difficult for an emotional Cancerian to sustain a love relationship with a coworker, particularly if it needs to be kept under wraps, perhaps because of company rules. You find it difficult to hide your feelings completely, which makes you exceedingly vulnerable, because there is also an extremely green-eyed and possessive side to your nature. This can make you too emotionally dependent on your lover, and that's never a good thing, no matter how well you may work together during office hours.

There is a highly tenacious side to the Crab's personality. You sometimes hang on emotionally to people and possessions for too long. This can create extremely awkward situations within your working environment if a love affair comes to an end, and if you are unable to accept the situation. There are bound to be relationships that do start in the workplace and that do progress toward a live-in relationship or marriage without too many stumbling blocks along the way.

However, there are also increasing amounts of sexual harassment cases being acknowledged in the workplace. It seems to be hard for some people to draw the appropriate line between paying someone a compliment and coming on too strong in one way or another.

Since you are someone who is acutely sensitive to the right ambience in *every* area of your life, try to ensure that a love relationship does not create unnecessary problems in your work.

You and Your Stress Factor

Cancer rules the breasts, stomach, and digestive system. When you suffer from stress, your stomach and digestion will often be affected, and too much stress can bring on an ulcer.

As I've said, you are one of the most emotional and sensitive signs in the Zodiac. Sometimes even the tiniest event can trigger a stress reaction within you. Nevertheless, if you're prepared to identify and start to recognize your own particular stress triggers, you will provide yourself with a powerful weapon for combating them.

Many of you seem to focus on your stomach when you're under stress, often by giving it too much food! This "comfort food" usually tends to be all the "sweet" things, which should be eaten only in moderation. Your energy level may go up momentarily, but you're soon back to feeling as stressed out as you did before.

It is almost impossible to avoid any kind of stress, especially if you are working overtime or worrying about firings and layoffs. Long hours may take their toll upon your body to such an extent that when you finally crawl into bed you find you cannot sleep.

Your stress factor is best kept at bay when you don't have to work in a noisy and distracting environment, and don't have to meet too many difficult deadlines. If there is an ongoing conflict between what you want from your work and what takes place on a daily basis, you are going to feel the stress! Naturally you cannot simply walk out of a job that provides you with the money to meet basic living expenses. However, occasionally you stick with a position that gives you neither sufficient security nor satisfaction.

In an earlier book, *Star Signs,* I devised a special meditation for you. Meditation will help you combat stress and hone in on your fine instincts and intuition to an even greater degree. This will enable you to develop a more positive attitude toward stress-creating issues and to become more protective toward your inner self.

You are often part of a very close-knit family, so that keeping in touch with all your relatives is extremely important to you. As a parent, you're one of the best—even though sometimes you're overprotective.

Most Cancerians I know are *incredibly* dedicated to their homes. You want to relax in the right atmosphere with every possible comfort, especially after a stressful workday. Many of you enjoy displaying your culinary talents in a well-equipped kitchen. Not the most energetic of souls, you're often happiest with a good book, a plentiful supply of your favorite CDs, and the perfect person to cuddle up to in a comfortable chair by the fireside.

Even if you don't want to stay at home all the time, you will usually enjoy catching up on romantic films or taking a walk along the ocean shore in the moonlight.

Remember that although stress cannot always be avoided, you must assume responsibility for keeping it at bay in your own life, which is why your leisure moments will always be crucial.

Your Attitude toward Making Money

Because of your determination to provide abundant security for your nearest and dearest (as well as for yourself), you have a skilled and pragmatic attitude toward your financial goals.

You're rarely tempted by get-rich-quick schemes. You are far too cautious for that. You prefer to put your trust in an accountant, a financial adviser, or a bank manager who has been giving financial advice to your family for years. The tried-and-true methods, and safest possible way of doing things, appeal to you, and you're always prepared to put in long hours at your chosen profession if you can reap the right rewards in the end. Long-term investments that give safe returns and provide something for your family after you are gone will interest you. Your intuition, combined with an excellent memory, serves you well in the stock market.

The sign of Cancer relates to the fourth house of the Zodiac, which is linked to the home and to domestic security and comfort. I have rarely come across many extravagant Moon Children—unless they were buying a gift for a loved one.

Since your long-term security is of major importance, try to make sure that any work contracts you sign will cover you for all the necessary benefits; and that you will be financially protected if your firm goes through a downsizing program. You may appear to be soft and sensitive on the surface, but there's usually a calculating brain working away inside your head!

When you're focused on your material goals, you will not allow anyone or anything to sway you off course. Even if some of you *do* sometimes display wildly fluctuating moods around Full Moon time, you will keep right on working to achieve the best you can. But don't ever become so centered on material issues that you start to miss out on the simple pleasures of life that money simply *cannot* buy!

How to Improve Your Work Relationships

As an imaginative, instinctive, sympathetic Cancerian, who can also be rather too touchy and moody at times, it's always important to cultivate the ability to get on even better with your coworkers.

The following guide will show you the best way to relate to all the signs, whether they are those of your boss, your peer, or an employee:

Cancer with Aries Boss: An Aries boss expects the work done ahead of time—not left sitting on the desk because you happen to be in a sulking mood! Avoid fighting back even if you're in the right. You wouldn't win!

Cancer with Aries Colleague: Keep your sensitivity under wraps and concentrate on being part of the team. Aries may be somewhat bossy, but you can hold your own. Express your ideas a little quicker to keep pace.

Cancer with Aries Employee: Be trusting, and you'll be rewarded with lots of loyalty, plus the work will be done right on time. But remember that Aries doesn't want to stay an employee for too long!

Cancer with Taurus Boss: Don't let your ultrasensitivity get in the way of working hard. Taurus expects everyone to do their duty—and to do it well with a minimum of fuss.

Cancer with Taurus Colleague: You can be a good team since you're both devoted and persevering where work is involved. But don't spend too long over gourmet lunches; they'll leave you tired by midafternoon!

Cancer with Taurus Employee: Be cautious about overloading the Bull with excessive amounts of work. Don't display too many negative moods because Taurus can be just as sensitive to atmosphere as you.

Cancer with Gemini Boss: This restless and versatile boss doesn't want to hear about any emotional upsets you may have had the night before! Gemini needs lots of organizing carried out in a highly practical way.

Cancer with Gemini Colleague: You will never be bored, but you may get frustrated trying to pin this colleague down to facts and figures. Enjoy the team spirit and the intellectual ideas flowing fast between you.

Cancer with Gemini Employee: You're tenacious in your approach to work, but Gemini is all over the place and needs to become more consistent! You'll appreciate Gemini's flair for innovative ideas.

Cancer with Cancer Boss: Watch out you're not so busy empathizing with each other that you forget that you're the boss! Maybe you should both stay at home when it's the time of the Full Moon.

Cancer with Cancer Colleague: You are so compassionate and protective about each other that this could be a mutual admiration society! Both of you must demonstrate sufficient fighting spirit to survive in today's aggressive workplace.

Cancer with Cancer Employee: You may feel emotionally drained with so much sensitivity around you. At least it will make you realize what you are like. Never be too bossy just because you're in a bad mood.

Cancer with Leo Boss: Don't be too much in awe of Leo's proud and domineering ways. The Lion is just a pussycat at heart. You may feel that you're doing *all* the work and Leo expects *all* the praise. Wait till *you're* boss!

Cancer with Leo Colleague: It could be party time all day if this colleague got his way! Remember that Leo likes to occupy center stage, but don't allow yourself to be intimidated. You have your rights too.

Cancer with Leo Employee: "Better a boss than an employee be" could be a favorite Leo maxim. Try to be more sensitive to Leo's difficulty in accepting orders, and you'll find you have an incredibly loyal staff member.

Cancer with Virgo Boss: Show that you can be as devoted to your work as any Virgo. Don't slip up just because you're feeling moody. Remember that Virgo is ultracritical of anyone's faults!

Cancer with Virgo Colleague: Your instincts and intuition combined with Virgo's powers of analysis can make you a winning team. Don't undermine each other's talents by nit-picking at each other too much.

Cancer with Virgo Employee: As a boss, you're often as much of a perfectionist as any Virgo, so you will be delighted with this employee's work. Don't be a slave driver, though, for Virgo likes to have some time at home too!

Cancer with Libra Boss: You won't need to complain about a difficult work environment when you have this boss, who is "charm personified." But be prepared for Libra to leave some tasks till the last minute!

Cancer with Libra Colleague: Remember that Librans don't have much patience with moodiness, and that you're not good at coping with indecisive people. In other respects, you should have a good work relationship.

Cancer with Libra Employee: How wonderful it is to have an employee who invariably smiles when greeting you each morning. Don't sulk even if Libra's organizational skills can sometimes be found wanting!

Cancer with Scorpio Boss: Remember that Scorpio is secretive, tough, suspicious, and highly disciplined. Any mistakes you make will be forgiven eventually, but probably never be forgotten!

Cancer with Scorpio Colleague: Both of you are ambitious and highly emotional. When you're competing with Scorpio for the same promotion, it's best to keep your tactics to yourself. Scorpio plays to win, with almost ruthless determination!

Cancer with Scorpio Employee: Always make sure that this employee respects you and the way you work, or she could become broodingly resentful that she is not the boss. Scorpio likes to be at the top of the ladder!

Cancer with Sagittarius Boss: This optimistic, positive, and self-confident boss is a joy to work for. Make sure you don't spoil the relationship by being hypersensitive if you're criticized for any mistakes.

Cancer with Sagittarius Colleague: Try to be as upbeat as your colleague, and you could make a good team. Sagittarius can be irresponsible and reckless, so your more cautious approach to projects will balance things well.

Cancer with Sagittarius Employee: Your mood swings won't usually bother this happy-go-lucky sign, but trying to cramp his style will. Respect the Archer's independent approach to life, and you'll be rewarded with excellent work.

Cancer with Capricorn Boss: Your opposite sign of the Zodiac is an ambitious workaholic with no time to deal with your fluctuating moods. Show you can be equally hardworking, and resolve to control your emotions!

Cancer with Capricorn Colleague: You both have traditional values and are aiming for material security. You work well together on the same team, but if you're vying for the same post, Capricorn is a formidable opponent.

Cancer with Capricorn Employee: See that Capricorn respects your working methods, or this employee could be fairly ruthless in aiming for your job. Keep your mood swings to yourself—it's more professional that way.

Cancer with Aquarius Boss: This boss may be absentminded, irrational, and unpredictable at times, but you won't get away with turning in sloppy work just because you're feeling down!

Cancer with Aquarius Colleague: Your Aquarian colleague is idealistic and imaginative, but not very practical. Working together could lead to some brilliant projects, but it's up to you to be the organizer.

Cancer with Aquarius Employee: An Aquarian employee isn't necessarily the best timekeeper in the world, and can be stubborn to boot. But you may be surprised at how often Aquarius devises brilliant ideas for getting you out of a fix.

Cancer with Pisces Boss: You're both sensitive Water signs, but don't expect too much tea and sympathy when there is work to be done. A Pisces who has reached the top means to stay right there!

Cancer with Pisces Colleague: The two of you are tempted to just sit around empathizing over each other's emotional ups and downs. Don't neglect the work that has to be done! Use your instincts and intuitions to the full, and you'll make a winning team.

Cancer with Pisces Employee: Don't be too soft and sensitive, even if you do recognize some of Pisces's insecurities within yourself. A practical approach produces the best results from this employee.

Getting Longevity out of Your Career

These days, it is harder than ever to map out one's future. More and more companies are merging, downsizing, or even going into bankruptcy. Workers can no longer count on having "jobs for life" but must rely increasingly on short-term contracts. This state of affairs is especially hard for you because you are focused on getting longevity out of your career, and because you become insecure at the very idea of anything threatening your basic stability.

I recently listened to a discussion on the radio where someone said that "jobs for life" had led to stagnation in the workforce, whereas the fear of being laid off was productive in keeping workers on their toes. However, the fear of losing one's job can have an extremely negative effect on people—and in the long run on the whole economy. They can become so petrified of making waves that they begin to fear expressing themselves creatively and consequently no longer give their best.

Try not to let the fear of being fired prevent you from giving *your* best. And when problems arise, make sure that you're not a crab who scuttles away from them, but someone who faces them head-on with a positive approach. Guard against becoming too tied to the treadmill; it may give you material security but will do little for your creative spirit.

Getting fired is never pleasant, but if it does happen to you, don't cling to the past, for this will be self-defeating. In some cases, your powerful Cancerian intuition will provide you with an early warning that layoffs are imminent, and you might be able to take steps to protect your job. Be sure to stay abreast of the latest information technology. Keep your résumé up-to-date and your eyes and ears open so you don't miss out on any openings in other firms.

Because you're such a practical sign, if you *are* fired, you don't have to be reminded of issues such as severance pay, health benefits, and pensions, nor that if you cannot sort these matters out satisfactorily, you can always consult a lawyer. As a security-conscious Cancerian, you probably have put aside sufficient funds to cover such emergencies as being fired. Be tenacious in your determination to find a new outlet for your talents and abilities. Believe in your ability to succeed—and succeed you will!

Many people like to continue working when they grow older, believing it keeps them healthier in mind and body. Even if you reach a stage when you feel your age might prevent you from continuing with your present work, it does not mean you cannot do something different. Switching careers does not come easy to a self-protective Cancerian, who finds it hard to leave a secure nest. But that's not necessarily because you're getting older; that's part of your nature!

If you are financially secure, why not take a short training course that will enable you to utilize your renowned instincts for helping people less fortunate than yourself.

Never think that because you grow older you can no longer achieve your desires. Your experience of life is invaluable, and combined with your particular talents and abilities, will still make you a powerful force in the workplace.

CANCER CAREER STRATEGIES—A CHECKLIST FOR EVERY AGE

- Always stay ahead of the game. Be forward thinking, and vow that you will never dwell in the past!
- Be self-motivated and creative, combining energy and imagination with your natural instincts and intuition.
- Be aware of, and strive to meet, the ever-changing requirements of today's workplace.
- Always try to find the best way to combine your domestic needs with your professional aims and ambitions.
- Never hide away in your shell. You need to play an active part in the workplace so that you're not overlooked.

- Make sure you're up-to-date on the technology within your company.
- Don't let your creativity slip because you start to fear the consequences of being laid off. You don't want to create a self-fulfilling prophecy!

LEO IN THE WORKPLACE

July 22 ☆ *August 21*

If you were born between July 22 and August 21, you were born under the sign of Leo, fifth sign of the Zodiac. You are a Masculine, Fixed, Positive, Fire sign, and your planetary symbol is the Lion. With the Sun as your planetary ruler, you possess great charisma and a sunny, sparkling personality. The sun is the center of our solar system, but this doesn't entitle you to center stage *all* the time—although some of you seem to think so!

You are one of the most powerfully positive signs in the whole Zodiac, with an inborn ability to light up the sky, and the workplace, with your creativity. Many of you also possess an underlying fear of failure, but your vulnerable side is often so brilliantly hidden that you come across as arrogant and egocentric at those very moments when you may be quaking with fear.

Leo the Lion is known as the King of the Zodiac. Your dynamic, proactive personality, with its leadership qualities and first-class communication style, is an added bonus in today's global marketplace. However, not every ambitious Leo can be the boss or end up as a president, like Leo Bill Clinton.

Unpredictable Aquarius, the sign of the humanitarian and truth seeker of the Zodiac, is your opposite sign. You can learn something not only from Aquarius but from all the other star signs. You might like to approach your workday wearing a different astrological hat once in a while.

Take a typical workday in the Leo life. You're delegated a difficult task by a superior whose work attitude and leadership skills you don't respect very much. The task provides you with a challenge for your own skills, but you're not sure you will be thanked for your efforts in the end.

Playing Aries:　You always rise to a challenge, even if it is given by someone you don't respect. You enjoy proving (if only to yourself) that you can do something better than anyone else.

Playing Taurus:　Although you may resent working under someone you don't respect, you are unlikely to show it. You're far too aware of unemployment figures, so unlikely to prejudice your long-term prospects.

Playing Gemini:　If you're not on the same mental wavelength as your superior, communication can be difficult. But you realize that the sooner this task is finished, the sooner you can get on to something more worthwhile.

Playing Cancer:　You're highly sensitive to atmosphere, and intuitive enough to know that making waves won't get you out of the task. Because you're motivated enough to see difficult tasks through to the end, you know you can do this one!

Playing Yourself:　You may be inclined to challenge authority here, even if you know it's the wrong strategy. Why not assume you can do the job brilliantly, and get on with it, even if you don't receive your rightful praise.

Playing Virgo:　You proceed with what needs to be done, even if you don't respect the other person involved. As a Virgo, you take all your duties seriously and derive pride from a job well done.

Playing Libra:　You decide that time wasted debating the relevance of the job is better spent completing it, so peace and harmony are restored all around!

Playing Scorpio:　Since you know instinctively that you're the best, you deal with the task at hand silently. But you'll never forget that you consider you've been treated unfairly.

Playing Sagittarius: You're far too confident of your long-term prospects to waste time worrying over a minor setback like this. You may be tempted to argue a little, but probably not for long.

Playing Capricorn: If you played the part of this workaholic sign more often, you'd never get behind with any work! In this situation, you are convinced that *you* should be the boss, but your Capricorn ethic keeps you silent.

Playing Aquarius: Learning from your opposite sign means that it's sometimes *impossible* to predict how you'd behave! One thing's almost sure: you hide your feelings and get the task over as fast as possible.

Playing Pisces: You are sympathetic to your superior's attitude, probably deciding she has enough problems already. You may not feel very happy about the situation, but your pride is less of a factor when playing Pisces!

The Positive and Negative Qualities of a Leo at Work

Among the most positive aspects of your Leo personality are your flair, tenacity, and ability to successfully drive a company forward. There is a wonderfully enthusiastic quality about your approach to almost everything you do—somewhat childlike but also inspiring. Sparkling and charismatic, you also have a larger-than-life quality that empowers you to become a major force in the workplace.

It was a Leo, Andy Warhol, who said that everyone is entitled to be famous for fifteen minutes. You have the potential to be famous for much longer than that! You have an amazing capacity to develop your mind and to trust the shining Sun which is the source of your power. You abhor the idea of failure and can be somewhat boastful when talking about your particular talents and attributes, but you have a warm heart and generous nature.

You might want to throw something at me when I say this, but you do possess a lazy streak. There are certain times when your somewhat laid-back and nonchalant approach to tasks means they are carried out in a less-than-diligent manner.

The sign of Leo relates to the fifth house of the Zodiac, the house of love affairs and creativity. Your creativity is unsurpassed when you're in top form. My partner is a Leo artist who never ceases to amaze me with his paintings. I continually see his art reach ever-greater heights.

The positive Leo has abundant creativity and leadership skills, with the vision and determination to be an enormous success. You are outgoing, enthusiastic, and wholly professional, with an entrepreneurial outlook. No one is more dynamic in approach than a positive Leo, since you possess the personal qualities and drive required to deal with almost every challenge you may encounter.

The negative Leo sometimes only sees his or her leadership potential and finds it hard to accept advice, even when necessary. In order to fulfill a high-profile role, even *you* may have to accomplish a few lowly tasks first. Sometimes you display an arrogant or boastful attitude to cover up your inner feeling of insecurity. But remember that it doesn't necessarily appear to the rest of us that you are feeling vulnerable. It is perfectly acceptable to have a natural sense of personal authority, but you must also recognize and accept that others have authority as well. (Remember what happened to Leos Mussolini and Napoleon!)

The wise Leo resolves never to become too egocentric, but rather to balance determination and the ability to be a real star with the ability to know when it truly *is* necessary to take second place.

Careers for Leo

Leos are often drawn to show business—especially the movie world (in front of or behind the cameras!), the stage, and theater management—public relations, painting, fashion or jewelry design, running one's own company, and almost any kind of high-level management such as department head or company director. Those of you who become big stars are determined to stay that way. Leo Mick Jagger seems to have been going forever and certainly shows no signs of disliking the spotlight of center stage. Leo Madonna has never seemed too happy when the spotlight has shifted from her and her activities. While Leo Henry Ford I, founder of the Ford Motor Company, is no longer with us, his name lives on with the Ford automobiles, as does the name of Leo Marshall Field.

Other famous Leos include Carl Jung, Aldous Huxley, James Baldwin, Coco Chanel, Norman Schwarzkopf, Neil Armstrong, Robert De Niro, Dustin Hoffman, Sean Penn, Arnold Schwarzenegger, Robert Redford, Alfred Hitchcock, Magic Johnson, Whitney Houston, Melanie Griffith, Pete Sampras, and Peggy Fleming.

Your Attitude toward Work

Naturally, your rising sign, together with all the other factors of your personal horoscope, will also influence your attitude toward work.

You often have a deep desire to become successful, which manifests itself early in life. While writing this chapter, I asked several Leo children what they wanted to be when they grew up, and they almost all came up with quite high-profile careers. Luckily for the rest of us, Leos also possess an inborn ability to be enthusiastic team players too.

In today's competitive workplace, charm and creativity may be less important at certain times than a deep understanding of corporate politics. It isn't always possible to start at the top of your chosen career. Even as a Leo, you must demonstrate a successful track record before you can truthfully say you're ready for a really high-profile role!

All the Leos I've ever met take immense pride in themselves and their achievements. You hate the very thought of failure, which perhaps is why you are so determined to succeed in the workplace. Your attitude toward failure could also explain why you don't apply yourself completely to anything you fear is beyond your capabilities. But the way to become more powerful in the workplace is to take pleasure in *all* your endeavors. When you enjoy what you do, you allow the power of the Sun, your planetary ruler, to shine through you. You are truly someone who can make your dreams come true, when you focus inwardly *and* outwardly on creating a high-profile image.

Since Leo is the regal ruler of the Zodiac, it would be fitting for you to work in a wonderfully elegant office with your very own Leo throne. I'm sure you'd like your office to be a showpiece, but if you insisted on this kind of treatment you wouldn't last very long, unless you owned the company. However, whether you have your own space or share one, psychologically it is important for you to create your own spot of luxury around you. (This does not mean you have to spend a fortune on furniture or having fresh orchids delivered every day!) If it's not possible to arrange something luxurious in reality, exercise some creative thinking: Tell yourself that your work space is fine for now, but that when you become more successful you will have the work environment of your dreams. Then put maximum effort into making your dreams come true.

It's hardly surprising that many of you become such forceful and shining personalities in the workplace. Your courage and enthusiasm, combined with your dreams of stardom, will always help to propel you to the top.

TIPS FOR A HEALTHY WORK ATTITUDE

- Never be too dictatorial, even when you *are* the boss!
- Always let your sunny Leo personality shine through, even if you do feel under pressure.
- Allow other people to take center stage once in a while.

Aiming for Promotion

I hope that what you have read so far will have confirmed what you already know deep down: that Leo's rightful place in the workplace is as a bright shining star at the top.

In today's highly competitive environment you cannot afford any setbacks in the way you carry out your responsibilities or in the way you build rapport at all levels. Aside from your Leo ambition and resolve to succeed, remember that you need to be able to understand and respond to the fast-changing needs of the workplace.

With your charismatic personality, you can be extremely dynamic when you're enthusiastic about something, and no one can top your leadership skills and strategic vision. When you're aiming for promotion, you must be totally focused on the end product. It's no use telling everyone (including yourself!) that you have unbeatable star quality if your actions do not match your words.

It's hard to suggest that you might sometimes try to keep a slightly lower profile. I don't think I've ever come across a Leo who isn't a born performer, grabbing our attention with almost every word or action. You have no problems with being assertive, but just because you're a Fixed sign it doesn't mean you always have to be *quite* so fixed in all your opinions. Remember that someone responsible for offering a promotion, and not aware of your inner vulnerability, might think you sing your own praises a little too loudly. Naturally, you must prove that you're the best person for the job in question, but don't imply that *everyone else* is inferior to you. Sometimes it really is best to leave center stage to the person you hope will offer you the job.

If promotion eludes you, through no known fault of your own, swallow your famous Leo pride and refrain from launching a tirade against the injustice of it all. Continue to believe in your own star quality, and remember that just because success eludes you once in a while, it doesn't mean you won't achieve it the next time around.

TIPS FOR PROMOTION SEEKERS

- Make sure your aura of self-confidence is strengthened by perfecting your skills, trusting your intuition, and understanding corporate politics!
- Always be realistic when analyzing your weaknesses and strengths—and make sure the strengths come out on top.
- Make every possible use of your networking abilities. That way, you'll know what promotions could be in the air.

How to Cope with Being Passed Over for Promotion

If you're a typical Leo, the very thought of being passed over for *any-thing* is enough to send your Leo heart fluttering wildly. But perhaps you aimed for a promotion without having all the necessary qualifications, making it inevitable that you were overlooked. Don't dwell negatively on the situation, but remember that there always is another a chance to direct your creative energies in an even more positive manner.

Because of your strong sense of Leo pride and your aversion to any kind of failure, it's difficult for you to realize that you cannot be the top dog *all* the time. You know that your inherent star quality always comes up trumps in the long run, and that you will have a chance to prove that you're the best!

Be glad that you were born under the sign of Leo, for your sunny disposition is unlikely to remain under a cloud for too long. Remember that the Sun, your ruler, is the source of all divine power, and make sure that you let this power flow within you, propelling you to the heights of greater success.

Ambition—or the Lack of It

Many of you seem to think that rising to the top of your chosen profession is your God-given right, and that you don't necessarily have to demonstrate an ambitious streak.

Naturally there are many ambitious Leos. President Clinton didn't get to the White House by simply saying to himself one day that that was where he wanted to be. Sean Penn would not have become a movie director had he not first proved himself as an actor in many movies. No one could say that Madonna is not ambitious, especially with her determination to play the role of Evita.

However, there are some of you who are determined to succeed in a particular situation, yet who seem to have no concept of how to plan your moves. It's as though you have failed to realize that today's workplace is more competitive than ever, and that you're not the only talented person around. You must continually demonstrate substantial achievements, and be prepared to challenge the status quo with maturity and pragmatism, as well as with your creative flair and vision.

When you are in an ambitious mood, no one can fault your drive and determination, and you will easily prove your ability to fit into the right high-profile slot for your Leo personality.

Always remember that your Leo strong points are your life force and your creative power, and that these will enable you to achieve your ambitions. Fear of failing to be a high-flier is no reason to renounce your aims. But avoid giving yourself a somewhat inflated air of grandeur along the way to the top. Just because the Sun is the center of the solar system, it doesn't mean that *you* are always the center of everyone else's world!

Ambition—and Your Love Life

As a Fire sign, you need to control your tendency to wear your heart on your sleeve and to be excessively romantic.

It's unlikely you would ever allow your professional ambitions to get in the way of your romantic life. You are more likely to spend too *much* time on your love life so that your ambitions take second place. This is not a good idea, especially when you should be thinking up new ways to gain greater visibility in the workplace.

Because you're such a warmhearted, larger-than-life person, it's easy to see how romantically attractive you are to other people. You get immense pleasure out of caring for someone special too. Your pride in yourself is equaled only by your pride in the person you love—as long as that person also loves and praises you sufficiently!

Sentimental and sensitive, you're also more vulnerable romantically than your independent and strong-willed bossy exterior makes you appear. I've known emotionally under-the-weather Leos who have found it difficult to concentrate on their work if they've been waiting patiently for a call from the love of their life.

If you're a Leo in love with someone whose ambitions are far more focused than your own, don't spoil things by being too pushy and demanding when your partner needs a highly disciplined approach to work.

TIPS FOR COMBINING WORK AND LOVE

- Resolve not to let talks *or* thoughts about your love life break into a busy work schedule.
- Try to schedule those extravagantly luxurious nights out with the love of your life only on weekends!
- Never allow a lover's interference to distract you from your ambitions—you'd be sure to resent this eventually.
- You can be a tireless pleasure lover. Make sure you're a tireless worker too!

Romance in the Workplace

Such relationships are not easy at the best of times, and extremely difficult at the worst. Given the prevalence of sexual harassment cases, it must at times be hard to be someone with as sparkling and shining a personality as yours. How do you know that a cheerful smile, offhand remark, or squeeze of a hand won't be interpreted by someone with a grudge against you as a sexual come on? The main problem is that in such matters, you tend to be childlike in your naïveté, never imagining that a friendly gesture could be misconstrued. I've noticed that many of you seem genuinely unaware of your alluring personality—to the extent that you're amazed when someone finds you immensely attractive. At the same time, you are also guilty of enjoying admiration just a little too much! Be careful that an innocently flirtatious line of chat doesn't occasionally put you in the line of fire of someone who doesn't expect to take no for an answer. Remember that there are a lot of emotionally lonely and perhaps even ruthless people out there in the workplace—and it may not be simply your job that they are after.

Since Leo rules the heart, there will almost certainly be times when you find yourself immensely attracted to someone with whom you work. I think it would be almost impossible for you to keep a romantic relationship with a colleague under wraps for very long. As noted earlier, if you're a typical Leo, you wear your heart on your sleeve for everyone to see. This may be fine in some circumstances, but it can be total disaster in others. Working in close proximity to someone you love will not be easy if you have to hide your feelings for whatever reason, or you realize that they are not reciprocated. You're the sort of person who wants to shout it from the rooftops when you're in love, and are always proud to be seen with the object of your affections.

You thrive in an atmosphere of team spirit and camaraderie, and your vibrant nature combined with the beauty, brains, and magnetic charm bestowed upon you by the Sun makes you unfailingly generous to the people you care for. It is wise for you to keep your love life and your working life separate, thereby avoiding the possibility of problems in either area.

You and Your Stress Factor

You are usually extremely careful about your outward appearance, rightly refusing to be tempted by the Sun's rays to hurt your body with excessive tanning, but not always so careful about burning yourself up inside with stress.

The roaring Lion and the docile Pussycat are conflicting aspects of the Leo character. To avoid the problems of stress, you must try to keep the two in balance. It doesn't always appear that you suffer from stress because you invariably display a positive personality which tends to hide any worries. But anyone who knows you well will notice how your energy level can slip from high to very low quite easily, and how you need constant praise and affection, to keep you from feeling insecure.

Perhaps because the Sun *is* your ruler, Leo men and women have always told me they feel more relaxed and more energized, inwardly and outwardly, in the sunny summer months. I wish I could tell you to simply hop on a plane to a hot and sunny location when you feel stressed out on a cold, gray winter's day, but life isn't quite that simple. However, there is nothing to stop you from visualizing the Sun's rays flowing into you. In one of my earlier books, *Star Signs,* I created a special Leo meditation to help you do this.

Astrologically Leo rules the heart, the spine and back, and the circulatory system. Remember that business lunches with rich, high-cholesterol food will make you sluggish both mentally and physically.

Leo is a pleasure-loving sign. Sometimes you exhaust your body by burning the candle at both ends. If you have a high-powered job involving long working hours, and yet still insist on going out to play at night, it won't be long before your body begins to react. Always listen to your inner voice, for it will give you advance warnings.

Although Leo relates to the heart, this doesn't mean you will necessarily suffer from heart problems. Still, it's wise not to tax your heart too much. Your back is another area that does not like to take too much strain. Remember this if you ever feel like yelling at a colleague, "Why don't you get off my back." Too often, what you feel psychologically can transform itself into a physical problem. Even if you're working in a highly competitive workplace, your first duty is to yourself. To deal successfully with stress, you must first recognize the signs. Next time your heart is pounding or your back is really aching, step back from the situation and identify and deal with whatever is truly wrong. Be good to yourself, and you'll do even better in the workplace too.

Stress can also occur when you become overly focused on your working life, allowing yourself insufficient leisure time. This doesn't give you carte blanche to become a self-indulgent hedonist at all times. But you are perfectly entitled to enjoy a good social life. A great way for you to relax is to take yourself off to a movie or the theater to catch one of your favorite stars, or simply get together with like-minded friends at a favorite restaurant.

You're not always the most energetic of signs. However, when you play any form of sport, your Leo pride usually ensures that you're good. Many of you prefer to enjoy a good massage or aromatherapy session, with someone else doing the work!

Make sure your life outside work is relaxing—whatever it is. A Leo friend, who works extremely long hours in the publishing world, never seemed to relax when she was in the city twenty-four hours a day, seven days a week. Now she has a weekend home on the water and is a new person. The relaxing weekend atmosphere has contributed to greater success in the workplace too.

Your Attitude toward Making Money

I don't think I've ever met anyone as kind and generous as you. Most Leos I know are extremely extravagant whether they have money or not! Often renowned as the last of the big spenders, Leos sometimes have a disdainful attitude toward money that borders on the ridiculous.

Your spending priorities include designer clothes, luxury restaurants, expensive vacations, and in many cases gold jewelry, which means that you need the income to pay for all of this. I've often felt that credit cards must have been invented by a Leo, and I've rarely come across any Leo who does not possess an assorted variety. It's not that handling money is beneath such a royal sign, but more that you simply forget to have sufficient cash upon your person or in your checking account.

It is important these days to make adequate financial provision for your retirement, especially because job tenure is less secure than in the past. It is often wise for you to find a reliable financial adviser, who will help you ascertain which investments are best for you. And I do mean a reliable one!

Your attitude toward making money will depend greatly on your priorities in life. Because of your flamboyant airs and love of luxury (astrologically, Leo is the ruler of gold!), you should probably aim for millionaire status! However, while you are one of the most creative signs in the Zodiac, you are not always sufficiently pragmatic in the way you follow through on ideas and projects. When you believe ideal-istically in what you're doing, you are totally dedicated to fulfilling your aims and ambitions. But sometimes you're more concerned with receiving praise for your efforts than actual payment in hand.

Spending money comes much easier to you than holding on to it, so it would make sense to work harder on formulating a way to save. Ensure that even if you're not interested in becoming a millionaire, at least you won't have to worry too much about whatever the future might bring.

How to Improve Your Work Relationships

Even a gregarious Leo will benefit from knowing how to get along even better with coworkers. Remember, it is not possible for you to take center stage *all* the time.

The following guide will show you the best way to relate to all the signs, whether they are those of your boss, your peer, or an employee:

Leo with Aries Boss: Although you find it hard to take orders from anyone, you respect the enthusiasm generated by this dynamic Fire sign. With Aries, you know you'll always be praised when you do something well.

Leo with Aries Colleague: Remember that both of you could be aiming for the top job, and Aries may be impatient to get it! Don't ever give way to indolence, or Aries will have a chance to beat you to the finish line.

Leo with Aries Employee: Never be too bossy and domineering with Aries the Ram, for this employee might challenge your authority even if it gets him fired. Just like you, Aries craves respect.

Leo with Taurus Boss: You can't afford to shirk your duties. Every-thing must be done extremely well, and careless mistakes will not be excused. Taurus demands a lot but is a loyal and appreciative employer.

Leo with Taurus Colleague: Never criticize Taurus for appearing to do things more slowly than you. This colleague is probably being a lot more thorough too. Your dynamism combined with Taurean dependability will take you far together.

Leo with Taurus Employee: Don't ever be too dictatorial. Taurus may appear to be a slow starter, but an ambitious Bull will almost always reach the top, and could be taking over your job one day!

Leo with Gemini Boss: This boss is a live wire, full of inventive ideas. Work efficiently, with a minimum of fuss. Your creative input will be gratefully received, plus you'll receive the respect you crave.

Leo with Gemini Colleague: Provided you don't waste time discussing your social lives, you make a winning team. But don't be so concerned with your professional status that you act like the boss.

Leo with Gemini Employee: Gemini may not be the best timekeeper in the world. But you'll get brilliant feedback on your plans and ideas from this communicative sign. So give respect where it's due!

Leo with Cancer Boss: Cancer is sensitive enough to realize that you're rarely totally happy as a subordinate. Be wise enough to know that you can't always be a boss, and you will get on fine.

Leo with Cancer Colleague: This colleague may sometimes seem to be crabby and hypersensitive, but Cancer has plenty of stamina too. Don't be fooled by that soft exterior—especially if competing for the same job.

Leo with Cancer Employee: Never upset Cancer's feelings if you want to retain her respect. Cancer needs to know you appreciate all her hard work, so don't forget this when it's *your* turn to give praise.

Leo with Leo Boss: Forget about the fact that you feel *you* should be the boss. Maybe next time you will! Meanwhile, let someone else be in the limelight, and study carefully what it took to get him there.

Leo with Leo Colleague: Once you stop giving each other orders and get down to work, you will become a formidable duo. A mix of creative dynamism and team spirit makes you *both* winners.

Leo with Leo Employee: How do you ever tell another Leo what to do? Keep your sense of humor, never be unnecessarily domineering, and *always* remember to give compliments for work exceptionally well done.

Leo with Virgo Boss: When you're working for this boss, you cannot afford ever to be lazy. Virgo expects excellent results. You may not get frequent praise, but you'll certainly get criticism if anything is wrong!

Leo *with Virgo Colleague:* Your creativity combined with Virgo's analytical accuracy could make you an unbeatable team. But if competing for the same job against Virgo, never let your standards slip.

Leo *with Virgo Employee:* Don't give too many orders to this employee. Virgo usually has an impeccable work record and always knows exactly what needs to be done and how.

Leo *with Libra Boss:* This boss may seem fairly indecisive, but don't be fooled. A Libran at the top will not be dominated by you. Your mutual charms will usually ensure that you work well together!

Leo *with Libra Colleague:* You both want easygoing lives, so don't rock the boat by assuming that you can be always in charge. If you're about to reach an unwise decision, Libra will always have a fail-safe alternative.

Leo *with Libra Employee:* This employee is tactful, diplomatic, and almost always willing to please. But just as *you* want praise for your work, remember that Libra feels the same way.

Leo *with Scorpio Boss:* Scorpio thrives on power and control, desiring allegiance at all costs. Never try to take over your boss's territory in any way, or you risk joining the ranks of the unemployed.

Leo *with Scorpio Colleague:* This colleague needs her own private space, mentally and physically. A formidable opponent, Scorpio knows how to play the power game, and how to ferret out your deepest secrets.

Leo *with Scorpio Employee:* Scorpio is unlikely to enjoy taking second place for too long. You'll have her undying loyalty if she respects you. If not, she could be devising a way to take over.

Leo *with Sagittarius Boss:* This self-confident and optimistic boss can be a joy to work for. But Sagittarians think they know everything and hate to be told they're wrong. They'll also be fairly outspoken about your faults.

Leo *with Sagittarius Colleague:* In a work relationship you probably need to go easy on the "old pals" routine. Your free-and-easy camaraderie needs toning down when projects require urgent attention.

Leo with Sagittarius Employee: A tactful way of telling this employee what to do will be infinitely more successful than playing the dictator. Sagittarius is great at devising creative ideas to complement your own.

Leo with Capricorn Boss: Ruled by Saturn, Capricorn is a tough taskmaster and won't put up with lethargy or careless mistakes. Make sure your social life never conflicts with your working hours.

Leo with Capricorn Colleague: Resist the tendency to play while Capricorn gets on with the work. Never be too dictatorial, for Capricorn will outsmart you. The Mountain Goat is the *most* ambitious sign in the Zodiac.

Leo with Capricorn Employee: Don't worry about telling Capricorn how to do the work. This sign is the workaholic of the Zodiac. If ever you're lazy or lethargic, Capricorn will be aiming to take over your job.

Leo with Aquarius Boss: Your opposite sign of the Zodiac could be the most unpredictable boss you've ever known. Be on your guard to avoid mistakes, and don't tell an Aquarian what to do.

Leo with Aquarius Colleague: This can be a mutual learning experience and a highly successful association. But don't be too high-handed in your manner.

Leo with Aquarius Employee: This employee may be as opinionated as you but has lots of creative flair and inventiveness. Aquarius will be happy and loyal if there isn't *too* much routine and drudgery in the work.

Leo with Pisces Boss: The Pisces boss never forgets your birthday or anniversary, and won't appreciate it if you forget his! Pisces may seem exceedingly impractical, but his intuition is right on.

Leo with Pisces Colleague: You're both equally creative, but in different ways. Pisces will give you all the praise you need, but you will need to be the more practical one if you're working together as a team.

Leo with Pisces Employee: Don't be too hard on this employee—unless you want to see floods of tears. Pisces will work long and hard to ensure that things are done well, but this *is* a highly sensitive sign.

Getting Longevity out of Your Career

Getting fired are two little words that can strike fear into almost everyone who is part of today's workforce. When you can't count on job security, you may be forced into retirement before you've had time to think about the financial implications, let alone contemplate what you might do with all your newfound leisure time. These days, retirees are not necessarily older individuals. I've known people who took "voluntary" retirement before they reached the age of fifty; it's called "voluntary" even if the person concerned is not terribly happy about the whole situation.

Your typical Leo pride will not take it lightly if it's ever implied that you're not pulling your weight sufficiently to be of ongoing value in your particular field. This is all the more reason to make sure that you never give anyone the opportunity to find fault with your work *or* with your personality!

Always remember that a large part of your time at work needs to be spent communicating and interacting with other people. Make sure that you never think yourself too important to do this. You can't afford to play it like a dictator too often, or you will lose the support of the very people you need on your side. Although you are usually brilliant at getting yourself noticed by those in high places, you need to remember that today's workplace can be a cutthroat environment. Make sure that you are always seen as an entrepreneur for whom no task is too difficult or beneath your dignity. Never allow your leadership skills to flag or your strong record of practical achievements to falter.

I know I have accused you of being lazy at times, but you also have great staying power when you are involved in something that fulfills your creative talents and abilities. There is no reason whatsoever why these should diminish with age.

Being fired is rarely the end of the road, especially for someone who is as dynamic, charismatic, and creative as you. More and more people change careers with a minimum of fuss, so why not you? If the workplace has become a jungle, never forget that the Lion is the symbol of your sign, and that the Lion is the *King* of the jungle. You're brilliant at networking, so you will always be one of the first to hear about new opportunities that are right for you. Professionally you're a real star, and there is no reason why that should ever change.

LEO CAREER STRATEGIES—A CHECKLIST FOR EVERY AGE

- Never let your fear of failure stop you from aiming for the top.
- Remember that the Sun—your ruling planet—is your very own divine power force. Believe in the magic of your dreams, and turn them into reality.
- Be proud of your leadership qualities, but never too proud to play a supporting role when necessary.
- Keep your love life and self-indulgent pleasures far away from the workplace.
- Put your heart and soul into showing that you will consistently be one of the brightest shining stars around.
- Even if you are the boss, it's wise to curb some of your spendthrift ways and cut down on some of your generous gestures, for Leos always tend to overspend.
- No matter how successful you become, never lose sight of how and where you started—and allow other people to take the limelight sometimes too!

VIRGO IN THE WORKPLACE

August 22 ☆ *September 21*

If you were born between August 22 and September 21, you were born under the sign of Virgo, sixth sign of the Zodiac. You are a Feminine, Mutable, Negative, Earth sign. Your planetary symbol is the Virgin. Your ruler is Mercury, Winged Messenger of the Gods, and the planet of communication.

It might seem as though being a perfectionist would allow you to reach the top of your chosen profession and stay there with ease. Although you are one of the most hardworking signs of the Zodiac—astrologically known as "the sign of service"—your dedication to your work does not always mean you have particularly high aspirations.

Of all the Zodiac signs, you are the most selfless. Mother Teresa, who always put caring for other people before her own needs, was a true role model for Virgo. Unfortunately in today's workplace, saintly behavior is unlikely to go hand in hand with success.

As one of the most businesslike and methodical signs, you pay attention to the finest details. This can be a big asset at work, but it is not something to worry about twenty-four hours a day. (You *rarely* make careless mistakes.) Sometimes you become unnecessarily fussy and don't use your imagination sufficiently to see the overall picture. Don't be so self-critical that your creative talents and abilities suffer. Learn to trust your intuition more, like your opposite sign, Pisces.

To learn something from each of the Zodiac signs, you can play a different sign once in a while. You'll discover new ways to deal with the day's events.

Take a typical workday in the Virgo working life. You worked late last night to complete a task that probably could have waited till the morning. You arrive at work to discover that your immediate boss, plus some other people, have all come down with the flu, and everything depends on you. Since this will involve a great deal of extra work, you probably will be working late again.

Playing Aries: Rising to a challenge is second nature to you. Impatient to get everything done as soon as possible, you won't have time to doubt your ability to be successful—as indeed you will be!

Playing Taurus: You will easily demonstrate your dependability without any Virgoan worries that you aren't clever enough to do three jobs. You don't waste time wondering if you will get everything done in time. You simply attack your work, task by task.

Playing Gemini: You probably heave a sigh of relief for there will be no time to feel bored. An action-packed day is the way you like it. Any initial nervousness soon disappears once the adrenaline starts flowing.

Playing Cancer: After you call the sick parties to make sure they are doing okay, you get on with the tasks at hand. Being immensely practical, you probably find someone else to assist you, rather than worrying how and where to start.

Playing Leo: How wonderful to have the chance to be in the limelight and prove that you have all the necessary attributes to play boss for a day. You never worry about doing something wrong; you know you're the best!

Playing Yourself: You probably regret working so late last night, now that you may do the same thing tonight! But you are proud of your track record, so you start on all the tasks—albeit with butterflies in your stomach and an unnecessary fear of failure!

Playing Libra: Weighing the situation, you soon realize that a few extra pairs of hands would get everything done a whole lot faster.

You tackle things in your uniquely cool, calm, and laid-back way—even if slightly worried underneath.

Playing Scorpio: That Scorpio strength means you can overcome fear and insecurity with ease. No task is too difficult for you, and you are ready to battle with anyone who thinks otherwise!

Playing Sagittarius: Playing this sign enables you to replace your fears and insecurities with optimism and self-confidence. So you cheerfully get down to work, happy to be called upon in any emergency.

Playing Capricorn: You are far too practical to lose time wondering how everything will get done. You cancel every unnecessary meeting, forget about coffee breaks, lunch, and maybe even dinner, and deal with the work until it is completed.

Playing Aquarius: The idea of being tied down to a day of relentless work pressures might fill you with horror. But you soon devise an inventive idea to make everything turn out just fine.

Playing Pisces: Your initial concern for the invalids could give way to sheer terror at the amount of work waiting for you. By voicing your fears, with the minimum of fuss, you soon cooperate with a willing bunch of helpers.

The Positive and Negative Qualities of a Virgo at Work

Logical, alert, bright, and exceedingly practical, you seem to be a paragon of virtue and a perfectionist in your work. You have an exceedingly bright mind that needs its freedom to explore new avenues. You are invariably brilliant at analyzing people and situations in a realistic and pragmatic way. You are also extremely adept at devising and carrying out creative projects. You will become even more successful if you allow your intuition and imagination to guide you too.

The sign of Virgo relates to the sixth house of the Zodiac, which in turn relates to work. Your highly developed analytical skills together with your sound strategic ability and understanding of business functions should make you a front-runner in today's competitive job market. You have what it takes to rise to almost every challenge, yet you often undervalue yourself and your talents. Sometimes you seem to settle for something minor rather than stretching yourself, content to work unobtrusively behind the scenes when you should be taking more of the limelight. Quiet, conscientious, and extremely responsible, you must feel needed—no matter what you do. Your ability to organize and systematize is renowned. I cannot imagine you losing anything or being anything but punctual for even the most unimportant meeting. You are brilliant at prioritizing your tasks so that your time is always well planned.

The positive Virgo develops more self-confidence. You place greater value upon yourself and your particular talents and abilities. Take a leaf out of Leo's book and appreciate the joy of being praised. Praise *yourself* once in a while too. You are pragmatic without losing sight of your ideals, dedicated without forcing yourself to work twenty-four hours a day, patient, persevering, and task-oriented—without constantly trying to force your own high standards on everyone else. You see clearly that you sometimes waste a great deal of energy when you do expect others to see things as analytically as you.

The negative Virgo takes on the worries of the world and is frequently too self-critical. Sometimes you are so worried about taking any risks that you undermine your creative skills. How can you ever develop your talents if you keep doubting yourself? Why do you have to worry about every slightest detail? It's almost as though you refuse to accept that to err is human. Stop taking your analytical qualities almost to the point of no return.

The wise Virgo will combine a strong record of practical achievements and business vision with initiative, tenacity, and flair. You will be able to demonstrate that you can understand and respond to fast-changing needs in today's competitive job market, and that your attitude toward service will be forward thinking at all times.

Careers for Virgo

Virgo men and women are often drawn to book writing, public service, government administration, the financial market, stockbrokering, pharmacy, science, bookkeeping, teaching, medicine (as doctors, nurses, and laboratory technicians), alternative medicine, and psychology. You also make excellent diet and nutrition experts, craftspeople, architects, artists, astrologers, book editors, secretaries, and proofreaders.

An unusually high proportion of Virgo men and women become highly successful writers, including Mary Shelley, Agatha Christie, Leo Tolstoy, D. H. Lawrence, William Golding, Ira Levin, Ken Kesey, Roald Dahl, Jorge Luis Borges, and Stephen King. Other well-known Virgoans include J. C. Penney, Leonard Bernstein, Karl Lagerfeld, k. d. lang, Patsy Cline, Ricki Lake, Lauren Bacall, Sean Connery, Michael Jackson, Tommy Lee Jones, and Jimmy Connors.

Your Attitude toward Work

Naturally, your rising sign, together with all the other factors of your individual horoscope, will also influence your attitude toward work.

You believe, rightly, that efficiency and dependability are major paths to success. However, there are times when a more entrepreneurial attitude might take you even farther along the path. With your alert mind, your highly developed verbal abilities, and your analytical skills, you could be a real star in the workplace by committing yourself to being more dynamic in your approach to your work.

You will always perfect your specialist skills and exhibit the disciplined approach required for every task, with the determination to achieve high standards. Sometimes you even allow coworkers to move up the ladder of success, as they take the credit for your efforts along the way.

You consider work as your function, but tend to forget that no matter how enjoyable, stimulating, and creative your work might be, it does not always have to last twenty-four hours a day. Work is only one part of your life. Don't let it take over to the extent of overlooking everything else.

Don't worry so much about everything you do. One of the most important factors of being successful in today's job market is to exude confidence in your own talents and abilities, and to *stay* confident. Stop being so self-critical. To inspire the trust of your superiors and your colleagues, you must also trust yourself more too.

You like to have a hands-on approach to everything you do. You have no problem in taking hold of the day-to-day details of your job.

The more details there are, the happier you are! You make sure you understand exactly what your job can lead to; you are always prepared to learn everything there is to learn about any new technology. You know that your efficiency and brilliant organizing skills will also be your ticket up the ladder of success. Performance reviews should not trouble you because you will have done your homework well enough to achieve more than satisfactory marks.

You are brilliant at planning your long-term strategy and specific goals. You require a sense of structure in order to feel truly secure, but sometimes you need to expand your boundaries and visions. Don't be so tied down to routine and order that you miss out on new opportunities. Try not to be quite so obsessed with details. Whether you work in a large or small company, or in a shop or laboratory, on your own or with other people, your main criterion is that everything must be neat, tidy, and exceedingly well organized. You cannot bear to have any mess around you, nor would you be happy trying to work with music blaring in the background. Your dedication to duty is so great that you could probably work in almost any conditions, but a tidy working space combined with your Virgoan concentration can produce miracles!

Your ability to spot a gap in the service market is unsurpassed. While writing this book in Italy, I took a day off to spend some time on a friend's boat anchored off a secluded bay, where a whole crowd of us had a picnic lunch. Italians love their espresso coffee after a meal, but this was the one thing missing. However, my friend reassured everyone that coffee would be arriving very soon. A small rowboat came into the bay, and it was shortly surrounded by people wading into the water. Coffee and cold drinks were immediately provided. This business enterprise was provided by a thoughtful local fisherman—who turned out to be a Virgo!

TIPS FOR A HEALTHY WORK ATTITUDE

- Resolve to be more positive and less self-critical.
- Stop letting other people take the credit for your ideas.
- Keep your feet on the ground when necessary, but allow your creative imagination to flow freely too.

Aiming for Promotion

I'm sorry to say that there are far too many Virgo men and women who do not aim for the promotions they justly deserve. And when they stay in the background, they run the risk of not only being overlooked for promotion but also being perceived as not pulling their own weight and thereby jeopardizing their current jobs.

Sometimes it seems to be your fear of failure or rejection that prevents you from seeking a promotion. You may even dwell on the past, talking about how successful you once were and how sad it is that things have changed. What you must realize is that *everything* changes and will continue to do so—it's called evolution. We're on the brink of a new millennium, which could mean that things will change even faster. Duty and service are what your sign is all about, but don't forget your duty to yourself to create the best situation for *you.*

Some of the best editors I have worked with in the newspaper and publishing worlds have been born under your sign, and a Virgo psychologist friend of mine in London is justly renowned as one of the leaders in his field. You all have what it takes to climb to the top of your chosen profession when you concentrate positively on your aims and ambitions and stop being so overly self-critical and judgmental.

I would never dream of asking you to stop being a pragmatist, but I would suggest that you become more idealistic about how you see yourself on a long-term basis. My psychologist friend believes that it is extremely beneficial for many people to have a five-year goal. I have a feeling that too many of you don't necessarily expect to be doing anything different in five years. However, with the constantly changing and fluctuating job market, and more and more people out of work, you may not even be able to maintain the status quo. As a hardworking Virgo you would, I'm sure, regret being made redundant before you were ready to step down.

If a patient and persevering, determined and dedicated approach to work were all that was needed to be a leading light in the workplace, you'd be there. Make sure that your talents are highly visible to the people who make the decisions when promotions are in the air. Start to become more of a trailblazer, plan to play a key strategic role in your work-performance driven environment, and don't be so afraid of the limelight. You will probably love it once you get there!

If promotion does elude you through no known fault of your own, that is no excuse to slide back into the background. Remember, there is always another chance to move ahead.

TIPS FOR PROMOTION SEEKERS

- Always be ready to take on new business challenges in a fast-moving environment without fear.
- Combine your business strategy skills with creative flair and imagination.
- Show that you can be a leader who is well prepared to challenge the status quo with maturity, pragmatism, and the resolve to succeed.

How to Cope with Being Passed Over for Promotion

Your tendency may be to analyze a missed promotion until you've spent more than a few sleepless nights. Self-critical at the best of times, you're sure to give yourself an unnecessarily hard time for not being good enough, without even considering the fact that there could be a whole host of other reasons as to why someone else received the promotion in question.

Stop giving yourself such a hard time, Virgo. Don't hide away with all your negative thoughts. Put on a more positive face, and find out whatever you can about the true situation. I'm sure it won't be that your work was not up to scratch. Regardless of what comes to light, resolve that it will not be a reason for you to hide away in the background. There is always a new time and a new place, and a truly ambitious Virgo will always find the right niche. Like the fisherman who provided the coffee in his little boat, you must be on the lookout for that opening which is just perfect for your own particular talents and abilities.

Ambition—or the Lack of It

In your slow but sure way, you are often extremely ambitious. The problem arises when you refuse to recognize this fact. Too many of you appear to prefer to sit back and allow other people to take the kudos for your efforts. In this way you also avoid any risk taking you feel would be involved in aiming higher than your current position.

I think you fear rejection in all its many forms more than any other sign. Because you are so dedicated to everything you undertake, it is a cruel blow if this dedication is undervalued in your particular workplace. However, this must not mean you get locked into a dead-end job, watching other people receive the positions that you would like. Always remember that the *way* you see the problem *is* the problem. With your keen eye and critical disposition, nobody can see problems quicker than you, nor come up with a more logical and practical way to overcome them. If you genuinely feel your ambitions are being thwarted for no obvious reasons, you must discuss the situation with your boss. Learn to distance yourself from your fears and to believe more strongly in yourself and your goals. There are times when you really do have to become more assertive, outgoing, and enthusiastic about your own talents.

Your ruling planet, Mercury, is a great asset to your powers of communication. It highlights your quick comprehension, together with your analytical and intellectual prowess. It enables you to analyze your strengths and your weaknesses, and communicate with your inner self and therefore understand your deepest feelings. Listen to Mercury and follow its guidance when you feel in a particularly ambitious mood.

See yourself as a star, and remember that self-fulfilling prophecies *do* work!

Ambition—and Your Love Life

I'm sure it's no coincidence that after a day of writing I called a married Virgo editor friend at 9:30 P.M. only to discover she had just then gotten home from the office. Fortunately, her husband is a brilliant cook and had a meal ready, but she works late too often as far as he's concerned!

If you're a typical Virgo, your devotion to duty at work can sometimes create problems when you have a partner who feels you're not around enough. Devoting yourself 100 percent mind, body, and soul to your job is therefore not always the best of ideas. If you are with someone who is as much of a workaholic as you, things will obviously work out a whole lot better. If not, make sure the balance in your life is not completely out of sync. Never become a martyr in the name of love or work, nor take your relationship too much for granted because you feel your partner understands the importance of your work. Remind yourself that love and romance are important too. There are plenty of happy Virgoans who manage successfully to combine a high-powered career and a good relationship. Be one of them.

If you are emotionally involved with someone who (regardless of his or her sign) has a work ethic and high ideals that are as evolved as your own, you will naturally understand your partner's allegiance to his or her career, even if you do not particularly like it.

Being overly critical can be negative, but one of the positive aspects of your Virgo personality is that you're usually prepared to go to the ends of the world to be with someone you truly love—even putting your own career on hold!

TIPS FOR COMBINING WORK AND LOVE

- Never be too analytical or critical about anyone or anything!
- Don't stay late at the office on too many occasions, especially if it will create problems at home.
- Always remember that even workaholics are allowed to have some time off—and some fun.
- Believe in yourself, your ambitions, and your love life in equal portions, and never become a martyr to any of them.

Romance in the Workplace

With your determined approach to work and sense of duty to your tasks, the idea of a romantic relationship in the workplace is not something that would appeal to many of you. While sex symbols Sean Connery, Sophia Loren, and Raquel Welch share your sign, there is a purity about you that would make it hard for you to conduct a love affair that had to be kept under wraps.

If something goes wrong in your love life, you tend to fall prone to a vast number of anxieties that gnaw away at and upset your equilibrium, affecting your concentration in the office.

As an Earth sign, with your feet very much on the ground, you would rarely indulge in an affair unless you felt deep down that it was true love. For someone who is often so desirable to other people, you tend to be extremely shy about your own sexuality—and I include those of you who are sex symbols. Virgo, the Virgin, is invariably portrayed as totally pure and virginal. I think you'd be too terrified at the very thought of sexual harassment to ever throw yourself at anyone else, no matter how much you were attracted to that person. It would be especially hard for you to embark on a workplace affair with someone who is married. Deep down, and whatever your circumstances, you truly believe that a virtuous life is best. Not only would you fear being hurt yourself, but you would usually find it very hard to be responsible for perhaps hurting a third party.

Your mind finds it easier to deal with material things than to follow flights of fancy. Although your planetary ruler, Mercury, is the same as Gemini's, you communicate your thoughts and ideas, including talking about your emotional needs, in a far more disciplined way than any Gemini I know. If workplace love affairs are frowned on by your employers, you are unlikely to take a reckless stand and allow any desires to dictate your actions. Even though you may have a scorchingly passionate heart and some seductively sensual ways below your cool demeanor and self-contained exterior, you prefer to get on with your work without risking any problems. Besides, you're usually too much of a worrier at heart to involve yourself in anything that might give you doubts and fears.

You and Your Stress Factor

Although stress is a normal human reaction to situations of which you are fearful, you tend to worry about something even when there is no crisis. You need to create the right balance between your mind, body, and soul. In one of my recent books, *Star Signs,* I devised a special meditation for your sign which can help you to relax and become less stressed.

Virgo, in addition to being the sign of work, relates to health. You like to keep tabs on the latest advances in the health fields, including traditional and alternative medicine. Some people unkindly refer to you as the hypochondriac of the Zodiac, but sometimes you do place an inordinate amount of concern on your well-being, and often the well-being of everyone else you know! Virgo rules the nervous system and the intestines, especially the small intestine. It also rules the digestive tract. When you worry excessively about things, you may suffer from stomach and bowel problems, which can be related to your nervous system. The right diet is extremely important, so that a hurried meal of drive-through junk food eaten while driving down the road is not the best idea if you wish to concentrate on achieving your maximum potential.

As a perfectionist, you often find it stressful to entertain the idea of delegating work to anyone because you worry that it might not be done to your high standard. You also tend to worry about your ability to adapt to today's more demanding and fast-changing work environment.

It is perfectly normal to feel anxious before important meetings or when under extreme work pressure. But don't put yourself under unnecessary pressure, allowing nervousness and agitation to take over your life, when what you really need is a chance to relax and unwind. When it's time to sleep, find a way to stop your thoughts and worries from churning through your mind, perhaps by listening to some calm music.

You also need to be able to switch off the pressures of the day and have some fun. Remember the phrase "Yes, Virginia, there is a Santa Claus"? Well, I would like to say, "Yes, Virgo, there is a life outside work." Your active and alert mind benefits from the opportunity to have its batteries recharged. If you find it extremely difficult to turn off your thoughts, even in your leisure time, why not take yourself to some interesting movies or plays. Losing yourself in a good plot will be like giving your mind a well-deserved vacation.

Sometimes you are so wrapped up in your work commitments that you find the idea of taking a *real* vacation beyond the realm of possibility. Aside from being unfair to yourself, this can be extremely unfair to a partner. If you live alone, I hope you have friends and family who will encourage you to go off and lie on an uncrowded beach or take in some different scenery. A good vacation will do wonders for your mind, body, and soul.

When you take up any kind of sport, you are as much a perfectionist at this as you are in your work. You're the kind of golfer who has a brilliant stroke and tends to get a hole in one while everyone looks on in envy—just think of Virgo Arnold Palmer.

It's praiseworthy to spend time looking after people as long as you're happy doing so, but don't make a martyr of yourself. Many of you are brilliant at helping on charity committees, but remember also that stress can be avoided when you are more charitable to *yourself*.

Your Attitude toward Making Money

A worrier and a planner by nature, you are unlikely to have an attitude toward making money that is in any way frivolous. You're more likely to be a compulsive hoarder than a spendthrift. You will not waste anything you have earned, for too much effort has gone into attaining it.

Considerate and careful, discriminating and analytical, you handle money much as you handle people. You want to know exactly where you stand in any given situation. Some of you still dislike the idea of buying anything with "plastic," and you feel much better knowing that paying on time means you pay no interest! Credit is not something you particularly enjoy, since it makes you feel vulnerable; nor do you relish the idea of being in debt. It is unlikely that anyone will owe you money for very long without receiving reminders.

Your realistic and careful attitude will rarely allow you to take risks. You are extremely efficient in dealing with financial matters, and you will certainly have a deep commitment to providing long-term security for yourself and any loved ones. Problems arise if you undervalue your own talents and abilities to the extent that you sometimes accept being underpaid for your job. Always try to ensure that your income relates fairly to your work contribution.

Your financial priorities tend to involve providing yourself with adequate health insurance (I've rarely met a Virgo who *doesn't* worry about health in some way), a comfortable home (but one that's rarely ostentatious, even if you reach millionaire status), and the knowledge that your bank account is never in the red. You often seem to feel uncomfortable spending lavishly on clothes. You are more likely to put spare money in a savings account than spend it on a new fall wardrobe.

Since job security is no longer a given, you are fortunate to have the ability to budget well and to possess a highly disciplined approach to saving. Your sound financial strategy will enable you to come out on top and to achieve the financial security you crave, even in today's highly competitive market.

How to Improve Your Work Relationships

As a Virgo with strong powers of analysis and discrimination, you are sometimes excessively critical of other people and of yourself. But never forget that it is extremely important to be able to get along well with your coworkers.

The following guide will show you the best way to relate to all the signs, whether they are those of your boss, your peer, or an employee.

Virgo with Aries Boss: Don't be intimidated by the Ram's somewhat aggressive techniques and tactics. Or too critical. This boss will listen to your practical advice with interest, even if still charging ahead with her own ideas.

Virgo with Aries Colleague: You seek perfection from beginning to end in every project. But Aries tends to start things with enthusiasm and get bored halfway through. Make sure you're not left with all the dreary jobs!

Virgo with Aries Employee: Remember that this employee secretly yearns to be the boss. While you're nit-picking about every little detail and criticizing every mistake, Aries is probably devising brilliant new projects.

Virgo with Taurus Boss: The Taurus boss may not be the most imaginative of souls, but you will both be on the same wavelength in many ways. Don't create waves by being overly analytical; Taurus is reliable and rarely makes mistakes.

Virgo with Taurus Colleague: Two dependable Earth signs working together are sure to get things done well. You may need to cultivate more of an entrepreneurial streak. Taurus is sometimes a bit slow to get projects off the ground.

Virgo with Taurus Employee: Restrain your urge to double-check everything. Learn to relax and get on with your own work, knowing that this employee is always efficient and never leaves a job half-done.

Virgo with Gemini Boss: Both of you are ruled by Mercury, but with different styles of communication. This boss is an inventive live wire who will appreciate your down-to-earth way of making sure nothing is ever overlooked.

Virgo with Gemini Colleague: Mental communication is rarely a problem; making Gemini sit still long enough to get on with the day's work is another story! Restless Gemini dislikes *any* criticism, but sometimes it's necessary.

Virgo with Gemini Employee: Be firm from the outset. Tidiness is not usually this employee's forté, and her organizing skills may never match yours. Talkative Gemini rarely concentrates on just one thing at a time.

Virgo with Cancer Boss: This boss is ultrasensitive and can be moody too. But you will receive plenty of appreciation for all your hard work, so don't be too faultfinding in your character analysis.

Virgo with Cancer Colleague: Your analytical prowess combined with the way Cancer feels things out will make you a formidable duo. Conversely, never underestimate Cancer's strength if you're on opposing teams.

Virgo with Cancer Employee: Try not to be too picky on Full Moon days! You can rely on this sign's devotion to duty, but you'll have to appreciate that he wants, and deserves, a home life too.

Virgo with Leo Boss: Let's hope this won't be a dictator-servant relationship! Leo has a heart of gold even if she likes the limelight a little too much! Your diligent and painstaking ways will be appreciated.

Virgo with Leo Colleague: Make sure Leo isn't holding court while you are left to get on with the nitty-gritty! Leo's creative flair combined with your pragmatic ways will make you winners in the workplace.

Virgo with Leo Employee: A workaholic Virgo with a pleasure-loving Leo? You may need to keep watch to make sure the work gets done, but Leo's bright and sparkling personality will inspire you.

Virgo with Virgo Boss: Now you will see what it's like to receive constant criticism, even when it's undeserved! This "mirror image" boss must thank his lucky stars to have an employee as perfect as you.

Virgo with Virgo Colleague: You may both appear to be dreary and self-doubting to others. Nevertheless, you'll be an extraordinarily efficient working team, provided you stop worrying about the long-term and get on with the now.

Virgo with Virgo Employee: Two paragons of virtue together! Do restrain yourself from being too critical when there probably won't be the slightest need. A Virgo employee *rarely* makes mistakes.

Virgo with Libra Boss: This boss may be somewhat indecisive but is wonderfully diplomatic and charming. Your hard work will be rewarded with praise and genuine admiration, so you should have few complaints.

Virgo with Libra Colleague: Your analytical ways combined with some Libran logic and charm can go a long way on the road to success. Be less nit-picking and more flattering—you will get on better that way.

Virgo with Libra Employee: Libra is anxious to please, so don't be too much of a dragon if this employee's work doesn't meet your exacting standards once in a while. Libra always works best in a harmonious atmosphere.

Virgo with Scorpio Boss: Remember the sting in the Scorpion's tail, and don't give this boss the chance to find fault with you. If you're hoping to take over, be aware that Scorpio truly believes she is unconquerable.

Virgo with Scorpio Colleague: If you're on the same team, this can be a powerful duo; but if Scorpio is your opponent, your work will be cut out for you. Scorpio is just as analytical and determined as you!

Virgo with Scorpio Employee: Just because Scorpio is renowned as the sex symbol of the Zodiac doesn't mean he can't be an excellent worker too! Don't be unreasonably critical. A Scorpio with a grudge could lead to a difficult working atmosphere.

Virgo with Sagittarius Boss: This self-confident and happy-go-lucky boss will be fun to work for most of the time. The Archer likes to be right, even when wrong, so be prepared to cover up any mistakes he might make.

Virgo with Sagittarius Colleague: Bright, bubbly, and bursting with ideas, this colleague has the entrepreneurial flair needed to inspire you to greater heights. But don't take the boring tasks while she has the fun.

Virgo with Sagittarius Employee: No way can Sagittarius be as painstaking as you. Try not to be overly critical. This employee's ways may not be neat and tidy, but he will support you with enthusiasm.

Virgo with Capricorn Boss: Ruled by Saturn, taskmaster of the Zodiac, a Capricorn boss won't put up with any nonsense. This is someone to respect, who usually reaches the top by dint of sheer hard work all along the way.

Virgo with Capricorn Colleague: Two hardworking Earth signs, careful and prudent in their ways. But you may both need to be more receptive to new technology to prove that you're geared for success.

Virgo with Capricorn Employee: If you weren't a natural-born worrier, you could sit back and enjoy life, knowing you have the hardest-working employee in the world! Stop fussing and rejoice in your good fortune.

Virgo with Aquarius Boss: Always remember that Aquarius got to the top being different from everyone else. This boss is unpredictable in many ways but amazingly appreciative of your diligent approach to your work.

Virgo with Aquarius Colleague: Your fastidious and exacting ways could drive Aquarius crazy. But your realistic appraisal of some of her unconventional schemes could lead to a successful working relationship.

Virgo with Aquarius Employee: The finished work may not look quite as you imagined, but be patient! Aquarius is friendly, loyal, articulate, and willing to learn. Too much nit-picking could cause this employee to look for another job.

Virgo with Pisces Boss: Your opposite sign is sensitive and impractical, but very caring too. You can learn a lot from this boss if you're prepared to be a little less exacting in your criticism of her ways.

Virgo with Pisces Colleague: Pisces tends to see the world through rose-tinted glasses, but don't be fooled! Professionally, Pisces can also be highly successful and you will work well together if you're not too patronizing.

Virgo with Pisces Employee: Be understanding if Pisces makes a mistake, for it's virtually impossible to live up to such a paragon of virtue as you. Pisces may be more caring than careful but would never want to let you down.

Getting Longevity out of Your Career

Getting longevity out of your career is really not something that should worry you unduly. Most Virgo men and women I know seem to continue working long past the usual retirement age, not necessarily because of the money but because they genuinely feel the need to be of service in one way or another.

The ability to remain passionate about service and quality throughout your working life, and to combine your disciplined approach to everything you undertake with the right blend of business and technical skills, is unlikely to fail you.

While your highly developed analytical skills and good record of practical achievement will not diminish over time, your unfortunate habit of undervaluing yourself and your talents can sometimes remain an ongoing, yet unnecessary, problem throughout your life—regardless of the heights of success you might attain. It is extremely important to retain a positive attitude throughout your working life, no matter how many knocks or disappointments may arise along the way.

It is impossible to predict the future of the workplace, but it is safe to say that people with business vision and outstanding interpersonal skills will always be needed. Just make sure that you are not so committed to getting on with your work *behind* the scenes that you end up being overlooked. Never risk losing your job simply because you have not made yourself as noticeable as other people in your company. Gaining visibility at the corporate level may not necessarily be your chosen aim in life, but it is becoming increasingly more important if you want to keep your job. And remember, information technology is the name of the game these days. Keep up-to-date.

Unfortunately, there are times when someone is fired unfairly. If this happens to you, find out what your legal rights are and hire an attorney if necessary. Keep your résumé up-to-date, and never hesitate to apply for something new. Being fired or laid off need not be the disaster of all time. People change jobs more and more often these days, and the age factor does not have to be a major barrier. When you have developed your own particular skills to a very high level, you will always be able to use them in one way or another. Keep believing in yourself and your talents, for then you will make everyone else believe in them too.

VIRGO CAREER STRATEGIES—A CHECKLIST FOR EVERY AGE

- Combine your dedication to duty with being more of a high-flier—it's sure to pay off well.
- Allow your mercurial mind to flow freely and to constantly generate imaginative and creative ideas.
- Resolve not to let other people take the credit for plans and projects devised by you.
- Be as good to yourself as you are to everyone around you. This often means finding more time to relax!
- Never let yourself get overstressed by being too much of a workaholic.
- Be a perfectionist by all means, but try not to criticize excessively those people who cannot live up to your high standards.
- Always define your goals. But don't get into a panic and waste important time worrying that you're not good enough to achieve them. I'm sure you are.

LIBRA IN THE WORKPLACE

September 22 ☆ *October 22*

If you were born between September 22 and October 22, you were born under the sign of Libra, seventh sign of the Zodiac, which relates to partnerships. You are a Masculine, Cardinal, Positive, Air sign. Your planetary symbol is the Scales. Your planetary ruler is Venus, Goddess of Love.

You are known as the sign of peace and harmony. An idealist with a logical mind, you need to see beauty all around you. You are prepared to work extremely hard in order to create that beauty. Because you are a born peacemaker, and appear on the surface to be so calm and laid-back, you are sometimes accused of not being competitive enough to be a major player in today's cutthroat business world. But surely no one could accuse Librans Lee Iacocca, Barbara Walters, or Ralph Lauren of having been too laid-back to achieve major successes in their lives. I hardly think that Libran actor Christopher Reeve would have fought back so strenuously and admirably from his horrific accident had he not possessed a massive amount of inner strength.

Libra relates to the laws of justice, harmony, and proportion, and almost every Libran I know is brilliant at weighing the pros and cons of any situation. Your Libran ability to be open-minded is an asset, but you must also be commercially astute and assertive, able to demonstrate a dynamic approach.

Your opposite sign, Aries, is as tough and determined as you appear to be soft and pliable. Aries can teach you to be more of a gung-ho leader in today's corporate world. Because you can learn something from *every* sign, you might try to play a different sign once in a while.

Take a typical workday in the Libra life. You are left in charge of a project that requires critical discussions with other members of your team. Unfortunately, they are unexpectedly unavailable. Some important decisions cannot wait for an answer, and everything is left in your hands. It may appear that everyone but you knows you can deliver the goods!

Playing Aries: Knowing it has to be "me" rather than "we" prompts you to be more assertive and even fairly dictatorial too! Keen to make a highly visible impact, you tackle everything with the minimum of doubts.

Playing Taurus: You'd never let your team down by taking too long to reach any decisions. Slow but sure in your methods, you are charm personified and study any problems with no hint of inner fears or self-doubts.

Playing Gemini: Gemini is another Air sign, so allow this double dose of Air to boost your lofty idealism. Listen to what your alert and intellectual mind tells you!

Playing Cancer: Your instincts and sensitivity help you reach the right decisions with a minimum of worry. You are determined to do the best you can for everyone on your team.

Playing Leo: A Leo never wastes time hesitating when fortunes can be made and lost in a mere moment! You grab the opportunity to become more of a star and resolve to have greater faith in yourself.

Playing Virgo: With a Virgo hat, your decision making is enhanced by your ability to analyze the pros and cons of *everything*. Provided you have sufficient faith in yourself, you will be a real winner here.

Playing Yourself: Be calm and forget about procrastination and vacillation. Resolve to externalize your inner sense of harmony and balance. You will soon make the right decisions!

Playing Scorpio: Forget any fears of not succeeding. With Scorpio's influence, you are unstoppable. Play fair but play tough too. Aided by Scorpio's sixth sense, there is no reason to doubt your ability to succeed.

Playing Sagittarius: When playing the Archer, your innermost doubts and fears give way to confidence and enthusiasm. You are so determined to make the right decision that there is almost no way you can fail.

Playing Capricorn: You put a great deal of effort into dealing with the situation conscientiously and prudently. Your feet are placed firmly on the ground, so you don't have to worry about anything.

Playing Aquarius: Wearing an Aquarian hat enables you to take a more unconventional approach. Your decision making is based on cool rationale, aided and abetted by an extremely alert and intelligent mind.

Playing Pisces: You are highly sensitive to the situation facing you and need to make sure you are not impractical. You don't hesitate over the pros and cons but listen carefully to your inner voice.

The Positive and Negative Qualities of a Libra at Work

Once you learn to overcome your tendency toward indecision, you are a major force to be reckoned with, whatever your position at work. Your Cardinal quality enables you to start projects with enthusiasm and ensures you don't then become too laid-back.

As an analytical Air sign, you are able to tackle issues with clarity and objectivity. You are a great negotiator, mediator, and a born peacemaker—with the ability to remain detached yet still show sufficient sympathy and understanding to others.

To attain *and* retain a high-profile role in today's highly competitive workplace, you must be as brilliant at working on your own initiative as you are at being a team member. Procrastination has become the root of all evil in the corporate jungle, so resolve now to be as gung ho and assertive as Aries!

Leadership skills are as important as your ability to form effective cross-functional relationships at all levels. Always keep up with the latest technology so that you can play a key strategic role at work.

To be a truly positive Libra, you must maximize your talents. Never become so soft and pliable that someone with less talent but more determination can overtake you on the road to success. Maximize your potential to turn situations to your advantage by using your Libran charm and diplomacy.

The positive Libra is harmonious and diplomatic, but also highly aware that the leaders in today's workplace are those who can perform exceptionally well under pressure. You are brilliant at taking the necessary time and trouble to understand the issues at hand, and perfectly capable of applying your own leadership skills in order to deliver results. The three Ls—lethargy, laid-back, and lazy—must be deleted from your vocabulary! Your intellectual ability is rarely in dispute, nor is your ability to interface with internal and external teams. By learning to seize the initiative more frequently, you can make an even greater contribution at work.

The negative Libra is sometimes too content to be overly influenced by other people. Just because you were born under the sign of partnerships, it doesn't mean you are not allowed to function alone! I've known Librans who have become so accustomed to using someone else as a sounding board that they have lost the ability to rely on their own good judgment. Stop being frightened to say what you want out of life; go ahead and work for it.

The wise Libran will develop new ways to define goals and keep evolving in his or her career. Combine your empathy and understanding with high energy, drive, and stamina. Never miss out on the opportunity to become more of a star; don't undervalue your talents or sit too long on the fence.

Careers for Libra

A high proportion of Libran men and women are drawn to the arts, especially writing books, painting, composing music, and working in the world of entertainment. You also make excellent art dealers, cinematographers, interior decorators, fashion designers, architects, diplomats, judges, counselors, personnel managers, public relations managers, stylists, hairdressers, and advertising executives.

Famous Librans include Nietzsche, Truman Capote, F. Scott Fitzgerald, Jimmy Carter, Brigitte Bardot, Jackie Collins, Donna Karan, Martina Navratilova (whom no one could ever accuse of lacking competitive spirit), Oscar-winning actress and political campaigner Susan Sarandon, Charlton Heston, Marcello Mastroianni, Jean-Claude Van Damme, Luciano Pavarotti, Arthur Miller, Gore Vidal, and Britain's Iron Lady, ex–prime minister Margaret Thatcher.

Your Attitude toward Work

Naturally, your rising sign, together with all the other factors of your individual horoscope, will also influence your attitude toward work.

Your sense of peace, harmony, and fair play can be a bonus when you are set among today's hardheaded businessmen and -women. Your element of Air makes you a sign of both reason and intellect, although sometimes you can be a bit of a snob if asked to do any work that you feel is beneath your dignity.

Libra is portrayed by the only inanimate symbol in the Zodiac: the Scales. You must ensure that your Libran scales are sufficiently in balance to achieve a harmonious and rewarding work life.

Sometimes your attitude toward work constitutes taking the easy way out. This happens when you are too inclined to appease rather than go into battle. Unfortunately, there are many occasions when today's workplace really does seem like a battlefield. Don't give away your power, Libra. Encourage your creative energy, identify your goals, and set out to fulfill them. Become a smarter player and promote yourself more so that you gain greater visibility.

In addition to your ability to analyze and rationalize, you have a great eye for detail. However, I feel that your attitude toward work should include setting yourself weekly goals, perhaps even daily ones. Avoid the "mañana" syndrome—that is, leaving something for tomorrow that needs to be completed *now*. Forget self-doubt. If you have done your homework, you will not need to worry about making mistakes.

When you are fulfilled in your work, you possess a deep commitment to your coworkers and inspire their trust. You are successful at fostering a collaborative spirit because you inspire trust from those who work with you. Teamwork is an indisputable fact of life these days. Often, before you are recognized for your own talents and abilities, you will be judged on the basis of your particular team's success.

Libran men and women do not necessarily demand their own private space in which to work. Because you are a sign that thrives on company, many of you prefer to work in tastefully decorated, open-plan areas, which need to be light and airy. You are sensitive, with a great sense of style and beauty, and would find it difficult to work within a depressing environment—or indeed with people who are depressing.

When you believe deeply in your work, there is no way you will give up, no matter what may befall you in your life. While writing this book, I was fortunate to meet and become friendly with the world-famous movie director Michelangelo Antonioni and his wife, Enrica Fico. Michelangelo is one of the most amazing Librans I have ever met. Even though he suffered a stroke eleven years ago, today, at the age of eighty-three, he is still directing with great enthusiasm. His last movie, *Beyond the Clouds,* with John Malkovich and Fanny Ardant, was highly acclaimed. To look at life through the eyes of a Michelangelo Antonioni is to truly appreciate the Libran love of beauty, for then even the foggiest of miserable gray days will contain wonderful elements of mystery or even mysticism.

TIPS FOR A HEALTHY WORK ATTITUDE

- Never sit on the fence when decisions need to be made.
- Enjoy functioning as part of a team, but always remember you have the talent to be a leader too!
- Remember that the most powerful people are empowered from within. Accept and love yourself for who and what you are. The rest will follow naturally.

Aiming for Promotion

When it comes to aiming for promotion, your laid-back approach does not serve you well. If you're being totally honest, you will admit that although the idea of climbing higher up that ladder of success is immensely appealing, you do not always take the steps to ensure that the next level is within your grasp.

Your debonair charm, your understated sensitivity, and your ability to weigh the pros and cons of just about every situation you encounter are all admirable traits; so too is your ability to cope with virtually any problem without losing your Libran balance. I simply don't believe you if you shrug your shoulders philosophically and say you don't care very much about aiming for promotion. All my Libran friends and clients have, at some point in their lives, wondered whether they should be higher up the ladder and making greater use of their particular talents.

Occasionally you have a tendency to be somewhat complacent in your attitude. This may allow inertia to set in, which is definitely something to avoid when a promotion may be in the cards! Sometimes I think you have a secret fear of failure which upsets your equilibrium and prevents you from striving for the success you desire. If you don't feel inwardly right about something, it's fine to let it go. But don't let it go when you *do* feel it's right.

Because Libra is the first sign of fall, when the Sun's force is waning, it is sometimes difficult for you to portray the fiery enthusiasm of your opposite sign, Aries, which is the first sign of spring. Since you are invariably brilliant at encouraging other people to become more successful (I have a wonderful Libran agent myself), I have never understood why more of you don't encourage yourselves in the same way! It really does all start from within. When *you* believe you are worthy of promotion, it is much easier to convince your superiors of this fact. Identify where your future lies and then take the steps to move forward.

Your Air element makes you extremely good at devising strategies, plus, as a Cardinal sign, you should be equally enterprising and determined. Think of the benefits of combining these qualities with your ability to negotiate. Never sit back and allow other people to take the promotions that you rightly deserve. Make sure you are an energetic and innovative Libran with the vision, drive, and enthusiasm so vital in today's corporate world. Demonstrate your ability to work as part of a team and to work individually within tight time frames. Remember that your diplomacy, persuasion, and independence of thought are extremely worthwhile Libran traits. Combine them with an insuperable determination to succeed, and a new Libran star will soon be born.

TIPS FOR PROMOTION SEEKERS

- Combine your team-building and motivating skills with greater entrepreneurial ability.
- Always try to make your personal contribution highly visible and influential.
- Prove your ability to develop creative, yet workable, solutions based on your sound Libran analysis.

How to Cope with Being Passed Over for Promotion

Sometimes, being passed over for a promotion gives you the opportunity to reevaluate your life, to consider that perhaps you were aiming in the wrong direction in the first place. It then becomes a blessing in disguise, giving you the opportunity to change your life for the better.

You cannot blame anyone else if a promotion has failed to materialize due to your own lack of motivation. In such situations, you must take a long hard look at your attitude toward work.

Don't be afraid to aim for the very top of your career. The workplace will always need people like you—people with strong communication skills who are able to work diplomatically within any corporate culture, at all levels, and across all disciplines.

Most Librans have a dream they long to fulfill. If yours is winning a promotion, never let a putdown put you off! There will always be other opportunities, but you'll only find them if you're actively looking for them.

Ambition—or the Lack of It

While you don't necessarily possess the get-up-and-go, enterprising attitude of your opposite sign, Aries, perhaps this is the moment to tell you that your sign includes Alexander the Great, Bishop Desmond Tutu (winner of a Nobel Peace Prize), Mahatma Gandhi, Juan Perón, and David Ben-Gurion, founder of the State of Israel. None of them were prepared to take second place.

Most Librans have ambitions to fulfill, but they are sometimes so busy being nice to everyone else that they neglect what *they* want out of life. Your ability to weigh both sides of a situation means that sometimes you are too inclined to accept the status quo. In today's fast-paced environment, you must prove you can be an entrepreneurial achiever with shrewd negotiating skills, able to explore and capitalize on every possible new opportunity.

Your motivational and interpersonal strengths will be of paramount importance in the workplace. Your sense of fair play is admirable, but sometimes you are not completely fair to yourself by underestimating or underplaying your talents and abilities.

Learn to project greater self-confidence, and don't allow yourself to slip behind in the technology race. Never drift aimlessly through the workplace. Rejoice in the benefit of your ruling planet, Venus. She allows you to see the beauty in your life. Visualize how your life can become even more beautiful when you fulfill some deep-rooted personal ambition—*whatever* it may be.

Ambition—and Your Love Life

Because you are the sign of balance, relationships, and partnerships, it sometimes becomes difficult for you to concentrate on your ambitions if your love life conflicts with your work. Interestingly enough, you can often cope with the effect of breakups without losing your Libran balance. But because of your inherent desire for peace and harmony at all times, it is often extremely hard for you to cut your mind off from any ongoing emotional upsets between a partner and yourself in order to concentrate totally on your work.

When everything is sweetness and light in your romantic life, you rarely have a problem with your work. Although you thrive on being in a good relationship, you don't necessarily feel you must talk with the love of your life half a dozen times a day. For you, it is sufficient to know that someone special is there. Creating the right balance between work and love is exceedingly important to you. It is all a question of balancing your Libran scales so your mind is clear and your heart is content.

I have known several Librans who have worked extremely well in business partnerships with their husband or wife. It becomes part of the "togetherness" that you enjoy so much. However, I have also known some Librans who have allowed a partner to have almost too much interference in their working lives, resulting in their being far too indecisive about certain work issues. If you are involved with a Libran, don't try to push this person too much one way or another. Librans need to learn how to balance their own scales without having them constantly balanced for them!

TIPS FOR COMBINING WORK AND LOVE

- Always strive for peace and harmony in every area of your life.
- Try to be tolerant with a partner who could be jealous, but never lose sight of your professional objectives.
- Never bury your head in the sand if problems do arise; deal with them diplomatically, remembering that you're a born peacemaker.
- Be committed to your career and your emotional life, without letting one take over from the other, unless you know that's what you *really* want.

Romance in the Workplace

Of all the Zodiac signs, I think yours is the most flirtatious. With Venus, Goddess of Love, as your ruler, your eye for beauty is renowned, and you can rarely resist a pretty face or sexy smile.

I don't want to tell you that you're not allowed to smile at anyone with whom you work, or even to indulge in a little harmless flirting. I merely want to remind you that what may be flirting in *your* mind could constitute sexual harassment in someone else's—especially in these days of "political correctness."

There is nothing wrong with starting a relationship with an office-mate when you are both free and wish to take it farther. But if you're a typical Libran, you are not very good at dealing with any kind of love triangle. You can be as jealous as any Scorpio, Aries, or Taurus. Jealousy makes it difficult for you to balance your Libran scales, and must never be allowed to interfere with your work!

A love affair in the workplace may sound wonderfully romantic, and I'm sure that on occasions it can be. But weigh the pros and cons of indulging in this particular exercise. Achieving peace, harmony, and companionship in your life doesn't necessarily mean that you should try to balance an office love affair with a job that is already demanding, time-consuming, and often stressful.

You rarely need advice in the art of seduction and many of you never stop searching for a perfect soulmate, no matter how long this may take, or where you are. But using your Libran charm to attract lovers is not what you should be doing in the workplace! It is great to enjoy day-to-day companionship with people who are on the same wavelength as you, but use your Libran scales to weigh things carefully and consider the outcome when you are contemplating a sexual relationship with a coworker.

You and Your Stress Factor

Stress is a normal reaction to situations that you fear; it can be beneficial by giving you a rush of adrenaline that will enable you to fire on all cylinders when you're feeling too laid-back. But in today's fiercely competitive workplace, there is an ever-growing number of people who suffer from stress-related problems.

A balanced approach to your work, your emotions, and the other aspects of your life is the key to keeping stress at bay. Creating the right balance within your mind, body, and soul is of paramount importance. In one of my recent books, *Star Signs,* I devised a meditation that will help you to achieve this, by calming your mind and enabling you to rise above any emotional imbalance.

Libra rules the bladder and kidneys, organs that regulate the body's liquids and eliminate waste. Both these organs will react to inner stress and to overindulgence. Because healthwise Libra also relates to the body's nervous system, when you lose your equilibrium you may also risk the possibility of ulcers. Keep a careful eye on your diet, and regulate the amount of alcohol you drink.

If you are feeling stressed out, getting out in the fresh air and eating a proper meal will do you far more good than ordering out for a sandwich and gulping it down at your desk. Taking a break, however short it may have to be, will also give you a chance to clear your mind and recharge your batteries. Keeping yourself physically and psychologically fit will always help to allay stress.

Your Libran desire for peace and accord can be a bonus, since it means you will rarely indulge in unnecessary arguments that could send your blood pressure rising sky-high! You are not afraid to stand up for your beliefs but would rather resolve disagreements in a calm manner whenever possible. Harmony around you helps to create calm in your inner world. But today's corporate world is often a cutthroat one, where peace and harmony may be too quickly misinterpreted by some people as being lazy and lacking in leadership skills.

Stress is bound to arise if you deny yourself sufficient time to unwind and enjoy some leisure time. Your inherent ability and desire to balance your life on *all* levels should ensure that you manage to enjoy a life outside work.

Social get-togethers with friends will always please you, especially when they take your mind off the pressures of your job. Most Librans are interested in the arts, so you will enjoy going to plays, movies, concerts, and exhibitions. Listening to music is also a joy to many of you, and you usually have extremely eclectic tastes.

You're not the most physically active of signs. When you are feeling particularly stressed, visiting a health club that allows you to indulge yourself in saunas and aromatherapy massages may be the best present you could ever give yourself!

Your Attitude toward Making Money

Making money is rarely your major motivation in life, although you may be brilliant at inspiring others to part with it for something you believe in. This is precisely what Libran Bob Geldof did when he helped the starving people of Ethiopia with his Live Aid concerts. But many of you are far too inclined to sit back and hope that the money will simply roll in. Gone are the days when raises were automatic. We're living in a time when performance reviews are more goal-related than ever. If your own performance is not up to par, you are highly unlikely to receive a raise—and could find yourself searching for a new job instead.

You are often more concerned with doing a "meaningful" job than with the amount on your pay stub at the end of the week or month. If you have dependents who are relying on your salary, you cannot afford to be too laissez-faire in your attitude toward money. Sometimes your generous nature means you allow other people to take advantage of you, lending cash to colleagues who are short a few dollars and then forget to pay you back. You're the sort of person who is always prepared to toast a coworker's good fortune with a bottle of champagne, even if it means economizing yourself.

It is important to have realistic salary goals during your working life. These will also act as an incentive for you to keep the field in perspective and to set your sights on the top. Always exploit your innovation and flair in order to accelerate your career. Focus your activity on the right targets—which must also include making enough money to cover all your expenses and still have some to spare for personal enjoyment. With your Libran love of beauty (never forget that you enjoy looking beautiful too!), I defy you to deny that you enjoy going on vacations, keeping up with the arts, and having a busy social life outside work; yet how do you expect to pay for all of that—unless you're relying on someone else to pick up all the tabs!

Always try to make sure you have a good savings plan in place so you don't have to worry when it's time to retire.

How to Improve Your Work Relationships

I know from personal experience that you're a master of tact and diplomacy, with a natural ability to be sweeter and more charming than almost anyone else. However, you may still have something to learn from this guide for getting along well with your coworkers. It will show you the best way to relate to all the signs—whether they are those of your boss, your peer, or an employee.

Libra with Aries Boss: If you always remember that an Aries boss expects you to complete tasks with the minimum of fuss—and the maximum of speed—you'll get on fine. Aries lacks patience, but maybe you can calm him down!

Libra with Aries Colleague: While you evaluate everything carefully, this colleague is inclined to rush ahead impulsively. Together you can move mountains if you learn more about each other's strengths and weaknesses.

Libra with Aries Employee: Don't forget you are the boss, or Aries will try to take over. Aries thrives on challenges, so try to give her at least one a day. Always thank her for her efforts, and you'll have the undying support of this employee.

Libra with Taurus Boss: You are both ruled by Venus, and the Taurus boss will generally be patient and understanding. Watch out you're not too indecisive or laid-back. The Bull can be a stubborn and demanding taskmaster.

Libra with Taurus Colleague: Be happy that peace and harmony flow between you. Taurus may be somewhat slow moving, but you're not the most energetic soul either! The Bull is a loyal colleague, so you make a good team.

Libra with Taurus Employee: This hardworking employee will never let you down, so don't criticize him for being too set in his ways. Taurus is dependable and unflappable, even when major problems arise.

Libra with Gemini Boss: With a live-wire intellectual Gemini boss, you will never become bored. But be prepared to deal with a myriad of tasks in the fastest possible time—and do them brilliantly too!

Libra with Gemini Colleague: Two Air-ruled colleagues have plenty to talk about. But don't spend too long discussing your different points of view, or the work will pile up in front of you and never get done.

Libra with Gemini Employee: Don't let Gemini talk too much or her tasks will be left unfinished. Be fair but firm and never indecisive. Gemini will soon consider you the perfect boss and provide you with brilliant backup.

Libra with Cancer Boss: This sensitive Lunar boss can sometimes be moody. Maybe you'd better check the phases of the Moon each day! Cancer can be quite a workaholic, so make sure your work is up to scratch.

Libra with Cancer Colleague: You think things out with logic and analysis, while Cancer feels them intuitively. Combine the two, and you can make a winning team. Remember that the Crab cannot help feeling ultrasensitive at times.

Libra with Cancer Employee: Once you've accepted that Cancer suffers occasionally from crabby moods, be thankful you have an employee who makes allowances when *you're* feeling down—and who is hardworking too.

Libra with Leo Boss: Forget about Mussolini and Napoleon—Leos aren't all dictators! Prove that you're prepared to work hard, and this boss will make you feel *almost* as important as her, as long as you don't try to take over!

Libra with Leo Colleague: Leo's self-confident approach will fire you with enthusiasm. Your ability to debate your different points of view will be equally well received. Together you make a successful team.

Libra with Leo Employee: No Leo likes to take orders from anyone, but when they're given with Libran charm and diplomacy you will soon be his favorite boss! Especially if you praise him in return.

Libra with Virgo Boss: When laid-back Libra works for the critic of the Zodiac, you'd best be on your toes and make sure your work contains no mistakes! Analytical Virgo wants perfection at all times.

Libra with Virgo Colleague: Always take a positive approach. Virgo's critical ways combined with your ability to weigh all the pros and cons should mean you *rarely* make mistakes and both of you will be winners!

Libra with Virgo Employee: A Virgo employee is a paragon of virtue who would almost faint at the idea of making mistakes. This service-oriented sign would never let you down, but don't overload Virgo with work just because you feel lazy!

Libra with Libra Boss: This is not a great combination, unless your Libra boss has a strong Ascendant and powerful planets in her chart to compensate for a laid-back tendency. Otherwise you could spend too much time being charming to each other!

Libra with Libra Colleague: This can be a wonderfully easygoing partnership, provided you are both more decisive and spend less time chatting about your social lives. The workplace has no space for dilettantes!

Libra with Libra Employee: Being a kind and considerate boss is commendable, but watch out you're not encouraging your Libran employee to take too much of a relaxed approach to everything.

Libra with Scorpio Boss: A Scorpio boss expects the best and hates any kind of excuse. This sign has justly earned its reputation of being invincible. Scorpio requires respect and work that is *always* done well.

Libra with Scorpio Colleague: Always remember to look behind you; this colleague could be after your job if he thinks it's better than his own. Scorpio can be very loyal and supportive—but you're never totally sure!

Libra with Scorpio Employee: Most Scorpio men and women are always striving to be more successful. Watch out you're not too laid-back, or *you* could end up as the employee with Scorpio as *your* boss!

Libra with Sagittarius Boss: On the surface Sagittarius appears to be the most informal and relaxed boss you've ever known. But the Archer thinks she knows all the answers and hates to be told she's wrong!

Libra with Sagittarius Colleague: This lovable, friendly colleague is brimming over with team spirit. But Sagittarians hate to be tied down and you're indecisive, so you need a well-organized schedule.

Libra with Sagittarius Employee: If this employee doesn't think you're doing something properly, don't be surprised if he tells you tactlessly. Both of you are languid at times, but make sure you behave like a boss!

Libra with Capricorn Boss: Capricorn is the uncrowned workaholic of the Zodiac, and sometimes a bit of a martyr about work too. Don't slip off early or take too long for lunch when working for such a highly disciplined and ambitious boss.

Libra with Capricorn Colleague: Remember that a Capricorn colleague probably aspires to become a boss soon. The Mountain Goat never neglects her duties, even when exhausted, so make sure you don't either.

Libra with Capricorn Employee: Having a hardworking Capricorn employee who will never let you down is no excuse for *you* to take off and have fun. Always be well-organized and have a businesslike approach to your work.

Libra with Aquarius Boss: Don't expect this flexible boss to behave the same way for more than a day at a time! Mentally you should be on the same wavelength, but get used to an unpredictable work schedule!

Libra with Aquarius Colleague: Since you're both "idea" people, you are a highly creative duo. Watch out you don't talk so much that insufficient work is done. If you're on opposing teams, remember Aquarius can be secretive too!

Libra with Aquarius Employee: Aquarius comes up with an innovative approach to everything. But this sign's concern for humanity at large means he doesn't always concentrate sufficiently on one person at a time.

Libra with Pisces Boss: This sympathetic and understanding boss provides you with a shoulder to cry on whenever the going gets tough. But even a soft and sensitive Piscean won't put up with sloppy and unfinished work!

Libra with Pisces Colleague: You are sometimes lazy and Pisces is not always practical. But your Libran ability to analyze, combined with a Piscean's intuition can also make you front-runners on your team.

Libra with Pisces Employee: Always be fair but firm with this employee, who tends to get emotional about any little upsets in her life. If you want perfect work on time, don't accept any weak excuses.

Getting Longevity out of Your Career

Because I have sometimes accused Librans of being too laid-back in their approach to work, you may assume that now I am going to accuse you of not even *wanting* longevity from a career. Not at all. I know Librans who have continued working to a ripe old age without ever wanting to stop! One good friend of mine, who was the owner of an English-language school in Italy, still enjoys giving lessons to private pupils, long after she could have retired and enjoyed a more leisurely life.

However, job security can no longer be taken for granted, whatever your age or position. I've known newspaper editors to be fired simply because the management decided it was time for a change, hoping that a change of editor could boost a flagging circulation. Having a good track record does not always guarantee you longevity in your job or career. Your inherent Libran traits of charm and diplomacy will not necessarily impress a management who cares a whole lot more about the financial results at the end of the year than how those results were obtained. But your ability to lead through persuasiveness and diplomacy certainly helps you to fit into most work environments without upsetting other people. You rarely have a desire to become embroiled in work politics, even though your ability to see both sides of a situation is highly commendable, as is the ease with which you can put out fires when tempers flare and disagreements arise.

Always make sure that your shrewd negotiating talents and business acumen continue to be combined with the entrepreneurial ability to work on your own initiative, not simply as part of a team. Never allow yourself to fall short of energy, enthusiasm, or leadership skills, or to lose the irrepressible desire to succeed at your chosen career. Be sure to learn and understand as much as possible about computers and any other new technology that pertains to your field. Since teamwork is an ongoing fact of working life, you are one of the most fortunate signs in the Zodiac, for being part of a team is highly desirable for Librans of every age. Networking is also extremely important, and because most Librans have a natural ability to be extremely popular among their peers and colleagues, you should have no difficulty in keeping up-to-date with whatever is happening in your particular field.

Resolve you will never become too easygoing in your working life, but that you will always strive to climb as high up the ladder of success as possible. Then if you *are* fired, at least the financial recompense should help to make up for some of your loss of pride.

It is said that most people change careers these days at least three times in their lives, so even if you are laid off from your present employment, there will always be something else you can do. You're sure to have sufficient charm to convince a new employer that you're indispensable. So don't waste time worrying about the future. Get on with living your working life *now.*

LIBRA CAREER STRATEGIES—A CHECKLIST FOR EVERY AGE

- When you need to be more gung ho in your approach, think about your opposite sign, Aries, and wear the Ram's hat for a while!
- Witty, lively, and utterly persuasive, you can be the perfect diplomat at all times. But don't sit on the fence for too long. At critical moments your response times will be vital.

- Make the most of your gregarious personality and networking skills to ensure you're never left out in the cold. You need to know *everything* that's going on.
- Never be so lazy as to not become totally conversant with the latest technology, no matter how often new developments come along.
- Be proud that you're a brilliant team player, but make sure you're a skilled leader who can seize the initiative too.
- Always keep your first-class communication and presentation skills up to scratch, and make sure you can perform well under pressure.
- Remember that Venus, Goddess of Love, gives you the ability to charm the birds off the trees. But don't forget that romance in the workplace will often lead to trouble.

SCORPIO IN THE WORKPLACE

October 23 ☆ *November 21*

If you were born between October 23 and November 20, you were born under the sign of Scorpio, eighth sign of the Zodiac. You are a Feminine, Fixed, Negative, Water sign. Your planetary symbol is the Scorpion. The Serpent and the Eagle are also linked with Scorpio as planetary symbols. You have two planetary rulers: Mars, God of War, and Pluto, Lord of the Underworld.

Aries is also ruled by Mars, and like Aries you sometimes consider life to be a battlefield. You are described as the most invincible of all the Zodiac signs, but there is a darker side to your personality, which makes it hard for you to forget a slight. I've always felt that you are the most maligned and misunderstood sign in the Zodiac, mainly because people cannot forget about that "sting in the Scorpion's tail." What these same people fail to take into account is that while you are supposed to be invincible, the truth is that you don't necessarily always feel that way! I know many highly successful Scorpio men and women who feel insecure at their core.

You have extremely deep and intense feelings. You're a highly sensitive Water sign, just like Cancer and Pisces, but you are far more private, holding everything inside you, until you're almost fit to burst. You may start to hold grudges against other people whose only faults are to carry on with their own lives in their own way; or you may become unreasonably jealous of someone you think is after your job.

We all have something to learn from our opposite sign in the Zodiac. Your opposite sign is Taurus—calm, dependable, hardworking Taurus. Taurus can be just as stubborn as you but is more prepared to take the time and trouble to find acceptable solutions to problems if and when they arise. You can learn something from every sign, which is why you might try to play a different sign once in a while.

Take a typical workday in the Scorpio life. Perhaps you arrive in the office in a really bad mood. The memory of a nasty disagreement with a coworker the night before still bothers you. You're convinced you were in the right, and you can't let it go. The receptionist tells you that your first appointment has arrived early. So what do you do?

Playing Aries: You act as though nothing was wrong—especially since you've probably been involved in a few other dramas since then! Someone who arrives early for an appointment always makes you smile; you're normally an early bird yourself.

Playing Taurus: Inwardly you may still feel you were right last night, but you act fairly cool about the whole thing. You convince yourself the other party will come around to your way of thinking in the end. You are never fazed by someone turning up early.

Playing Gemini: You haven't lost any sleep over the situation with your coworker. You are happy that the appointment will start early; it will enable you to cram extra activity into the rest of the day.

Playing Cancer: You are sympathetic to an opponent's reasons for disagreeing with you, and sensitive to the opponent's feelings too. You feel in tune with someone who has turned up early, knowing you'd do the same.

Playing Leo: You don't let any wounded pride carry over to this day, although you don't necessarily lose your love of power. But you refuse to let the disagreement with your coworker affect your attitude toward an appointment; you have too much pride for that.

Playing Virgo: You hate to let it show that you're worried or unsure about *anything*, even if you are. The typical Virgo soon becomes engrossed in the new day's work, regardless of what it entails.

Playing Libra: Being more Libran means taking a far more balanced view of each and every situation. You probably wouldn't have even fought with your coworker! This morning you make sure you are sweetness and light personified.

Playing Yourself: As you pass your colleague, you ignore him even though he smiles and says hello. But such behavior could make it obvious to the person waiting for you that this is the wrong time and place for an appointment!

Playing Sagittarius: The consummate actor—you don't show anyone that you're still in a bad mood. You're convinced you were right last night, but you also made sure you both went home good friends.

Playing Capricorn: Your professional sense of duty makes you determined to let bygones be bygones. No working time is lost going over old ground. It's unlikely that anyone else would arrive at the office (or leave it) before you!

Playing Aquarius: Still fixed in your opinions, you are far more forgiving of someone else's mistakes than Scorpio is. You find it easier to detach yourself from unpleasant situations early on than to have a fight. You never show your inner feelings.

Playing Pisces: You are tolerant of someone else's mistakes—even if that person is unable to admit them! You are also willing to accept that *you're* not infallible. You immediately put at ease the person who is waiting to see you.

The Positive and Negative Qualities of a Scorpio at Work

Because of your incredible inner strength, you are able to convince yourself and others that nothing is too difficult. You have exceptional instincts and intuition, and rarely have any difficulty in being assertive.

Your strong reasoning power, sound strategic ability, perception, and intelligence give you an edge in the success stakes. It makes total sense to me that both Bill Gates and Ted Turner are Scorpios! You are a brilliant tactician and operator who is able to demonstrate substantial achievements in an extremely competitive environment. You possess a unique and highly developed scanning system, which enables you to know what is needed to realize the maximum potential.

However, some of you have a power complex that makes you extremely difficult to deal with in certain situations. Don't forget the benefits of negotiation and of being a good team player! You will benefit from listening to your heart rather than your ego. Sometimes you seem to thrive on living "on the edge," rather than in creating a balance between your strong desires and your inner need for a peaceful life.

You work best with people who are prepared to accept your determination and loyalty without question—and who don't try to get under your skin.

The sign of Scorpio commences in the fall, when summer is over but winter is not yet upon us. It relates astrologically to death, regeneration, big business, investments, and inheritances. You're a sign of great extremes, sometimes fluctuating between deep suffering and deep joy. You possess a warrior spirit that can also help to bring you your heart's desires.

The positive Scorpio has an almost uncanny knack of knowing just how and when to strike, in order to make an upward leap toward greater success. You have an amazing ability to rise above difficulties and turn them into advantages. You are definitely goal-oriented and are extremely fortunate in possessing a charismatic personality, a brilliant memory, and strong powers of concentration.

The negative Scorpio can become ruthless and manipulative when a power struggle is taking place. Assertiveness then becomes hostile aggression, and you become almost too desperate to succeed. Sometimes your mental toughness and killer instincts can make you unpopular among the very people you need on your side. Always try to focus on the long-term consequences of your actions and not simply on the short-term advantages.

The wise Scorpio will learn to combine excellent instincts and intuition with the flair, tenacity, and skills needed to be a bright star in today's fast-moving work environment.

Careers for Scorpio

In the workplace, many Scorpio men and women enter the business and financial world, and their know-how can often lead them to the top. Often brilliant researchers, Scorpios are also attracted to the fields of psychiatry, psychology, counseling, police work, politics, science, law, medicine (as surgeons, pathologists, lab technicians, gynecologists), and religion. As a writer, you often have a way with words that makes the reader feel 100 percent involved with every situation you create. Scorpio Pat Conroy achieves this brilliantly with *The Prince of Tides* and *Beach Music*.

Marie Curie, Dr. Jonas Salk, Dr. Christiaan Barnard, and Carl Sagan were all born under your sign. Other prominent Scorpio men and women include Dostoyevsky, Billy Graham, Pablo Picasso, Richard Burton, Mark McCormack, Calvin Klein, Bruce Jenner, Boris Becker, Tina Brown, Anna Wintour, Naomi Wolf, Martin Scorsese, Johnny Carson, Dominick Dunne, Roseanne, Whoopi Goldberg, Jodie Foster, and Julia Roberts.

Your Attitude toward Work

Naturally, your rising sign, together with all the other astrological factors of your personal horoscope, will also influence your attitude toward work.

If you're a fairly typical Scorpio, you will have plenty of energy, willpower, and determination to succeed. Scorpio rules the reproductive system and the sexual organs. In many ways your sexual desires and your desires to achieve success at work seem to interrelate. Many of you get a real burst of renewed sexual energy if you've been involved in a power struggle that takes you higher up the ladder of success.

Because your sexual and physical energy *is* so potent, you often set yourself a major goal or challenge in your working life, knowing that when you strive to reach it, you will not give up halfway through. Indeed, your work may become all-consuming, especially if it involves something that truly stretches your mind. Your tremendous drive and above-average powers of concentration are great assets on the job.

You *will* need to beware of your inherent desire for power and control, especially if don't know how long a work position will last. Your stamina and determination to succeed—regardless of what odds lie ahead—will always be something to be proud of.

Since you're basically an extremely private person, you will usually prefer to work on your own. It's not that you have something to hide, or that you want to waste hours of your working time on the telephone to friends. It's just that ever since you were a child you have needed your own little space. You often do your best work alone, in silence with your intuitive thoughts.

You have amazing self-control. Even if you are fearful of tackling certain work-related tasks, you are unlikely to show your fear. Your insight will be a great help in enabling you to focus positively on the cause of your fear and to realize that you can overcome it. This insight is an added bonus, for at critical moments when your response times are vital, it will enable you to make important decisions based on your gut feelings with a minimum of delay.

Ruled by the element Water, you throw yourself wholeheartedly into whatever you believe, and you are passionate about both service and quality. You delve deeply into life and pass your discoveries on to the rest of us. Your self-driven warrior spirit will sustain you, and as you fulfill your burning desire for greater knowledge, you will enhance your aura of self-confidence. You thrive on solving a variety of challenging tasks, and when you truly trust your Scorpio intuition, success will be yours.

TIPS FOR A HEALTHY WORK ATTITUDE

- Try to lighten up more—don't be quite so intense!
- Retain your power without ever letting it become self-destructive.
- Always believe in the strength of your Scorpio sixth sense; it's one of your greatest assets.

Aiming for Promotion

I've rarely met a Scorpio who hasn't had a goal of some kind, or who wasn't sassy enough to achieve a desired promotion. You have amazing inner strength, which, when used positively and productively, will allow you to rise above almost impossible odds to prove that you're one of the best workers out there.

You appreciate the benefits of networking and know that the office grapevine will often be the source of worthwhile snippets of information. You're brilliant at keeping your own thoughts to yourself, never divulging your finds to anyone who might be competing for the same promotion as you. Because of this, you might sometimes be accused of being selfish, but hardheaded business strategies are becoming increasingly more important in these days of job layoffs.

Since Scorpio is often drawn to the political area (Theodore Roosevelt, Jawaharlal Nehru, and Indira Gandhi were all born under this sign), you should be at your best when it comes to understanding corporate politics. By means of your Scorpio sixth sense, you know what makes people tick, and what is the best way to deal with people in order to advance in your particular company. If ever you feel victimized by discrimination, you have the inner strength necessary to bring it to the attention of those in a position to do something about it.

However, although you're never afraid of a power struggle, you sometimes need to watch yourself. You have a tendency to react badly toward anyone whom you feel is unworthy of your respect. In a perfect world, it would be wonderful to have respect for everyone with whom we have to deal. Your Scorpio instinct enables you to know better than any of us that this is impossible much of the time. Never spoil your chances of promotion by going into battle so ruthlessly that you antagonize the very people whose respect *you* need.

I wouldn't dare advise a Scorpio man or woman to keep a low profile. I think that's almost impossible for someone with a personality as magnetic as yours. Make sure, therefore, that your attitude never becomes a turnoff rather than a turn-on. Adept as you are when it comes to being the sex symbol of the Zodiac, you're not always so brilliant at being diplomatic. Don't forget that some Scorpio feelings are best kept to yourself!

If promotion eludes you, through no known fault of your own, remember that these days most companies are more likely to be reducing their staff than increasing them. Don't overreact by immediately threatening to walk out from your current position, without being at least fairly confident that there is something else waiting for you out there.

TIPS FOR PROMOTION SEEKERS

- Acknowledge that teamwork is essential—especially if you think your own promotion chances may be judged in the framework of your particular team's success.
- Always keep up-to-date in your field, which means keeping up with your research.
- Remember, sex with your coworkers is NOT the best way to advance!

How to Cope with Being Passed Over for Promotion

Your initial tendency may be to withdraw immediately into your own little world, filled with resentment about being passed over. This is a no-win tactic, especially for someone who is supposed to be forceful and astute.

Here is a better plan: (1) Find out from your superiors if you've made mistakes without being aware of them. If this is the case, resolve to learn from these mistakes. (2) Make sure that your contribution to your company becomes even more visible and influential. (3) Don't fall behind on the information highway, and (4) always focus your activities on the right targets.

You're a person of vision, born with an insuperable determination to succeed. When someone or something dies in a Scorpio's life, there is always a rebirth to come. You may feel devastated that you didn't get the promotion you wanted, but soon you will be empowered to start afresh in your climb up the ladder of success.

Ambition—or the Lack of It

It is extremely difficult for me to imagine a Scorpio who is lacking in ambition—not unless your personal chart contains an extraordinarily major influence of less aggressive signs and conflicting planetary configurations.

An ambitious Scorpio, especially in the workplace, will be stiff competition for coworkers. It isn't just that you're renowned for being indomitable on so many occasions; nor even that you sometimes apply yourself ruthlessly to achieving your ambitions. It's usually much deeper—a feeling within you that there must always be something more to the mystery of life. Your renowned Scorpio insight is a great aid when you have to navigate any career ups and downs, for it enables you to steer clear of major problems. It also teaches you to appreciate the value of good timing, allowing you to pick the right moment to discuss promotion with your superiors.

Remember it is *you* who are in charge of your career, and that you are the one who has to care about it. When you do care sufficiently, you will throw yourself completely into getting to the top. Make sure you never misuse your Scorpio power by becoming too controlling. Never forget Scorpio is a sign of extremes, relating not only to the Scorpion but also to the Serpent and the Eagle. To be truly successful, you must learn to soar like the eagle on higher currents, and to find your spiritual center so that you will neither fear rejection nor become too ruthless in your desire to achieve your goals.

Just as you must avoid being too hard on other people, you must also remember to be good to yourself. Never become overly obsessive about your ambitions. With the aid of your two ruling planets, Mars and Pluto, you will always have the ability to reach greater heights in your chosen career.

Ambition—and Your Love Life

Of all the Zodiac signs, you are the one for whom sexual gratification is one of the most important aspects in life. As a rule, you know from an early age that you're also one of the most sexually charismatic signs around!

No matter how ambitious you are in the workplace, I don't think you'd want to lose out on a good relationship for long by devoting yourself mind, body, and soul to your job.

However, because you devote yourself so intensely to almost everything you undertake, there is sometimes a conflict over which area of your life should take precedence. A highly sensitive Water sign, often you're completely controlled by your feelings and by your desire for physical contact. It is highly important for you to understand this aspect of yourself. Sometimes your love life will simply have to take second place to the demands of the workday!

Any partner who is involved emotionally with you needs to understand that there will be times when your energy will be directed 100
percent to your work. Equally, you must accept that there will be times
when your own needs and physical desires may have to take second
place to your partner's working life. Sometimes you seem to wear your
heart on your sleeve, taking everything so personally that you become
your own worst enemy. Don't allow this to create an imbalance
between your working and your domestic life.

TIPS FOR COMBINING WORK AND LOVE

- Always allow lovers and coworkers the privacy you desire
  yourself.
- Don't shut off your emotional feelings, but keep them apart
  from your work.
- Remember to listen to your intuition, never do things simply because of your ego.
- Avoid power struggles. It's far better to achieve the right
  balance in a calmer way.

Romance in the Workplace

Perhaps it was no mere coincidence that actress Demi Moore played
the female lead in the movie of Michael Crichton's novel *Disclosure,*
for Demi Moore is a Scorpio! I don't wish to infer that every Scorpio
man and woman is likely to be involved in a sexual harassment case,
nor that you would flaunt your sexuality before you like a red flag.
Nevertheless, some of you allow your sexual desires to come pretty
near to the surface.

If you find yourself violently attracted to someone who shares your
feelings, it is best to talk things over together carefully, making sure
you are each aware of the circumstances in which you could find yourselves. Although you are renowned for your ability to keep secrets, not
everyone possesses the same ability. Insinuations about your sex life
can be counterproductive to achieving your professional ambitions.

Highly emotional, you thrive on the art of seduction, temptation,
and mystery. For you, love is an all-consuming flame that burns bright
and long, but sometimes you satisfy your passionate desires only to

leave your soul hungering for something deeper. Doesn't this sound like a prelude to disaster if you set your sights on someone with whom you work?

A romantic relationship in the workplace is especially difficult for you because you can be extremely possessive and jealous—to the extent where it becomes more difficult to hide your feelings. This makes the situation even more tricky if either party is married or in an existing partnership. One of your baser negative traits is sometimes a desire to manipulate others. Resolve not to use your sexual skills to manipulate your way higher up the ladder of success. Think seriously about the karma this will produce, and know within your deepest soul that you are worthy of far better things. You can achieve your ambitions without resorting to sexual strategies along the way!

You and Your Stress Factor

Scorpio rules the reproductive system and genital organs in general, and the bladder, urethra, descending colon, anus, rectum, and prostate gland in particular. Problems can arise in these areas if you hold back your deepest feelings and refuse to let go of negative patterns. A great deal of stress is created by such "holding back" and "refusing to let go."

Mars and Pluto, as corulers of your sign, combine to give you huge reserves of energy. Pluto, in particular, endows you with amazing powers of recuperation should you fall sick.

Stress is the normal way in which we all react when we encounter circumstances and situations that appear to threaten us in some way or that we feel we cannot deal with successfully. When your normally brilliant concentration seems to slip, or you find you are unable to relax or let go of problems, you may be showing some of the first symptoms of stress.

The highly private side of your nature makes you likely to fight inwardly against any sign of stress. But hiding away your feelings does not mean that they will disappear; instead, they may become more aggravated. Face up to what you're feeling, rather than try to suppress it.

Stifling feelings of anger or depression over a work problem doesn't mean the problem will go away. Your external behavior may be perfectly fine, but what have you achieved if you are churning away inside? It's better to share your true feelings with someone you know you can trust.

At times, there is a self-destructive side to your personality. Unfortunately, a stressed-out Scorpio is sometimes more likely to be involved in drug abuse, alcoholism, and even to contemplate suicide, than many of the other signs.

When you are able to make contact with the spiritual center within you, it will be much easier for you to combat stress and all its side effects. It is extremely important for you to achieve the correct balance between your mind, body, and soul.

Because you feel *everything* in life so deeply, it's not surprising you sometimes worry too much. That's why it is often vital for you to lighten up and see the brighter side of life—rather than just focusing on those parts that appear so dark.

Don't be a workaholic all the time. No matter how hard you work or where, you're entitled to have some enjoyable leisure moments too. You are unlikely to allow your sex life to suffer because of a heavy agenda, but remember this is only one aspect of your life away from work!

You often have an exceptionally wide range of interests, ranging from tai chi and karate to classes for astrology and tarot. Games that tax your mind, like bridge and chess, are also brilliant ways for you to cut yourself off from the pressures of your workload and to reduce the threat of stress—unless you become too competitive of course!

Your Attitude toward Making Money

You appear to thrive on the buzz that making money brings your way, even if you are rarely the most money-centered of signs.

You are usually willing to put in overtime at work, without using this to influence your employers into giving you a raise; unless you feel you are being treated unfairly. You know just how and when to strike and to make an upward leap. This asset is especially useful when combined with your inherent entrepreneurial streak.

As a Fixed sign, with great staying power, you won't lose sight of the end product, although your tendency to be ruthless and manipulative might make you a few enemies along the way.

You are prepared to work hard and to formulate a realistic strategy to become a financial success. You are brilliant at devising ways to increase both your earnings and your savings, with planning skills and a sixth sense second to none. Because Scorpio is astrologically linked to business, investments, and inheritances, you will quickly learn how to make your money work for you in the best possible way. This is a great advantage now that job security is becoming more tenuous, making it even more necessary to ensure you have sufficient money put aside for your long-term security.

Your attitude toward making money will depend greatly on your needs, aspirations, and priorities in life. But your Scorpio instinct will *always* be an added bonus, especially when you must decide just how much time, energy, and money you will need to invest to make your finances grow faster.

Your intuition will prevent you from being hustled by unscrupulous people trying to take your money. You're rarely interested in risky schemes no matter how brilliantly they may be promoted, since you much prefer to see your money grow under your own control.

Always believe in yourself and in your moneymaking abilities. You have the power to rise above incredible odds, and even if you suffer a bad financial patch, your warrior spirit will take you through it. You will have the strength to start afresh, with sufficient patience to weather the worst storms and come out on top financially once again.

How to Improve Your Work Relationships

As a Scorpio, with strong likes and dislikes, plus the tendency to be something of a loner, it's important to cultivate the ability to get along well with your coworkers.

The following guide will show you the best way to relate to all the signs, whether they are those of your boss, your peer, or an employee:

Scorpio with Aries Boss: This could be a challenge for both of you. Don't create unnecessary battles. An Aries boss will not appreciate being walked over by a subordinate, especially an invincible one!

Scorpio with Aries Colleague: Learn to be a little more open with your thoughts. It will enable you both to cooperate much better with each other. Being ultrasecretive makes it harder to keep the team spirit going strong.

Scorpio with Aries Employee: Try to keep your power complex in check. Remember that an Aries employee will one day want to be the boss too. Learn to respect each other now, and keep it that way.

Scorpio with Taurus Boss: Your opposite sign has much to teach you. Don't bring your emotional intrigues into the office. Taurus is interested in getting the work done well with as few dramas as possible.

Scorpio with Taurus Colleague: Both of you will sometimes display a stubborn streak. You're both committed to reaching your career goals. You have plenty to learn from the workings of each other's mind.

Scorpio with Taurus Employee: Here you have one of the most loyal and hardworking employees in the Zodiac, even if he does sometimes seem slow. Don't take advantage of Taurus the Bull by pushing him too hard.

Scorpio with Gemini Boss: Your deep-rooted intensity could drive this mentally active live wire totally wild! Try to be more open and to come up with creative ideas on a regular basis.

Scorpio with Gemini Colleague: Don't spend too much time discussing what you both do *outside* work. Your intuitive faculties combined with Gemini's creatively innovative ideas can make you a powerful team.

Scorpio with Gemini Employee: Try not to show your frustration if Gemini's sense of order doesn't measure up to your requirements. If you continually demand a highly organized working style, Gemini may not last long with you!

Scorpio with Cancer Boss: Since you are both emotional Water signs who are highly sensitive to atmosphere, you will start off on a good foot. Use your intuition to gauge when your boss is in a bad mood, and you'll do fine.

Scorpio with Cancer Colleague: You will benefit from having such a compassionate coworker. Don't upset the balance by being too much of a ruthless power player, even if you are both hoping to be the boss one day.

Scorpio with Cancer Employee: This employee is very protective. No one will barge into your office or reach you by phone unexpectedly. But Cancer is ultrasensitive, so watch your Scorpio sting!

Scorpio with Leo Boss: Leo wants to feel like the boss at all times and won't appreciate someone she feels could stab her in the back! Besides, Leo will always praise you for your efforts and give credit where it's due.

Scorpio with Leo Colleague: Try never to undermine the confidence of a Leo colleague, for underneath a somewhat bossy exterior is a vulnerable heart of gold! Besides, you can be just as bossy at times.

Scorpio with Leo Employee: It seems that Leo always hates to be given orders, but that is not totally true. When you have the respect of a Leo employee, you will also have a wonderful working relationship.

Scorpio with Virgo Boss: Remember that this boss is a true perfectionist, and more analytical even than you! Resolve never to lay yourself open for flak, either about your work or by being sexually flamboyant in the office!

Scorpio with Virgo Colleague: Scorpio's strong intuition combined with Virgo's analytical powers could make you a powerful working team. However, outside the office you may part company feeling you have little in common.

Scorpio with Virgo Employee: Virgo has high work standards, so you should have few complaints. If a mistake does occur occasionally, try harder to forgive and forget! A Virgo employee will be very loyal.

Scorpio with Libra Boss: You couldn't wish for a more charming and diplomatic boss, who is rarely too demanding and never too pushy. But you may have to point out when certain things have been overlooked—tactfully, of course!

Scorpio with Libra Colleague: Scorpio doesn't cope easily with Libra's somewhat laissez-faire attitude and somewhat indecisive ways. But Libra can be just as ambitious as you—even more manipulative too.

Scorpio with Libra Employee: Stress the importance of getting to the office on time. Diplomatically point out you need someone who won't misplace important files. (Libra is not always tidy.)

Scorpio with Scorpio Boss: The number one rule is to respect each other's privacy and working methods, while remembering who is the boss. Since you work best with someone as intensely loyal and determined as you, this relationship should be good!

Scorpio with Scorpio Colleague: There could be lots of back stabbing if you're ruthless adversaries climbing to the top. But you *will* understand each other's working methods and might even learn something new!

Scorpio with Scorpio Employee: You know what it was like to be a Scorpio employee once upon a time. So be aware of the difficulties that this can create. Remember this employee needs to respect you in every way.

Scorpio with Sagittarius Boss: Life will never be dull. This friendly and easygoing boss is one of the most optimistic signs of the Zodiac. But Sagittarius does like to think he is *always* right.

Scorpio with Sagittarius Colleague: You will appreciate the Archer's positive input and team spirit. Sagittarius may seem to be born lucky—but don't be fooled. She also works hard at getting where she wants to be.

Scorpio with Sagittarius Employee: This employee brightens up those days when your Scorpio intensity tends to see the darker side of life. The Archer will usually adapt to your working schedule, even to unexpected overtime.

Scorpio with Capricorn Boss: Capricorn is the workaholic of the Zodiac. Don't let your nightly sex life be so exhausting that you're useless in the office. Capricorn demands nothing less than the best you can give.

Scorpio with Capricorn Colleague: Stolid, reliable, ambitious, and persevering—that's Capricorn. Capricorn is a wonderful team member, unless you're both aiming to be the boss. Then your work will be cut out for you!

Scorpio with Capricorn Employee: You never have to worry that Capricorn will forget something or make careless mistakes. This employee won't take unnecessary risks or leave work early.

Scorpio with Aquarius Boss: Unpredictable, unconventional, brilliantly creative, but often absentminded, this boss could be a handful. Use your intuition well. Sometimes you may feel as though *you're* in charge.

Scorpio with Aquarius Colleague: The Aquarian creativity will inspire you to find new ways of dealing with projects, solving problems, and using your imagination. Don't be too intense with this more detached sign.

Scorpio with Aquarius Employee: Aquarius always comes up with a fresh approach to the most mundane task. Since this sign has a low threshold for boredom, Aquarius may not adjust easily to the routine of a nine-to-five job.

Scorpio with Pisces Boss: A Pisces boss not only listens to your problems but also tries to help you out. Don't imagine that you're dealing with someone too lightweight to be a boss, for Pisces can be as tough as you.

Scorpio with Pisces Colleague: Two Water signs should have plenty of empathy, but you may consider the Piscean romantic idealism too sloppy for words. You can work well together if you both concentrate on the tasks at hand.

Scorpio with Pisces Employee: You'll get the best results from this employee by not coming across as a megalomaniac power player! Pisces is incredibly sensitive to atmosphere and needs lots of encouragement, and some praise too!

Getting Longevity out of Your Career

Getting fired is something that you would rather not contemplate. However, in today's corporate world there are more and more layoffs because of the scaling down of companies and advances in technology that make humans more expendable.

Your keen intuition and perceptive analytical powers will help you sense what is going on around you in advance of many other people. Highly resourceful, you are also particularly adept at acquiring additional learning skills, which will enable you to keep up-to-date with what is happening in your particular field.

Learn to take any defeats in stride. Resolve not to succumb to the dark side of the Scorpio nature, which brings with it those underlying feelings of brooding resentment and revenge, jealousy, and self-destruction. Remember that you need to resonate at a high level, to be like a phoenix rising from the ashes, rather than to lock yourself unnecessarily into negative emotions deep down below. If you concentrate on the insuperable side of your personality, you will be able to rise up, above all odds, and find the self-renewal so essential to your sign.

If ever you have to face being laid off from a job, it's always a good tactic to analyze the reasons why. If the layoff was due to merger mania or to other reasons that are no fault of yours, don't give yourself a hard time. If you were dismissed unfairly and legal advice has convinced you that you have a good case against your company, plus the money to deal with it, you must of course take the necessary action. However, if you feel, deep down, that you may have perhaps been responsible for your own downfall, try not only to accept this but also to learn a lesson from the situation.

Never get into a panic worrying about the longevity of your career. You know that you will always survive, and that you could end up in an even better job in the future. When you do make a mistake in your work, never go into denial and refuse to accept that it was your fault. Try also to be a little more forgiving (yes, also to yourself) and resolve to forget slights, imagined or real. *Forgiving* and *forgetting* are among the hardest things in the world for many Scorpios to master, but both are sometimes essential, especially in today's competitive workplace.

If you have to adjust to life after being fired, make sure you have a decent letter of reference and the correct amount of severance pay. You must then resolve to sharpen your skills so that you have the very best to offer when job hunting again. Always believe in yourself and in your ability to climb up from the bottom of the darkness into the brightness of a wonderful new job.

Getting longevity out of your career does not mean that you should have to fear getting old. Your invincibility doesn't fade as the years go by! If you want to continue working late in life, you are sure to do so. You're more likely then to be the boss of your own company than an employee; or perhaps you'll even decide that self-employment fits better into your lifestyle. With your thirst for knowledge, and with more time on your hands, you may decide to take up a course in psychology or counseling, or involve yourself in social work.

I once knew an older Scorpio lady who enjoyed writing, but who had always been entrenched in a business management career. Once she retired, she took a course in short story writing and ended up publishing some of her stories in magazines. At the age of seventy-five she achieved a heartfelt desire. So even a Scorpio doesn't always know *everything* the future has in store!

SCORPIO CAREER STRATEGIES—A CHECKLIST FOR EVERY AGE

- Always remain highly disciplined, but never overly intense.
- If you find yourself in a tough situation, always remember to listen to your instinct. It will rarely let you down.
- Since you demand the right to privacy, make sure you give others in the workplace that same right.
- Never be too ruthless and manipulative, for it can work against you in the long term.
- Keep your sexually charged magnetism out of the office— remember the movie *Disclosure*!
- Don't show resentment if someone is promoted over you, even if you can't understand why.
- Never forget you *are* invincible, even if you don't achieve your ambitions overnight!

SAGITTARIUS IN THE WORKPLACE

November 22 ☆ December 20

If you were born between November 22 and December 20, you were born under the sign of Sagittarius, ninth sign of the Zodiac. You are a Masculine, Mutable, Positive, Fire sign, and your planetary symbol is the Archer, or Centaur, which is half man/half horse. With Jupiter, planet of good fortune, as your planetary ruler, you possess a self-confident and optimistic personality, but sometimes you enthusiastically aim your Archer's arrow so high that it may be almost impossible for it to reach its goal.

Energetic, positive, and idealistic, Sagittarius relates to the ninth house of the Zodiac, which in turn relates to long-distance travel and the higher mind. The Sage and Counselor of the Zodiac, you are on a perpetual journey to uncover the truth about life and to impart its message to the rest of us. You would like to leave a lasting legacy upon the world through your name, rather as Sagittarian Walt Disney did with his. Because you need to feel that you're a free spirit, sometimes you lack the discipline that is so vital in today's highly competitive workplace.

Your enthusiasm, innovative ways, good humor, and ability to communicate on all levels are major assets when you want to become a trailblazer in the workplace. However, while brilliant at telling others how to behave, you must also understand that you cannot always be the teacher; sometimes you will also have to be the student!

We all have something to learn from our opposite sign in the Zodiac. Gemini, sign of the mind and of mental communication, is yours. Both of you are great thinkers, but since Gemini is an Air sign, whereas you are Fire, Gemini has a more reasoned approach. You could benefit greatly from this approach, for it would prevent you from rushing fearlessly ahead into something that could be extremely risky. You can learn something from *every* sign, which is why you might try wearing a different astrological hat once in a while.

Take a typical workday in the Sagittarius life. You've just heard about a great scheme or project that could make millions for your company and bring you a promotion with a marvelous raise. You're absolutely convinced it cannot fail and cannot wait to get on with it.

Playing Aries: You could be equally enthusiastic and almost *too* impulsive with the Ram's influence. But luckily the more vulnerable side of the Aries nature means that you won't be afraid to ask for input from your coworkers.

Playing Taurus: Wearing a Taurus hat, you temper your optimism and enthusiasm with a more down-to-earth and pragmatic approach. You move a little slower and view the project with a more realistic eye.

Playing Gemini: You analyze the best way to tackle this project, and come up some ways in which it might just *not* work out. Strategy and organization are important to Gemini.

Playing Cancer: When playing Cancer, you are not so obviously self-confident about your chances of success. You soften your approach and use your intuition to help you plot your moves—which means less risk.

Playing Leo: A double dose of ego means a double dose of determination to succeed! With Leo's conviction that being a star is the only thing to be, you leave no stone unturned to achieve success.

Playing Virgo: Wearing the Virgo hat enables you to see more analytically the way to move ahead. Everything is clearly signposted so that you can become more constructive in your efforts to succeed.

Playing Libra: Playing Libra means you can balance your tendency to be excessively optimistic and ambitious with the ability to weigh every pro and con. A Libran hat would stop you from being a reckless gambler.

Playing Scorpio: You gain an even greater determination to succeed when playing Scorpio. Your Sagittarian tendency toward risk taking is tempered by Scorpio's intense desire to avoid any risk of failure.

Playing Yourself: Watch out you don't gloss over all the nitty-gritty details necessary to make the project work. You're often too inclined to take risks and shortcuts, ignoring the more realistic issues at stake.

Playing Capricorn: This serious and highly practical sign never takes the slightest risk. The Capricorn tendency to be highly structured and organized means you won't miss the slightest thing.

Playing Aquarius: With an Aquarian hat you are even more original and creative in your thinking and make the most unlikely project turn out well. But you also need to be highly organized and not too idealistic.

Playing Pisces: Too much self-confidence in a head that may be way up in the clouds doesn't necessarily spell success! But a Pisces hat makes you highly sensitive and enhances your intuition too.

The Positive and Negative Qualities of a Sagittarius at Work

There is an immensely positive attitude about your sign when you truly believe in something. Sagittarian Steven Spielberg knew what *he* wanted to do from a very early age, and has never looked back.

Ruled by Jupiter, you see possibilities where others may see only difficulties or limitations, and project yourself toward new horizons with the attitude that life is a constant adventure. A good friend of mine, Gerry, was a perfect example here. This Sagittarian was fulfilling his objectives even while battling a life-threatening illness.

Your optimism, versatility, and enterprising ways, combined with your honesty, will help you go far in today's competitive workplace. You are able to operate on your own initiative with flair and entrepreneurial ability.

A fearless Fire sign, you are rarely afraid of new challenges in unknown territory. Your talent for generating ideas and concepts is excellent, but seeing them through to fulfillment is not always your greatest forte. You may need to concentrate on becoming more results-oriented.

The positive Sagittarian is optimistic, adaptable, versatile, open-minded, and idealistic, with a wonderful sense of humor. Savvy, sincere, and self-confident, you get on well with almost everyone. There is a wonderfully childlike quality about the way you look at life.

The negative Sagittarian sometimes exhibits careless and irresponsible behavior, brought on by the belief that the Archer can do no wrong. You may also be prone to exaggeration, extravagance, extremism, and excessive embellishment of the truth! Although basically extremely frank and honest, you tend to gloss over the brutal facts if things go wrong. Some of you find it too easy to tell other people (often somewhat tactlessly too!) what to do, while refusing to allow them to give *you* any advice, even if it's needed. Try to accept criticism and advice with better grace.

The wise Sagittarian will not insist on having things your own way all the time. You will continue to see life as a perpetual quest for knowledge, without jumping to conclusions or traveling too fast. You will seek and speak the truth, but will resolve not to hurt others through being too outspoken. Combine your dynamism with greater diplomacy, and you can be a big star.

Careers for Sagittarius

A high number of Sagittarian men and women are drawn to careers in philosophy, law, teaching, sports and sports promotion, diplomatic work, social administration, and politics. Also appealing are travel-related careers, whether in travel agencies or as couriers or long-distance truck drivers, flight attendants, pilots, or cruise ship hosts, travel writing, journalism (especially in the travel and sports fields), and almost anything in show business.

Sagittarians love to teach others about the world they live in. If she were alive today, I'm sure that Sagittarian Jane Austen would delight in the newfound publicity her books have received since they have become internationally celebrated movies.

Some of you may feel that you're more suited to follow some free-lance specialty that allows you to come and go as you please, rather than to apply yourself to a career that involves lots of routine. What is always of major importance is for you to feel *inwardly* free regardless of the commitments you face on the outside.

Famous Sagittarians include Nostradamus, Beethoven, Edith Piaf, John F. Kennedy, Jr., Joe DiMaggio, Kirk Douglas, Frank Sinatra, Lee Trevino, Monica Seles, Phil Donahue, Woody Allen, Jane Fonda, Kim Basinger, Tina Turner, and Bette Midler.

Your Attitude toward Work

Naturally, your rising sign, together with all the other factors of your individual horoscope, will also influence your attitude toward work.

You will always find ways to make your working life enjoyable, exciting, and adventurous. If it gives you the chance to make new friends too, that suits you even better. When you enjoy your work, you will throw yourself into it wholeheartedly. Problems seem to arise only if you're stuck in a dead-end job that bores you to tears. You find it hard to settle down to discipline unless it is a discipline of your own making!

Always perfect your skills with determined conscientious practice. Knowing your job duties is simply not enough; you must carry them out effortlessly and efficiently. Take a more down-to-earth and dispassionate analysis of your weaknesses and your strengths. Being positive is fine, but never trust *too* much to luck.

With the lucky planet Jupiter as your ruler, good fortune seems to be on your side. Your optimistic and outgoing personality is a fantastic bonus when you are aiming for the top. When *you* believe in yourself, you can make the rest of the world believe in you too. It's not surprising that Dale Carnegie, with his books on positive thinking, was a Sagittarian!

You can be as savvy and exceptionally plugged in to what is expected of you in the workplace as any other star sign. But sometimes you are too inclined to favor the shortcuts to success, which necessitate taking crazy risks that would turn most people's hair gray overnight.

Never be backward in learning about the new technology that is taking over all our lives. Remember that becoming superorganized and efficient not only will help to make your particular job more secure, but will also be your ticket to moving upward.

To forge a successful career, it is important to be a good team player. Bonding with coworkers and creating a collaborative spirit among team members is often one of your strongest suits, so don't set yourself up as a know-it-all or your popularity will take a nosedive! Prove that you're a hands-on natural leader with the personality and communication skills to galvanize your particular team to reach new levels of performance.

You often prefer to work in a group-oriented environment so that you never feel alone for long. Even a party-hearty Sagittarian must know how to behave like a veteran member of the working rank and file. Always demonstrate that you have sufficient maturity and credibility to establish and maintain working relationships at all levels. Keep your agile mind focused analytically on your work, instead of wasting valuable moments gossiping when major deadlines await you.

If you are forced into a corner and *must* find work, you will rise brilliantly to the occasion, managing to remain optimistic in situations that would floor many other people. This inherent optimism will take you a long way down the road to success.

TIPS FOR A HEALTHY WORK ATTITUDE

- Learn the art of tact and diplomacy—even when you're standing up for your convictions and cannot resist speaking your mind.
- Be self-confident, but never be so blindly optimistic that you become a reckless gambler.
- If you feel totally constricted by an office job, study for something that will enhance your life and bring you greater success.

Aiming for Promotion

You're crafty and clever enough to achieve the heights of success. Just like your opposite sign, Gemini, you're the master of the fast line, sometimes able to talk your way into filling the post you are after, without even needing to demonstrate you have the necessary talent!

I've sometimes been amazed at the way you are able to bluff people into believing you're a brilliant strategist. I don't deny that you're one of the most creative signs of the Zodiac, but I would like to point out that impressing the higher-ups with your ideas isn't all you have to do to win a promotion. You must also turn your concepts into feasible projects and then get those projects completed!

Aiming for promotion will challenge your mind and enable you to expand your boundaries. Both of these exercises are appealing to almost every Sagittarian friend or client I've ever met. There is a wonderful never-give-up quality about your sign. I know a Sagittarian who was determined to become an editor in a publishing company, when jobs of this kind were seldom advertised. She constantly wrote interesting letters and sent them with her résumé to the company for which she hoped to work. Her focused application toward her goal paid off, and she is now a successful member of her particular department.

It takes a special commitment to achieve a great future in the changing world of work. You must always make the best use of your time—which means concentrating on your goals without getting sidetracked or leaving the office early to go to a party. While writing this chapter, I read an article which implied that ambitious executives should not stay in the same job for too long, because lengthy service was out and diverse résumés were in (perfect for your sign!). It appears that many companies now require a wider and wider range of skills when they are recruiting, skills often obtained by working in a variety of jobs. This means that a Sagittarian who prefers to be on the move rather than sit still for any length of time will have a great deal to offer.

However, you will still need to prove not only that you are adaptable but also that you have a proven track record and have not been a job hopper simply out of boredom. When aiming for promotion, always present the most relevant aspects of your work experience in the best possible light—but don't embroider the facts. There's little danger of the latter since Sagittarians are usually far too honest to be good at lying!

Balance your strong entrepreneurial flair with an absolute commitment to quality service, and, as an enterprising Fire sign, you will not fail.

TIPS FOR PROMOTION SEEKERS

- Always focus your activity on the right targets, and make sure you are credible at the highest levels with a strong work ethic and disciplined approach.

- Show that you have an enthusiastic and irrepressible desire to succeed, with charisma and commitment.
- Never alienate your supervisor or aggravate coworkers by implying you always know best.

How to Cope with Being Passed Over for Promotion

You have an extraordinary ability to rise above disappointments, even if you are highly sensitive to any form of criticism. You show a great sense of humor, even when hurting inside, and you have the ability to pick up the pieces and start over again even when you miss out on a promotion.

Another side of you hates to think you could ever be passed over for *anything,* and you tell yourself that the only reason you didn't get a promotion is because someone in a high position doesn't like you. The idea that you simply didn't measure up might not occur to you. This is your dark side—the side that gives you delusions of grandeur, making you gamble irresponsibly even when aiming higher up the ladder of success.

Never just assume that something else will turn up. In today's business climate you have to always understand and respond to the fast-changing needs of your own particular company. Don't lose a high-profile appointment simply because you have been insufficiently committed to your goals.

Ambition—or the Lack of It

Some Sagittarians have confessed to me that their major ambition has been to earn sufficient money to allow them the liberty to do what they wanted with their lives without the need to work. They were not particularly lazy, but their freedom-loving personalities rebelled against the thought of being fenced in.

Other Sagittarians seem to glide through life so easily, achieving one success after the other, that they appear to be born winners, making it hard to imagine that they might have found it difficult to get their first break. I read that Steven Spielberg knew from the time he was twelve years old that his world would be the movies. At seventeen, he managed to walk onto a studio lot, take over an empty office, and call himself a producer, with no one the wiser. But then he was a *Sagittarian* kid with the ambition and drive to turn his childhood dreams into major realities. When you focus on *your* deepest needs and desires, you will also find you have the ambition to achieve them.

Sometimes you recklessly scatter your energies too far and too wide. In your mind you have a concept of what you want to achieve, but tend to forget that concepts need practical application to bring them to successful fruition. At other times you charge ahead from one harebrained scheme to another, with the blind faith and optimism of a child, convinced you cannot fail.

Today's workplace is not for innocent children. It's a place where you must keep your wits about you at all times. If you demonstrate a highly noticeable lack of ambition in your work, by sitting back and allowing coworkers to play the key strategic roles in your company, you might soon be looking for something else to do with your life.

Ambition—and Your Love Life

Perhaps for you, this section should have been entitled "Ambition—and Your Social Life," for if you're a typical Sagittarian, you're one of the friendliest and most sociable signs in the whole Zodiac. You could easily become the best of friends with half the people in your workplace and consequently allow your work to take second place to your interesting conversations.

It is not always easy to create the right balance between work and love, especially if you are involved with a partner who is jealous of the time you spend apart from each other. But in the corporate workplace these days, working under pressure is becoming more and more the name of the game. Always remember that you are the only person who is in complete charge of your career, and the only one who truly cares about it. Although you are not necessarily thought of as a workaholic, there will be occasions when your love life may have to take second place to a pressing work project. You may be involved with someone who truly *is* a workaholic, and it will then be you who has to take second place.

More than most people, you hate to feel hemmed in by anyone or to be pressured with too much work. If you're a typical Sagittarian, your professional ambitions and your love life can be equally important to you. You will need to discover how to make them fit easily together, side by side!

TIPS FOR COMBINING WORK AND LOVE

- Don't work too hard at being everyone's best friend when there is more pressing work to do.
- Resolve to be more tolerant if you're involved in a relationship with someone who is a real workaholic and keeps much longer working hours than you.
- Be the life and soul of the party by all means—but draw the line between the workday and your social life.
- Don't be quite so determined to do what you want *whenever* you want to do it, even if you do prefer a free-and-easy life!

Romance in the Workplace

Although you tend to be an incurable optimistic, prepared to gamble for high stakes in love and romance, you will usually step back from getting emotionally involved with someone at work, especially if this person is married. Because you are basically so frank and honest, it would be extremely difficult for you to be part of a triangle. Although you may consider yourself a freedom-loving person who would never want to put chains on anyone else, I've had several Sagittarian friends and clients who have admitted being unable to cope with their feelings when they were in love with a married man or woman. You have a great dislike of jealousy in others, and often a tremendous fear of finding it hidden deep within yourself.

As a Fire sign, just like Aries and Leo, your heart often rules your head. There may be times when you feel a lightning attraction to someone you might never have met had you not been working in the same place. Naturally, a certain number of successful relationships have started off this way. A smile, a joke, a drink together after work—all these things are harmless in themselves and may bode well for a pleasurable future together. I'm only suggesting that you go easy, because the powers that be in today's workplace are generally only interested in your work output, not in the state of your emotions.

Of course there will be instances when an executive or manager is obviously having a passionate affair with whomever is working for him or her at the time. But how many of these affairs end up being mutually satisfying, long-term relationships? Remember that you're the sign of the higher mind, the Sage and Counselor of the Zodiac, and you should be aiming a whole lot higher in your life. Besides, I've known more than a few of you who are also extremely moralistic and narrow-minded in your own attitude about what other people do!

It is wise to remember that overfriendliness to a coworker might be misinterpreted as sexual harassment and be used against you.

I don't mean to imply that a romantic liaison at work can *never* turn into a warm, loving, and lasting relationship—of course it can— but it isn't always easy!

You and Your Stress Factor

You're a positive survivor and an eternal optimist, brimming over with such amazing enthusiasm, good sense of humor, and buoyant spirits that it's hard to imagine you could ever suffer from anything remotely resembling stress. Nevertheless, if you find yourself caught up in situations that create a conflict between what you want and what is actually taking place, you *too* will be prone to stress. Insecurity at work plus insufficient time for your home and family can soon add up to a point when you begin to feel you cannot cope with *anything* anymore.

An optimistic risk taker, you will sometimes push yourself to the brink of exhaustion simply because you refuse to give in to any sign of weakness. Thinking you can do everything is all very fine and noble, but your body needs a say in this too.

Listen when your inner voice tells you that you need some time to rest, relax, and recharge your batteries. Creating the right balance between your mind, body, and soul is especially important when you're driving yourself excessively hard in the rat race. In one of my recent books, *Star Signs,* I devised a meditation especially for you, which will help you achieve greater balance by allowing the stress to drift out of your body, so that you feel clear-headed and energized once more.

Sagittarius rules the hips and thighs; also the femur, ilium, coccygeal and sacral regions of the spine, veins, and sciatic nerves. If you don't eat a healthy diet, but snack on cookies and sugar-filled drinks on the job, don't be surprised if your hips and thighs are the first areas to gain excess weight. Exercise is important for you and will also get rid of excess stress. If you don't have time to attend a weight-training or aerobics class, you can always obtain a good exercise video and work out at home—provided you don't overdo it.

Quality of life, including job satisfaction, is of immense importance to you. Too many hours of routine work at something that does not stimulate you will increase your stress factor. So will the frustration and anxiety that can arise from feeling unprepared to work under extreme pressure in today's fast-paced work environment.

Always focus on the unique things that you have to offer, that are also right for you. Ask yourself what is important in the long run, rather than ending up burned out by stress through focusing only on the short-term gains.

Since you are a highly sociable sign, your lifestyle outside work will invariably be crammed with different events. But you don't necessarily like to book yourself up for weeks ahead, preferring instead the freedom to avail yourself of an exciting invitation at the last moment. Many of you enjoy an outdoor life—from long hikes in the mountains to summer picnics by the ocean.

Because you are the sign of the "higher mind," many of you will also have an interest in psychology, philosophy, or counseling. Sometimes one of these interests may even become a new career. I have a Sagittarian friend who worked in the corporate world for many years, until deciding to leave it in order to study psychology. She has all her degrees now and is able to practice as a qualified psychologist with the necessary letters after her name. She learned all about stress in her previous work; now she is helping the rest of us to overcome ours.

Your Attitude toward Making Money

When it comes to making money, you will frequently take more risks than many other signs. You usually dislike sticking to any budget, and running up debts is often looked upon as an adventure. Credit cards seem to have been invented just for you, for when you're spending plastic it doesn't seem like real money. Invariably more spendthrift than saver, financially you are at times your own worst enemy!

With Jupiter as your ruler, Lady Luck does seem to influence your sign, and some of your risks do pay off. No one could ever say that Sagittarians like Andrew Carnegie, J. Paul Getty, Frank Sinatra, Richard Sears and Steven Spielberg were naive where money was concerned, but often you are too laid-back in your moneymaking attitude and too inclined to overly trust to your own good luck with every new scheme that comes along. Even those of you who don't bet on the horses or in the casino tend to be gamblers by instinct.

In your job, you are sometimes too fond of shooting for the Moon without first knowing how to stand on terra firma. Some of you see only the big picture ahead of you, failing to look at the crucial details in a pragmatic way. You need to have real vision and savvy negotiating talents in order to make money these days. Your self-confident presence, drive, and leadership skills are admirable qualities, but they must go hand in hand with solid experience of the latest developments in your field. To be financially astute, you must also be able to formulate sound commercial strategies and to understand the workings of the business world.

You're a wonderfully energetic self-starter but not always so great at following through on moneymaking ideas.

Your personal sense of freedom is often more important to you than your paycheck. This attitude is fine if you don't have to work for a living, but somewhat foolish if you need every penny you earn. You are one of the most generous signs of the Zodiac, but you must keep your sense of self-preservation too. Never sell yourself short when negotiating for a raise you know you deserve. Even if you do enjoy being a spendthrift, don't spend so recklessly that you forget to provide for any rainy days that may lie ahead!

How to Improve Your Work Relationships

Adaptable, open-minded, freedom-loving, and dependable at the best of times, you can also be a real pain in the neck if you become tactlessly opinionated, gamble recklessly, or are too full of self-importance. Teamwork and team spirit are extremely important at work. The following guide will show you the best way to relate to all the signs, whether they are those of your boss, your peer, or an employee:

Sagittarius with Aries Boss: You soon learn to respect the energetic way this boss gets down to business. Keep your mind on the job and don't insist on giving your views on how something should be done. Aries enjoys being boss!

Sagittarius with Aries Colleague: Two fiery, enthusiastic, and free-spirited signs working on the same team can achieve a lot. But watch out you don't spend so much time talking that nothing gets done.

Sagittarius with Aries Employee: Don't be too free and easy with this employee, or you may have him striving to take over your job. You must always work hard yourself to gain Aries's esteem, or his own work ethic could slip.

Sagittarius with Taurus Boss: Beneath a somewhat stubborn, stolid, disciplined, and well-organized exterior, there lies a boss who will genuinely appreciate the efforts you put in to ensure your work is always up to scratch.

Sagittarius with Taurus Colleague: Try to be less of a know-it-all and be thankful that Taurus's pragmatic approach to life will prevent you from working on too many grandiose pie-in-the-sky schemes.

Sagittarius with Taurus Employee: Lady Luck *has* smiled upon you, because this loyal and dependable employee will never let you down when work needs to be done. Don't push her too hard or tactlessly accuse her of being slow.

Sagittarius with Gemini Boss: Your opposite sign has a mind even speedier and more innovative than yours. Don't forget that Gemini is the boss, so won't appreciate your wasting time or flaunting your supposed superior knowledge!

Sagittarius with Gemini Colleague: You're both brilliant at devising ingenious schemes that could have far-reaching results. But you must become much more organized to be successful in today's competitive workplace.

Sagittarius with Gemini Employee: Behave more like a boss and less like a buddy, or you'll never get any work done from an employee as chatty as this one! Both of you will benefit from a touch more discipline.

Sagittarius with Cancer Boss: This boss can be moody and hyper-sensitive, often depending on the phases of the Moon! But Cancer will be loyal and fiercely protective, so always do your best work.

Sagittarius with Cancer Colleague: Cancer's need for empathy and a peaceful atmosphere may sometimes make you scream for loud music and a stiff drink! But Cancer's intuition will prove invaluable when you're not sure if you're on the right track.

Sagittarius with Cancer Employee: Try to be sympathetic and understanding if this employee confides in you about any personal problems. Cancer is the most home-loving sign in the Zodiac, but also ambitious to get ahead at work.

Sagittarius with Leo Boss: Remember that this boss thinks big and can be very dictatorial. Knuckle under, get on with your work, and don't imply that you know best—because you're not a boss yet!

Sagittarius with Leo Colleague: You both have great social skills, but don't spend so much time admiring each other that the work is left undone! A dose of reality will help you both be even more creative.

Sagittarius with Leo Employee: Leo the Lion is rarely good at taking orders! Try to give yours with tact and diplomacy and lots of praise—when it's rightfully due. But don't be overruled since you are the rightful boss!

Sagittarius with Virgo Boss: Remember you're working for the faultfinder of the Zodiac! Never be too lackadaisical in your ways. Don't sit and gossip when there is important work to be done.

Sagittarius with Virgo Colleague: This nit-picking colleague could be a blessing in disguise when some of your grandiose-sounding schemes require practical analysis! Do try to be more organized in your ways.

Sagittarius with Virgo Employee: Your positive approach to life will help encourage Virgo to be more positive too. Be glad that this hard worker will always check your work first and never send out anything with the slightest error!

Sagittarius with Libra Boss: Try to avoid the tendency to take advantage of this charming, easygoing boss. There is logic involved in taking time to make important decisions—and Libra can show you why!

Sagittarius with Libra Colleague: Libra thrives in good company, so there should be plenty of team spirit here. Organize yourselves well, making sure you don't simply talk about your plans—with insufficient action.

Sagittarius with Libra Employee: You think you know all the answers, while Libra prefers to debate the facts. Provided you're not too caustic and impatient, you will have a wonderfully diplomatic employee who thinks you're great.

Sagittarius with Scorpio Boss: This boss is more likely to brood over your mistakes than smile at them. Scorpio never forgets, even if he does occasionally forgive! Be a better timekeeper and concentrate harder.

Sagittarius with Scorpio Colleague: You tend to take excessive risks with projects. Scorpio prefers to ferret out the hidden problems. You can work well together, but on opposing teams a Scorpio could beat you hands down!

Sagittarius with Scorpio Employee: Don't forget about the sting in the Scorpion's tale. If you upset this employee by being too outspoken, or accuse her unfairly of being at fault, it will never be forgotten.

Sagittarius with Sagittarius Boss: You may be constantly ordering each other about—no matter which one of you is the boss! But if this boss made it to where she is, you surely know you can get there too.

Sagittarius with Sagittarius Colleague: There is no shortage of ambitious schemes when two enthusiastic Archers work together in harmonious bliss. But the results may not be brilliant, unless one of you is financially astute.

Sagittarius with Sagittarius Employee: Don't trust too much to luck and expect everything to be done just the way you want it. Remember this employee is a Sagittarian too! Don't forget you are the boss and not your employee's best buddy!

Sagittarius with Capricorn Boss: A Capricorn boss takes himself more seriously than most. Never fool around when you have work on your desk. Capricorn may be a hard taskmaster but knows that hard work takes you to the top!

Sagittarius with Capricorn Colleague: Forget about trying to take any shortcuts when working alongside the Mountain Goat. Work that is worth doing is *always* worth doing well—that is the motto of this colleague.

Sagittarius with Capricorn Employee: Your flexible ways could come as a surprise to this employee, who will have an extremely organized working life. You might enjoy getting Capricorn to relax a little more, knowing the work will still get done!

Sagittarius with Aquarius Boss: You know you'll have fun once you're working with a boss who appreciates your suggestions and enjoys your humor. Don't try to take over, or you'll soon know who is in charge.

Sagittarius with Aquarius Colleague: This could be a mutual admiration society—two like-minded colleagues encouraging each other's plans and projects. Just make sure it's not all talk and no positive actions.

Sagittarius with Aquarius Employee: Since you know what it's like to feel inwardly free, never try to confine this employee's open mind and inner spirit. Always give praise when it's due; it will bring the best results.

Sagittarius with Pisces Boss: The Pisces boss may appear to be more of a dreamer than a doer but will soon see through *you* if you try to take over. You will be glad that you have such a sympathetic and understanding boss.

Sagittarius with Pisces Colleague: You're the daring and dynamic risk taker, but when you're working together you will definitely benefit from Pisces's sixth sense. Try to organize yourselves with weekly goals—perhaps some daily ones too.

Sagittarius with Pisces Employee: Don't terrify this shy and reserved employee by bellowing out your orders in a really bossy way, even as a joke! Be firm but always kind—and you'll get total loyalty in return.

Getting Longevity out of Your Career

In these days of ever-increasing layoffs and downsizings, it is advisable to be prepared for whatever might happen. Even though you seem to thrive on risk taking, the danger of suddenly finding yourself out of work is rarely something you would choose, especially if you can ill afford it.

One of the great things about being born under the sign of the Archer is that you never stop aiming your arrows high. Fear of failure rarely stops you in your tracks for very long. You possess an abundance of self-esteem which will never let you down. Besides, it doesn't have to mean your career is over just because you encounter setbacks. Ensure your résumé is always kept up-to-date, and if you sense an unsettling atmosphere at work, endeavor to find out what is going on, then get to work promoting your skills in the right direction.

You have great advantages over many other signs, for you are flexible, fast on your feet, a born networker, and always ready for what life has to offer you. If you're good at what you do, you know full well that you also have more than enough self-confidence and optimism to pick up the pieces of the past and propel yourself forward into something new.

You could easily change careers a few times because the idea of being tied down too long in one place rarely appeals. Naturally, you feel much better if the timing of such changes is left completely up to you. Being fired unexpectedly is rarely pleasant. Some people have compared it to suffering a bereavement. However, even midlife career changes should never be feared by Sagittarians, whose creativity rarely diminishes over time. Some of you thrive on the opportunity to do something completely new when you grow older. In one of my previous books, *Star Signs,* I mentioned a Sagittarian who had her first painting accepted by the Royal Academy of Art in London at the age of sixty-four.

If your aim is maximum achievement throughout your life, with the minimum risk of being laid off through any faults of your own, it is essential not only to remain passionate about the service and the quality of your work but also to develop and retain strong work relationships at all levels. Keep abreast of the latest advances in technology, and ensure that you know exactly how it all works. You never want to run the risk of a machine knowing more than you!

Make sure that your flair, tenacity, and ability to successfully drive a company forward will always drive *you* forward too. Allow your independent spirit to take you into the next millennium, secure in the knowledge that getting longevity from your career is not something you need to worry about. You're a natural philosopher, a great believer in making this "the best of all possible worlds," and your Sagittarian skills will always find the right outlets—no matter what your age or situation.

SAGITTARIUS CAREER STRATEGIES—A CHECKLIST FOR EVERY AGE

- Remember that creating concepts is not enough these days. You must ensure they come to fruition by being a pragmatist who can analyze the big picture too.
- Always be sufficiently empowered to take on new business challenges in a fast-moving environment.
- Never create the impression that you know *all* the answers to problems in the workplace. Your coworkers will soon resent a know-it-all.
- Ensure your business acumen is based on solid results, for one-shot successes don't produce a good résumé.
- Always be true to yourself and to your ideals. Aiming your Sagittarian arrow in the direction of a fast buck will rarely satisfy your soul.
- Combine a thorough understanding of business strategy skills with a knowledge of the latest information technology.
- Be confident that you will always have the ability to add exciting new dimensions to your career.

CAPRICORN IN THE WORKPLACE

December 21 ☆ January 19

If you were born between December 21 and January 19, you were born under the sign of Capricorn, tenth sign of the Zodiac. You are a Feminine, Cardinal, Negative, Earth sign. Your planetary symbol is either the Goat with the curling fish's tail or, as often portrayed, the Mountain Goat.

With Saturn, known as the "Task Master of the Zodiac," as your planetary ruler, you possess a determination to succeed in your ambitions that is unsurpassed by any other sign. Saturn teaches you self-discipline, patience, and responsibility. Saturn's influence requires you to work long and hard for what you want to achieve, but in return will bring you the greatest rewards.

You are driven by your goals almost from your very first breath, and, on reaching adulthood, you possess a devotion to duty that is rare to find. You are the natural builders of the Zodiac, and whether your aim is achieving major material success like Capricorns Conrad Hilton and Howard Hughes, or working for peace like Dr. Martin Luther King, Jr. and Anwar Sadat, you rarely lose sight of your objectives.

Sometimes you are so focused on achieving material success that you lose sight of your inner needs and spiritual desires. However, many Capricorns have had great spiritual leanings, including Paramhansa Yogananda, Gurdjieff, Maharishi Mahesh Yogi, Louis Pasteur, Joan of Arc, and Albert Schweitzer.

We all have something to learn from our opposite sign in the Zodiac. Cancer, the home lover, who is instinctive and nurturing but also ambitious, is your opposite sign and can teach you a great deal. To learn something from every sign, you might try to wear a different astrological hat from time to time.

Take a typical workday in the Capricorn life. You are part of a team responsible for finding out information on a company that your own company could be interested in taking over. Although this information is not required for a few weeks, you are determined to get all the details long before then. But your partner has arranged an important dinner party, and you have promised to be home by 6 P.M.— unusually early for you!

Playing Aries: You make sure you arrive at work extra early, tackling everything with Aries enthusiasm and a positive attitude. You also make sure you are home at precisely 6 P.M., promising to be at work early again tomorrow.

Playing Taurus: With a Taurus hat, you have a double dose of loyalty toward your work *and* your domestic life. You explain the situation to your coworkers, enlist their help, and slip away on time without a problem.

Playing Gemini: The more to do, the merrier—for anyone who wears the Gemini hat! You won't lose your highly developed sense of responsibility, but you won't be so hard on yourself for taking off on time for once.

Playing Cancer: In this role, you find it much easier to balance your personal and professional life. You understand that it is as important to support your partner when he or she needs you as to be married to your work twenty-four hours a day.

Playing Leo: With a jolly expression on your face, you soon relay your directives to everyone else on your team and cajole *them* into working late if necessary. There is absolutely no way you'd be late for any sort of social event!

Playing Virgo: You may be so worried about letting down your partner in any way at all that you end up taking work home and doing it after the guests have left. Somehow you manage to do everything required!

Playing Libra: With a sprinkling of Libran tact and diplomacy, you charm everyone around you into doing twice as much work as usual, so that you don't have the slightest fear about leaving early enough to get home by 6 P.M.

Playing Scorpio: You tackle the day's work in an unbeatable way. Fear of failure would not occur to you for an instant. Your instinct tells you that leaving early once in a while is no offense!

Playing Sagittarius: You are fairly nonchalant about the whole thing, knowing the necessary information will be ready in time anyway. You don't worry about not being the last to leave the office for once!

Playing Yourself: Unfortunately, the odds are you'll go on working past the time you were supposed to leave. Stop being such a martyr to your work; you are allowed to enjoy some free time too.

Playing Aquarius: Even if worried about leaving slightly early, you could devise an ingenious excuse—like an unexpected meeting with someone important. But the Aquarian influence makes you more likely to be truthful from the start.

Playing Pisces: With a Pisces hat, you are ultrasensitive to your partner's wishes. You might simply explain to your boss and your coworkers—with the strength of your convictions—that today your personal life must come first.

The Positive and Negative Qualities of a Capricorn at Work

Serious, self-disciplined, and strong-willed enough to persevere through thick and thin, you possess the ability to turn mere concepts into successful realities.

I know two wonderful Capricorn women, both in their seventies, who started their own businesses from scratch and still control them brilliantly. You *like* to be in control—it's an integral part of you!

Saturn, your ruler, is also known as "Old Father Time," and will teach you the importance of timing in your life. In an earlier book, *Star Signs,* I wrote at length about Saturn's influence upon you.

Grounded by your element, Earth, you don't like to take risks or shortcuts to achieve results. You plan every action meticulously and rarely worry about the number of hours your tasks will take you— sometimes working long after everyone else has gone home.

The positive Capricorn is fully conversant with the latest technology, always keeping up-to-date in his or her field. You perfect your working strategies and concentrate on your specific goals, keeping the field in perspective and setting your sights on the top.

You possess patience, clarity, mastery of details, and brilliant administrative skills. In business you have mental toughness and a killer instinct with an extraordinary ability to deflect disadvantages and turn them into advantages. Your task-oriented approach, with your ability to influence and direct both colleagues and clients at all levels, is extremely desirable in today's workplace. Your determination to succeed, combined with your ability to work within a strongly established corporate culture, is highly positive.

The negative side of your personality is that you tend to find it hard to balance your personal and your professional life. I have known many of you, both as clients and friends, who seem to feel inferior without reason. You can be too much of a perfectionist and much too hard on yourself. Sometimes you are too fond of judging other people by your own high standards. Try to be less concerned with the face that you show the world, and resolve not to come across as quite so intrinsically materialistic. Your negative side makes you ruthless when thwarted in your aims, or when your status, power, and image are less than you desire. As I wrote in previous books, both Richard Nixon and John De Lorean succumbed to these qualities.

The wise Capricorn will be levelheaded and serious without becoming overly narrow-minded and pessimistic. Even if material success *is* the primary goal for many Capricorns, you will try to develop more of a sense of humor—directed not only toward yourself but also toward life itself.

If you're a typical Capricorn, you entered the world as a born executive with sky-high goals. Never lose sight of your inner values along the way.

Careers for Capricorn

A high number of Capricorn men and women are drawn to careers in politics (in front or behind the scenes), construction (as architects, surveyors, builders), big business, retail sales, teaching, science, the money market, banking, accountancy, insurance selling, and tax collecting. You also make excellent secretaries and production assistants—on your way to the top!

Famous Capricorn men and women of the past include Helena Rubinstein, Louis Pasteur, Al Capone, J. Edgar Hoover, and Elvis Presley. The media is also full of Capricorns who have used their talents with great success. Mary Tyler Moore and her former husband, TV tycoon Grant Tinker, are both Capricorns, as are *Rolling Stone* magazine founder Jann Wenner, Diane Von Furstenburg, and Vidal Sassoon. Dolly Parton, Kevin Costner, Mel Gibson, Denzel Washington, Anthony Hopkins, Nicolas Cage, Janis Joplin, Tracey Ullman, David Bowie, Diane Keaton, Faye Dunaway, George Forman, and Tiger Woods were also born under your sign.

Your Attitude toward Work

Naturally, your rising sign, together with all the other factors of your particular horoscope, will also influence your attitude toward work.

Your basic attitude toward work is serious. Your concentration and single-mindedness are not deflected when you encounter problems that could throw other signs into a blind panic. Your self-confidence is shaped by an abundance of knowledge and preparation every step of the way. On the surface, you are able to take a realistic and dispassionate analysis of your weaknesses and your strengths—even when you are guilty of being exceedingly hard on yourself.

You are born with the ability to turn concepts into concrete realities, to take defeats in stride, and to turn obstacles into success. Like Taurus, you are one of the builders of the Zodiac, with a deep need for security. You know that you must lay the foundations correctly in order to build *anything*. As a Cardinal sign, you have both initiative and resourcefulness. Capricorn is the tenth house in the Zodiac, and it relates to your prestige and standing, as well as your career and ambitions in the workplace. Your attitude toward work coincides, in many ways, with your attitude toward material issues. You are highly concerned about your future and are rarely a risk taker. It's not that you *always* gravitate toward the job that pays the most, but more that you consider your work as the one constant in your life that enables you to plan for the future. You will often work long hours at the dreary behind-the-scenes tasks that would drive many other people crazy. You do them because your determined sense of discipline enables you to see the larger picture beyond the dreariness. When you are paid to do a job, you consider it your duty, no matter how long it takes.

It is unwise to remain too much or too frequently in the background, even if you do generally prefer to have an office or workspace to yourself! Aside from presenting a strong record of practical achievement, you must also be a savvy communicator with lots of style and presence. While you rarely lack a lofty work ethic, sometimes you do need to be more dynamic in your approach and attitude, proving that you have the stature and charisma needed to build rapport with workers at all levels.

To achieve and maintain maximum success, try to develop more of an entrepreneurial outlook, while remaining a pragmatist with a high energy level who can operate under pressure. Invariably commercially astute and assertive, sometimes you are insufficiently open-minded to new techniques. By nature you are a conservative traditionalist; but we're on the verge of the next millennium, and you must move with the times or risk being left behind.

In order to climb like the Mountain Goat to the top of your chosen peak with the minimum of discomfort along the way, remember that teamwork is a fact of working life today. Before you achieve recognition for your own work, the performance of your particular team will be often assessed. Strongly self-disciplined, you are more than capable of motivating and leading a team toward success; but you're not always flexible enough to follow someone else's orders. Even though you are highly ambitious, it is not always possible to be the leader of the team.

TIPS FOR A HEALTHY WORK ATTITUDE

- Balance your sense of discipline, determination, and serious view of life with a sense of humor and a few more smiles.

- Always use your work talents to the maximum, but don't neglect your innermost needs and desires on your way to the top.
- Cultivate lots of team spirit. It's often just as important as being the last to leave the office at night!

Aiming for Promotion

It's almost as though you were born to be boss, possessed with a business sense that has you aiming at a promotion from your very first breath! As a child you were probably determined to be at the top of your class. In your first job you might have grudgingly accepted some menial position only because you knew you'd soon be moving on. Intelligent and realistic, patient and disciplined, you will carefully formulate your game plans to advance higher up the ladder of success.

I have rarely met a Capricorn who hasn't had a business plan of one kind or another, whether for the immediate future or perhaps for five years' time. In the workplace you will almost *always* have a goal. When seeking a promotion, you are adroit at putting together an excellent analysis and conveying a clear picture of your expectations, but underneath your somewhat imperious and self-assured facade lurks a person who is often as insecure as any other sign.

Aiming for promotion involves not only having the know-how to do the work entailed, but also perhaps convincing the board of a major corporation that no one else could match you. Always ensure that your communication skills come up to scratch. The strength of your personality, your diplomacy, persuasion, and independence of thought are always on trial. You must show that you are capable of bringing all of these *and* a dynamic approach to a new role from day one.

Don't wait until you're aiming for a specific promotion before you have thoroughly analyzed and assessed all the new technologies, techniques, and products out there. Never fail to keep up with developments in your field, for there are sure to be lots of equally bright competitors for every promotion that comes along.

Sometimes you may have to move *around* in order to move up, perhaps even spending time overseas, which will allow you to gain a wider perspective of global markets. Always promote yourself well.

Selling yourself today involves thinking like an executive and then becoming sufficiently visible at executive levels. Never take the pessimistic view that because of your particular circumstances you don't have what it takes to climb to the top. Many highly successful Capricorn men and women, including the late Aristotle Onassis, come from a poor background. It only served to make them even more determined to achieve their goals.

Combine your Capricorn devotion to duty with sufficient pragmatism, trailblazing energy, and enthusiasm to face the next millennium, and you will aim at promotion in the best possible way.

TIPS FOR PROMOTION SEEKERS

- Prove that you're a thinker who takes the time to understand the issues, and then show that you have the highly developed leadership abilities needed to deliver results.
- Demonstrate that you have first-class communication skills, and ambitious long term goals.
- Make sure you have a good record of tackling the wide range of complex issues that can arise in today's workplace.

How to Cope with Being Passed Over for Promotion

With your cautious approach to life plus a deep-rooted need for security, it can be difficult for you to cope with being passed over for a specific promotion—even if you were fairly pessimistic about it from the outset.

However, Saturn will always be your greatest ally, teaching you to make the most of delays and limitations by viewing them as learning experiences. Never allow yourself to feel down or depressed for long. Your potential for success is not diminished even if it does take longer to reach that mountain peak.

Try harder to retain a sense of humor. Never blow the situation out of proportion. Don't put up your defenses to the extent that you refuse to let anyone see that you're disappointed. It is not a sign of weakness to shed a few tears if it will make you feel better! Stay in touch with your emotions and stop playing it quite so cool, calm, and collected, even if you *are* a Capricorn.

Keep your eyes fixed on that mountain peak—you know you will get there soon.

Ambition—or the Lack of It

I have rarely come across a Capricorn man or woman lacking in professional ambition. Your Capricorn temperament makes you resolute and decisive in almost every area of your life. You have the ability to turn even the loftiest aspirations into reality, aided by your common sense and your willingness to work conscientiously almost until you drop! Your inborn sense of timing makes you a genius at moving ahead. But sometimes you become obsessed with your career goals, insensitive to the needs of others, and horribly full of your own self-importance. Never forget that Joseph Stalin, Al Capone, and Idi Amin were also Capricorns.

Your ambition goes hand in hand with your desire for abundant material security, especially if you have suffered difficulties in your early life. Astrologically, due to Saturn's influence, the first twenty-eight to thirty years of a Capricorn's life are the hardest and then everything becomes easier.

Be aware that Capricorn will not be the only sign aiming for the top of the success ladder. Never become so wrapped up in your own little world that you fail to see what is going on around you. Remember that you can always learn something new to help you advance, but don't lose sight of your inner needs and desires along the way. In my last book, *Success Through the Stars,* I pointed out that Howard Hughes's millions didn't seem to make him happy. Always try to ensure that your ambitions don't make you sad.

Ambition—and Your Love Life

You are often more concerned with status than the rest of the Zodiac signs put together. You know precisely what you want from your love life and are prepared to wait patiently for the right person to come along. You may even put your love life on hold until you have reached a point in your career when you are convinced you're ready. However, I have known several Capricorn men and women who were so avidly ambitious at work that, on reaching their late thirties, they found they didn't like the life they were leading. Although they had achieved their professional goals, their social life was flagging and their love life nonexistent.

Creating the right balance between work and love is not always easy, especially for a workaholic Capricorn. Nevertheless, you are the only person who is totally in charge of your career, and in total charge of your love life too. Don't be so ruthlessly disciplined in your approach to work that you lose out on personal happiness; for then you will have no one to blame but yourself. If you're involved with someone who is as much of a workaholic as you, at least you will know the rules of the game and will have no reasons to be jealous or to feel left out.

Your desire for status and a materially secure domestic life could mean that once you are happily settled in a permanent relationship your interest in working hard could lessen. I have also met Capricorn women who, for financial reasons, have had to be the sole breadwinner in the family and who rarely complained about the hours they put in.

TIPS FOR COMBINING WORK AND LOVE

- Always remember to listen to the dictates of your heart as well as to your head—you can't snuggle up cozily to your desk at night!
- Never complain about how hard you always have to work. It was inevitably your choice in the first place!
- In work you're acclaimed as a move-ahead genius—so why not in love? Don't be quite so cool, controlled, and calculating!
- Learn to balance your career goals with a more relaxed approach to other areas of your life.

Romance in the Workplace

Your feet are placed firmly on the ground, and you are usually more determined to achieve your lofty goals than to daydream about love and romance.

While you are undoubtedly attracted to wealth and power (and often admit to being turned on sexually by these), I'm not sure you would necessarily compromise your professional ambitions by conducting an illicit affair with your boss or by marrying the boss's son or daughter to get ahead.

However, there seems to be a contradiction within your carefully controlled personality. Although you may be highly moralistic, with traditional values of marriage, you can also be fairly ruthless about going after someone you find attractive—even if that person is married to someone else. If someone at work *does* turn you on, your moral ethics may be somewhat diminished. Unlike most other signs, if you conduct a supposedly secret office affair, it is *sure* to remain a secret. Cool, calculating Capricorns rarely gossip, even to other Capricorns.

Because you are so ambitious, you can also be ruthless if you believe you're not getting where you want to be because of *someone else*'s affair. Let's say a coworker is having an affair with your boss and, for this reason alone, is getting better evaluations of her work than you are. Then it might be you who starts to spread the gossip.

Many companies frown on liaisons between employees and make their views plain from the start. Sexual harassment cases appear to be on the rise, but as a highly disciplined Capricorn you are unlikely to put yourself in a position where you could be accused of harassing anyone or to leave yourself open to unwanted come-ons.

When people are working closely with each other for at least eight hours a day, there will be times when a jokey flirtation does turn into a love affair. But as a brilliant disciplinarian, you would be wise to set yourself some pretty strict ground rules. Although you are renowned for your cool demeanor, remember you would still have to live with how you were feeling inside, especially if things went wrong.

With your careful and conscientious attitude toward life, perhaps it's best to leave the dubious risk taking involved in an office affair to a more adventure-loving sign.

You and Your Stress Factor

As one of the most career-minded and business-oriented signs, you dedicate yourself with amazing discipline to the tasks that face you, sometimes becoming a virtual prisoner of your work. You seem to think you were born for long hours and work overload, almost forgetting you have a domestic life too. With your conservative way of thinking, you may think of *stress* as a dirty word—something to which no well-brought-up Capricorn should dare succumb! But bear in mind that stress is simply the body's normal reaction to events that seem threatening, or which you feel unable to cope with for one reason or another.

While writing this chapter, I heard a radio discussion about a new health problem called Information Fatigue Syndrome, which arises when people are inundated with so much printed matter, e-mail, faxes, and so forth, that they can never keep up. With the syndrome comes a growing fear that your competitor will learn more than you. As a Capricorn, you may be particularly susceptible to this health problem. Your commitment to your work is awesome, but you must make a commitment to yourself that you will not burn out on the way to the top.

Sometimes, you are so busy concentrating on your long-term goals and ambitions that you lose sight of what your inner voice is telling you about your body's needs. In one of my earlier books, *Star Signs,* I devised a meditation especially for Capricorn, which will help you reach that calm and still place deep within you. You will then be able to achieve greater balance by allowing the stress to drift from your body.

Capricorn rules the knees, the structural elements in the body, the spine, teeth, bones, joints, ligaments, and the skin. Astrologically, it is said that when you become too set in your way of thinking, you can sometimes develop arthritis or rheumatism because of the crystallization that then takes place. If you make up your mind that there is only one way of doing something or no one but you who can do it, you leave yourself open to stress.

It is so important to create a balanced way of life. When you are constantly used to working under pressure (often of your own making), it even becomes unsettling to think about taking some leisure time for yourself.

As you grow older, you usually come to terms with the fact that rest, relaxation, and enjoying yourself in a leisurely fashion are not banned from your life! But you are allowed some leisure time when you are young too. It's all part of creating a balanced life for yourself. I'm sure many of you would love to travel more, especially when it gives you an opportunity to indulge your interests in different cultures and architecture. Enjoy going to good restaurants, and don't worry unnecessarily about the cost. Don't make yourself a martyr by missing the latest theater productions, music concerts, and films, and take some time to visit art galleries and museums. Pamper your body with a great massage, or spend some time in the sauna.

Above all, dedicate some time to *you*. It's one of the best ways to avoid succumbing to stress.

Your Attitude toward Making Money

Your attitude toward making money is rigid rather than reckless, carefully controlled as opposed to careless. You are a supreme saver and rarely a spendthrift.

Many of you are inordinately concerned about your savings and checking accounts. I'm sure you know all about money market accounts and that you have made certain you possess sufficient health insurance in case you're sick. Cautious and often anxious to extremes, you will always aim to have sufficient funds invested for the future, for yourself and any dependents.

If you are a typical Goat, you may be frugal in the amount of spare cash you spend on yourself, which is totally unfair considering how hard you work. I think your attitude toward your finances should include the ability to enjoy not only making money but pleasurably spending some of it too. Don't allow unreasonable fear of financial failure in the future to prevent you from getting on with your life in the now. You know, deep down, that although you're often pessimistic in your views, you are a born survivor, who would never let any financial obstacle set you back for long.

Be happy that you were born with a natural bent for money. Intrinsically materialistic, you have a great talent for handling money profitably. Indeed, some Capricorns are brilliant managers in investment companies and as administrators of estates. Use your financial skills to ensure you get the best deals for yourself too, without losing sight of your normal scruples in order to do so.

You have the ability not only to analyze the big picture but also to make tough commercial decisions. Combined with your astute business mind, and financial awareness on all levels, this decisiveness should make you a seasoned professional when it comes to making money.

All that remains is to remind you not to sell yourself short when you're selling *yourself.*

How to Improve Your Work Relationships

As a reliable, disciplined, ambitious, and conscientious Capricorn, you rarely have problems in carrying out your work diligently and sure-footedly. However, you can sometimes be almost as critical as Virgo in your assessment of the way other people perform their work.

It is always important to cultivate the ability to get on well with your coworkers. The following guide will show you the best way to relate to all the signs, whether they are those of your boss, your peer, or an employee:

Capricorn with Aries Boss: Your Aries boss has brilliant ideas but is rarely so great at following them through. Make the most of your ability to organize and to willingly carry out orders, and you'll get on really well with this boss.

Capricorn with Aries Colleague: Don't end up *doing* all the nitty-gritty work while Aries merely talks about how much there is to do! Your pragmatic analysis of ideas offsets the Ram's headstrong approach.

Capricorn with Aries Employee: It must be hard to remain patient with an impulsive and sometimes undisciplined Aries. Be thankful that Aries will be honest, loyal, and respectful when working for a boss as disciplined as you.

Capricorn with Taurus Boss: A Taurus boss is just as disciplined and hardworking as you. You will enjoy working for someone whose ideas you respect, so impress the Bull with your willingness to work late when necessary.

Capricorn with Taurus Colleague: Two determinedly ambitious Earth signs on the same team will produce successful results. If you're on opposing teams or aiming at the same promotion, keep your wits about you all the time!

Capricorn with Taurus Employee: Taurus may sometimes be slow, and dislikes being rushed in any way at all, but will always do things to perfection. Loyalty to the Bull will bring you unswaying loyalty in return.

Capricorn with Gemini Boss: You're concerned with the outcome of one project at a time, but this boss may want you to deal with myriad different things. You will learn from Gemini's flexible ways—including how to be less rigid yourself.

Capricorn with Gemini Colleague: Your single-minded devotion to duty combined with Gemini's constant need for mental stimulation could bring problems. But together you will devise brilliant projects if you sit down and really talk.

Capricorn with Gemini Employee: Be prepared to be a little less rigid in your work rules—like allowing your employee to leave on time at the end of a heavy day. Otherwise you'd be better off hiring a different sign!

Capricorn with Cancer Boss: Underneath Cancer's soft and sensitive exterior lurks an ambitious streak as powerful as yours. Cancer gets to the top by dint of sheer hard work, so don't start to think you can suddenly take his place!

Capricorn with Cancer Colleague: Astrologically, it is said that opposites attract, and you both have traditional values and are searching for security. You may have to try harder to be sympathetic toward the Crab's up-and-down moods.

Capricorn with Cancer Employee: Accept that this employee does have a home to go to at the end of the day. Cancer will always work hard but resents feeling put upon just because *you* like to stay late at the office.

Capricorn with Leo Boss: This boss is a charmer, sweet-talking you into overworking, while she goes off on three-hour lunches charged to her expense account! Because of your ambitious goals, you'll probably grit your teeth and aim for promotion.

Capricorn with Leo Colleague: Make it clear that you're not prepared to be the workhorse while Leo goes out and has fun. Never hide in the background too much; you don't want the Lion to take the credit for *everything.*

Capricorn with Leo Employee: You know you're rarely the easiest of bosses, but do try to praise a Leo employee when praise is due. Then you'll have a worker whose loyalty is almost impossible to match.

Capricorn with Virgo Boss: Be thankful for a boss who recognizes and appreciates your workaholic ways. Admit you greatly respect his business acumen, even if sometimes you're a little jealous that you're not yet the boss!

Capricorn with Virgo Colleague: On the same team, you and Virgo are two kindred spirits aiming for a common goal. But if the two of you are aiming for the same promotion, it could be hard to predict which of you determined Earth signs will win!

Capricorn with Virgo Employee: Never worry that the work won't get done or that Virgo will take a long lunch break. Rejoice in your good fortune, and don't offend Virgo by searching for mistakes you're unlikely to find!

Capricorn with Libra Boss: Since Libra wants everything done perfectly, and won't rush you into impossible deadlines, you should get on well. Don't believe stories about "lazy Librans." Most Libran bosses will be as hardworking as you.

Capricorn with Libra Colleague: Never be fooled into thinking that Librans are not ambitious. You will enjoy working with such a peaceful, and diplomatic colleague. Don't expect too many instant decisions, though!

Capricorn with Libra Employee: Although Libra may seem laid-back and indecisive, this employee will be loyal and determined to do her best. Libra also possesses a cool ability to handle difficult people.

Capricorn with Scorpio Boss: You have to admire Scorpio's incisive mind and ruthless determination to get to the top. Never try to cut any corners with this boss. Mistakes may be forgiven, but never forgotten.

Capricorn with Scorpio Colleague: This charismatic colleague will be your equal in the power struggle, so tread carefully if you're both aiming for greater success. Scorpio is highly secretive, so could be plotting moves behind your back.

Capricorn with Scorpio Employee: A power-hungry Scorpio prefers to be the boss and makes a formidable enemy. Never give this employee the chance to stab you in the back; remember that sting in the Scorpion's tail!

Capricorn with Sagittarius Boss: This boss's somewhat disorganized style may differ from your disciplined approach, but you will enjoy his positive view of life. Don't be offended by his outspoken ways; Sagittarians are not renowned for their tactfulness!

Capricorn with Sagittarius Colleague: Appreciate the Archer's ability to come up with brilliant-sounding projects, and use your pragmatism to bring her down to Earth. You could make some great music together!

Capricorn with Sagittarius Employee: Try to get Sagittarius to stick to more of a routine, and you'll achieve a minor miracle! Always listen to this employee's ideas, one of which could be a stroke of genius.

Capricorn with Capricorn Boss: Provided you admire and respect your boss's working style, you will get on fine. But be prepared for trouble if you interfere too much with the Mountain Goat's routine!

Capricorn with Capricorn Colleague: There should be little cause for criticism since you're both such perfectionists. If one of you is more ambitious than the other, I'm not sure which one would be more successful!

Capricorn with Capricorn Employee: Be thankful that you have such a conscientious employee, but be warned that he could be after your job before too long! Never take anything for granted with such an ambitious sign.

Capricorn with Aquarius Boss: Don't expect the traditional way of doing things, but be prepared to admit that this unpredictable boss can come up with some totally brilliant ideas at the most unlikely times!

Capricorn with Aquarius Colleague: This friendly and informal colleague will bring a breath of fresh air your way, and some inventive ideas too. Try to understand that Aquarius can rarely stick to routine or such long hours as you!

Capricorn with Aquarius Employee: This is not the greatest combination! You're a hard taskmaster in the workplace, and Aquarius works best when she feels totally free—not when she is being rigidly controlled.

Capricorn with Pisces Boss: Don't be fooled into thinking that every Pisces boss has his head in the clouds. There is a shrewd and calculating side to the Fish, so don't start to be devious and think you can take over.

Capricorn with Pisces Colleague: It may appear easy to convince this sympathetic and sensitive colleague that you're the cat's pajamas. But Pisces is also psychic and savvy enough to be assertive when necessary.

Capricorn with Pisces Employee: A contented Pisces will always work hard for you, even if she is not the best timekeeper around. Try not to be too be hard on this employee if she's feeling sad; Pisceans are ultrasensitive to atmosphere.

Getting Longevity out of Your Career

Throughout your life the influence of your ruling planet, Saturn, will inspire you to use the maximum amount of discipline and effort to reach the top. If you're a typical Capricorn, there is no way you will give up halfway or consider your career purely as a brief passage in your life. As the workaholic of the Zodiac, you're determined to get the maximum longevity out of your career—for as long as *you* want it.

In today's workplace, *downsizing, redundancy, getting fired, job termination, staff cutbacks,* and *reorganization* are all words that are heard with alarming frequency. Job security is no longer a given, even for a worker as reliable and responsible as you. You must not only focus on the unique things that you have to offer, but also make sure they are constantly visible to your bosses. It's a bonus to be appreciated for your unimpeachable integrity and administrative skills, but don't forget that there is a fiercely competitive labor market out there and that you cannot afford to let your standards slip.

Some companies have been cutting staff to the bare minimum, and they expect the survivors to pick up the slack. Working excessively long hours is rarely a problem for you, but try not to make yourself overly tired for then your concentration can slip. Always prioritize your tasks, for if you are overworked *and* overtired, you are more likely to make mistakes. It is highly important for you to keep up with all the new technology, but don't go to extremes.

You are someone who will always take responsibility for your errors, and make sure they do not happen again. You also appreciate the value of learning from your mistakes. You are brilliant at overcoming obstacles and setbacks, so that if for any reasons outside your control you are laid off, you must also believe that you will not be out of work for long. Obstacles can create power—the power to become even *more* successful in the future.

Just like the other Earth signs, Taurus and Virgo, you will remain committed to service and quality throughout your working life. If you are unfairly fired, you will be well aware that there are always legal avenues to take. Never get into a panic about getting older; if you're a typical Mountain Goat, you will have made sure that there is a nest egg for any rainy days ahead!

People change their careers more frequently these days. Don't cultivate the sort of stick-in-the-mud mentality by which you feel you have to stay in the same job forever. Often it is an advantage to move around in order to move up, for you gain new experiences all the time. Keep your résumé up-to-date, and don't neglect your networking so that you are conversant with everything going on in your workplace, and outside it too.

You're a genius at moving ahead, with the determination and discipline to achieve the highest goals. Never create unnecessary obstacles worrying about the longevity of your career. You're a born survivor, and I'm sure your working life will survive too!

CAPRICORN CAREER STRATEGIES—A CHECKLIST FOR EVERY AGE

- Set your sights on the top, but don't forget to keep the rest of the field in perspective too.
- Always look at the long-term consequences of your actions in addition to the short-term gains.
- Never lose sight of your spiritual needs in your search for material success.
- Make sure you're sufficiently prepared for the future with a confident and competent knowledge of the new technologies.
- Allow yourself to be seen playing key strategic roles at work.
- Add new dimensions to your career on a continuing basis.
- Show that you're a seasoned business professional—who will never give up!

AQUARIUS IN THE WORKPLACE

January 20 ☆ *February 18*

If you were born between January 20 and February 18, you were born under the sign of Aquarius, eleventh sign of the Zodiac. You are a Masculine, Fixed, Positive, Air sign. Your planetary symbol is the Water Bearer.

Uranus, the great awakener and the planet of invention, is your planetary ruler, and you are one of the most unique and inventive signs of the Zodiac. (Before Uranus was discovered in 1781, the planet Saturn was associated with Aquarius.) The influence of Uranus helps to put you ahead of the pack striving to make their marks in the corporate workplace. It is said that Saturn continues to influence you, acting as the calming influence that restrains your more rebellious tendencies.

You will leave no stone unturned to achieve success in your chosen field. The name of Aquarian Montgomery Ward is known to most American shoppers, while Aquarian Barry Diller is responsible for the Home Shopping Network on TV. You love to challenge rules that the rest of us meekly follow, seemingly caring little for the reaction that such behavior provokes. Original in thought and independent in manner, you are frequently an idealist and a rebel with a cause. Vanessa Redgrave, Germaine Greer, and Yoko Ono are all Aquarians.

Progressive in your outlook, and ultramodern in your techniques, you are the sign most likely to benefit from each new technological invention. Aquarian Thomas Edison not only brought us the lightbulb but also gave us the very first movie projector.

Originality of thought is an asset that often needs to be tempered with the ability to fit into a corporate workstyle. Prove that you have not only specialist skills and the ambition to succeed in your chosen field, but also the disciplined approach necessary to achieve a consistent record of practical achievement.

We all have something to learn from our opposite sign in the Zodiac. Leo, regal ruler of the Zodiac, is your opposite sign. Leo is more focused on getting the job done well and in time—even if only to receive all the praise! You can learn something from every sign, which is why you might try to play a different sign once in a while.

Take a typical workday in the Aquarius life. You have been used to working on your own initiative, with no fixed time frame provided your work is ready when it is needed. Suddenly there is a change of management, and everyone is expected to fit in with everyone else's hours, regardless of their rank.

Playing Aries: After the initial horror, the stark reality of life in today's workplace hits you. Having determined that you don't wish to lose your job, you decide to take up the challenge to see if you can be less unpredictable.

Playing Taurus: You have no problem with the new policy. Taureans are famous for their ability to stick determinedly to routine, believing it's the best way to achieve success in the long run.

Playing Gemini: Originality of thought combined with originality of action is wonderful. Unfortunately, Gemini can be almost as unpredictable as Aquarius, so you have your work cut out for you if you are to stick to the rules.

Playing Cancer: With your enhanced sensitivity, you can recognize and accept that sometimes it *is* important to try to fit in. Your instincts tell you to give routine a chance.

Playing Leo: Although you still feel that your way of working is best, your Leo pride makes you rise to the challenge of fitting into the new regime better than anyone else. You adore the praise you receive for your efforts.

Playing Virgo: Your unpredictability is toned down by the earnest and conscientious desire to do everything asked of you with the minimum of fuss. You'd never sleep a wink if you felt you could lose your job by failing to fit in.

Playing Libra: Balance at all costs! If keeping your place in the workplace means getting in on time and sticking to the rules, you'll do this. With Libra's influence you find it easier to be charming and diplomatic about it too.

Playing Scorpio: You might find it hard to compromise your attitude of "each to his own." But you are thankful that Scorpio's steely strength enables you to tackle this new situation with the determination to survive!

Playing Sagittarius: "You win some, you lose some" is the usual Sagittarian approach to life. Although you might make a lot of noise about having to fit in with everyone else, you follow your new routine with confidence.

Playing Capricorn: Capricorn's conventionality combined with Aquarius's unpredictability is an interesting match. You have no problems in sticking to routine, and you score top marks for turning your unique ideas into practical results.

Playing Yourself: Your determination to be the eternal rebel could land you in trouble. To succeed today, you must have the personal qualities and drive to rise to every challenge, including following routine!

Playing Pisces: You'd hate to think you were letting down your team. So you do your best to understand and respond to the new rules with the minimum of fuss. Your sixth sense helps you see the bigger picture.

The Positive and Negative Qualities of an Aquarius at Work

You're blessed with a special spark of pure genius, and your motivation springs more from your inner visions than from other people's opinions.

You are often wonderful when we expect you to behave like a monster, but insufferable when we think you're going to be sweetness and light personified. This is, perhaps, a major part of your unique charm.

You have a deep yearning for knowledge, and because you are the sign of the humanitarian, you believe deeply in creating a better world for everyone. But in today's often ruthless workplace there is rarely sufficient time to indulge in humanitarian beliefs and desires. We all have to watch our backs to make sure that someone else does not take over our job.

A positive approach to work must involve a willingness to fit in with the rest of the team. Sometimes you are too dogmatic as you try to force other people to see things your way.

The positive Aquarian is intellectual and independent, ingenious, offbeat and altruistic, high-flying, and versatile. You're a great believer in the truth, in fair deals and equality, and in preparing the way for the rest of us to follow. You will easily understand and respond to the fast-changing needs of today's workplace and display outstanding interpersonal skills with the necessary stature and charisma to build rapport at all levels. You will exploit your unique innovation and flair to accelerate your career, making your contribution even more visible and influential.

You will be at the forefront of the information highway. You probably visualized it even before others started navigating it. You possess strong communication skills which will be couched in a highly creative approach, as well as a flair for unorthodox ideas, which will often pay handsome dividends.

The negative Aquarian is sometimes *too* unpredictable and unconventional. Your insistence on "being different" and "standing out in a crowd" can leave you isolated. These days, being out of sync can also mean being out of work. The two words you hate most are probably *rules* and *regulations*. Rarely afraid of taking responsibility, you may dislike having it foisted on you by *someone else*.

You are at your best when left free to follow your dreams in your own unique way, with no one giving you orders—or even advice! This is rarely possible, especially in today's cutthroat workplace.

The wise Aquarian will balance idealistic thoughts, ideas, and causes with a more grounded and pragmatic approach to life in general and work in particular. You're the scientist, alchemist, academic, and reformer, but try to understand that some people won't be ready or willing to listen to your knowledge. Sometimes you must show a greater willingness to listen to theirs.

Careers for Aquarius

Ideal professions for your sign include anything that involves working with electricity (you make great inventors), television, radio, science, astrology, astronomy, computers (as technicians or inventors of programs), archaeology, sociology, charity organizations, writing (especially your outspoken thoughts in books, plays and movies!), aviation, and the space programs.

Famous Aquarians include Galileo, Abraham Lincoln, Franklin D. Roosevelt, Charles Dickens, James Joyce, Wolfgang Amadeus Mozart, Geena Davis, John Travolta, Paul Newman, Jack Lemmon, Tom Selleck, Joe Pesci, Zsa Zsa Gabor, François Truffaut, John Schlesinger, Jackson Pollock, Betty Friedan, Norman Mailer, James Michener, Angela Davis, Michael Jordan, Jack Nicklaus, Wayne Gretzky, Babe Ruth, and Greg Louganis.

Your Attitude toward Work

Naturally, your rising sign, together with all the other factors of your personal horoscope, will also influence your attitude toward work.

However, regardless of what profession you choose to follow, your approach is always carried out with great flair and style. One of my best friends, Aquarian Mark Hayles, is a leading makeup artist who always manages to make famous movie stars look more beautiful and interesting than they already do. Aquarian Helen Gurley Brown realized her goal of making *Cosmopolitan* the first women's magazine to be outspoken on matters of sexuality. Aquarian Oprah Winfrey continues to have a huge following with her television show, because she does not rely on slick humor and packaging to get her viewers tuning in, and unconventional Aquarian actor James Dean has never been forgotten by millions of fans all over the world.

Your work attitude sometimes comes across as too disinterested, especially if you are wrapped up in your own little world conceiving brilliant ideas that may be far ahead of their time. At times your behavior is erratic, and your attention to details spasmodic. You often present a cool, aloof, and unemotional exterior, but remember that too much detachment in the workplace can look like disinterest in your work.

You can be extremely stubborn and inclined to perform a whole song and dance if you are asked to do something by someone you do not sufficiently respect. You assume that sticking to your principles is the only way to behave. But *is* it sticking to your principles, or simply your determination to be different?

In today's tough workplace you may have to go with the flow on a short-term basis to achieve better long-term results. Sometimes it *is* necessary to take orders from a superior, and sometimes calmly discussing the reason for these orders will clear things up in your mind. You must be able to work under pressure and prove you are as effective a team player as you are a charismatic leader. Teamwork is more important than ever today, because often you will be judged not only on your work but also within the framework of your particular team. You must also show that you are able to work within a strongly established corporate culture and maintain positive business relationships at all levels.

Your multitalented skills are a bonus, provided you don't scatter them in too many directions. Brilliant at understanding what *other* people are all about, you are sometimes far too uncommunicative about what really makes you tick. You enjoy working in an office with an open floor plan or in a store with people and technology all around you. Even though you're not the greatest timekeeper in the world, you rarely mind working extralong hours when necessary.

In today's workplace you must make a highly visible impact, which should be easy for you as you are an expert at rapidly analyzing and assessing new technologies, and researching new techniques and products as required. Your ruling planet, Uranus, is the planet of invention, and you may have no problem in devising brilliant programs for your company's computer network.

TIPS FOR A HEALTHY WORK ATTITUDE

- Always use your brilliant imagination and flair for the unusual in a positive and constructive way.

- Balance your individuality within the workplace with the commitment and ability to be an effective team player too.
- Remember that you thrive on constant stimulation, change, and variety in your work.

Aiming for Promotion

When you are seeking a promotion, believe in yourself wholeheartedly. It may seem strange to say this to someone who appears to be so extroverted. However, I have known many Aquarians who are prepared to speak out forthrightly on something they believe in rather than on *themselves*. You're brilliant when arguing for causes, whether they be charitable or political, and at inspiring other people to get off their butts and do something positive about their own careers. Everything seems to change when the object under review is you.

Although you are such an individualist and invariably come up with innovative ideas, always make sure that these ideas (and where they came from!) come to the attention of the powers that be.

Try to strike the right balance between being unnecessarily outspoken or argumentative about your beliefs, and being slightly less restrained, though no less confident.

You rarely decide upon a long-term business plan because that would mean staying in the same place for a long time. Too much routine and regimentation is frustrating for a live wire such as you, and when you aim at promotion you can be almost as impatient as any Aries.

You are bound to encounter others up for the same position as you—even though they may not be aware of this! You have an important edge over the competition: you are able to keep your deepest thoughts to yourself while plotting your next move up the ladder of success. In this way you can outmaneuver your opponents because your Aquarian instincts are also sure to intuit their next steps.

Aquarians like to shock people, especially the establishment, by coming up with radical ideas. If you're set on a corporate or business career, remember that there are unlikely to be many companies that welcome too many ideas of this sort. You must show not only that you're a pioneer with an amazingly creative approach and flair for unorthodox ideas, but also that you can be a pragmatist with the skills required for implementing them.

Focus on the unique things you have to offer. If it becomes necessary to make an attitude adjustment to move up to the next rung of the success ladder, listen to your instincts and rise to every challenge. If anyone can be a bright light, it's you!

TIPS FOR PROMOTION SEEKERS

- Make an impact with the brilliance of your work, without being too unpredictable.
- Show that you have the necessary blend of business, personal, and technical skills.
- Don't be so obviously against routine; it's necessary for all of us at times.

How to Cope with Being Passed Over for Promotion

It might be difficult for you to contemplate that anyone could possibly turn down such an outgoing, positive, enthusiastic worker as you, particularly one with such strategic vision and leadership potential.

If you have made mistakes along the way, at least you will know what to do next time. Never let a turndown be a turnoff. It's tough out there in the workplace, but you're sufficiently savvy to navigate the ups and downs of your career. If being passed over for a particular promotion leaves you in a dead-end job with no changes in the foreseeable future, be your own public relations agent and send out your résumé to other companies where you would like to work, even if there aren't any current job openings there.

Don't get embroiled in office politics; valuable time can be wasted that way. Concentrate instead on acquiring and refining the specialist skills needed to get ahead in your field. Allow your Aquarian vision to focus on the promise of the future, rather than dwelling on any disappointments of the past.

Ambition—or the Lack of It

Whether your ambition consists of making sure you are noticed for reasons unrelated to work, or of being the best in your field, I am sure that most of you *are* ambitious!

Because you are a Fixed sign, you sometimes hold on stubbornly to your ideas even when you need to fit in more with other people. The eternal truth seeker, you care little for tradition if it conflicts with what you are convinced is the way to move ahead.

It is often said that Aquarius is endowed with a special spark of genius; certainly you're brilliant at coming up with new ideas and inventions, doctrines and theories. Sometimes your determination to express your views can create conflicts with your career ambitions, as Aquarian actress and political activist Vanessa Redgrave has discovered at times in her theatrical career. Sometimes your dislike and fear of routine prevents you from laying the groundwork necessary to fulfill your ambitions.

You need to find a way to stay motivated. You rarely aim primarily for material success, but you do require continual mental stimulation in your work. Don't waste your unique gifts, but turn them into stellar achievements in the workplace.

When you are truly ambitious, you won't allow anything to get in the way of your goals. I have a very good Aquarian friend who was the tour manager for a large travel group. She loved this stimulating work, which took her all over the world, but had to give it up after she got married. Nevertheless, she and her husband made it their goal to start their own luxury hotel in Portugal's Algarve. During the construction stage, she discovered she was pregnant, and before long there was a new hotel *and* a new baby to occupy her time. Both of them are flourishing, so now she has even more stimulating interests in her life!

Ambition—and Your Love Life

Because you are such an unconventional and unpredictable sign, it is particularly difficult for me to generalize on this subject. You are a law unto yourself, and although you're sometimes accused of being emotionally cold and analytical, it is often your determination to be free that is your most prominent trait.

If you're a truly ambitious Aquarian, this desire to be free, and uncluttered by emotional ties, will prevent you from letting your love life interfere with your ambitions. It's often difficult enough for you to stick to the routine of a regimented workplace, without having a jealous lover trying to keep tabs on your spare time.

Personal relationships on a one-to-one basis are not always your forte—usually because you are so unpredictable. You are often better at fulfilling the role of best buddy than lover. Naturally, there will be happily married Aquarians who also have fulfilling careers, but it is sometimes hard for you to balance a domestic routine with a professional one.

Anyone who is involved with you on an emotional level must often be prepared to put up with your unconventional way of life, and learn to intellectualize and theorize with you rather than suffocate you with too many invasions of your private emotional space. If you are involved with another Aquarian, at least you should understand each other. But other signs might find it hard to understand just why you are so fascinating and yet so fickle too!

TIPS FOR COMBINING WORK AND LOVE

- Don't close off your feelings totally. When you're at the top of your chosen career, you might enjoying sharing your success with someone special!
- Remember that being too outrageous could sometimes mean you're ostracized by someone you'd like to know better.
- Acknowledge that your motivational and your interpersonal strengths are of equal importance.
- Use your analytical skills on yourself to discover how to achieve the right balance between realizing your ambitions *and* enjoying good relationships.

Romance in the Workplace

It's often hard enough for you to fit into a regimented work culture without entertaining the thought of embarking on a love affair with someone in the workplace.

Because you tend to flee from any kind of binding emotional commitment, you're unlikely to go around looking for someone. You know that being an effective team player doesn't mean you are supposed to play the field with your coworkers.

With you, a sexual attraction is more likely to take second place to an attraction of two like-minded individuals. You thrive on good mental communication with someone who doesn't try to tie you down. Your ideal world is one full of ideas and intellectual arguments, rather than a torrid romance behind closed office doors.

One always hears of people who are presumed to have slept their way to the top of their profession, but I think you have too much pride in your individuality to be one of them. You are far too outspoken to keep quiet if ever you found yourself a victim of sexual harassment. A renowned champion of causes, you would, I'm sure, also be the first to offer to give advice and help to any other victim in your workplace.

Naturally, it is possible that you will be extremely attracted to a coworker and find yourself indulging in an affair you never expected to take place. Since you tend to reveal very little about your emotional feelings, even to your nearest and dearest, you'd be unlikely to allow this to become public knowledge. But secrets always have a way of coming into the open, and even if you are evasive about your private life you could find yourself with someone who *does* find it difficult to be unemotional about the situation.

If you find it difficult to be part of a structured corporate regime, it is wise to refrain from indulging in *any* activity that takes your attention away from your work. There are times when an exciting affair might appeal to your adventurous nature, especially since you enjoy having admirers. However, if fame and prestige are your major goals, it's best to concentrate on them.

You and Your Stress Factor

When you are under a great deal of pressure at work, your normal aloofness can turn to erratic and irrational behavior that becomes increasingly unpredictable. You may also become more dogmatically fixed in your own opinions. This combination is definitely not a good formula for success.

Remember that stress is not bad per se. It is a normal reaction of the body to events that seem to threaten you, or which you feel unable to cope with for one reason or another. Because Aquarius is known as a New Age sign, you are probably conversant with many aspects of alternative medicine and aware of the benefits of relaxation techniques such as meditation. In *Star Signs* I devised a meditation for Aquarius, which can help you shake off the pressures of the workday and find a balance between your sense of duty to the world and your sense of duty to yourself. I'm sure you have your own methods for releasing stress. Use whichever methods you prefer, so long as you don't bottle up your feelings inside you. You're the kind of person whose diet depends in part on the way you are feeling at the time; fortunately, while your tastes tend to be fairly eclectic, they veer toward the healthy side.

Your Aquarian temperament leads you to fluctuate between periods of frenetic energy and times of complete lethargy. Because you thrive on challenging the rules that others may follow meekly, you often land yourself in situations that are unnecessarily stressful. Your outspoken and unconventional way of expressing your thoughts will rarely leave you feeling cool and collected at the end of a busy day. To succeed in today's rat race, you must be able to work well at all levels and across all disciplines. Because you *are* such an individualist, you may decide that the corporate workplace is not for you, especially if you find yourself too stressed out too often. This will be a personal decision, but you may need also to ask yourself if some of the problems are due to your reluctance, rather than your inability, to conform to the structures of your particular workplace.

Aquarius rules the ankles and the limbs from knee to ankle. Some of you suffer from weak ankles, and varicose veins and hardening of the arteries are also Aquarian complaints. Because Aquarius also rules the circulation, make sure that you take special care in cold weather.

You're extremely gregarious, and your social calendar is usually full. Party-going and party-giving are favorite Aquarian pastimes. There is also a deeper side of your Aquarian soul which at times can make you quite a loner. Many of you have New Age interests and find yoga is a good way to keep you free of stress. The movies, especially those with exciting special effects, help you forget the pressures of work. Many of you enjoy trying out new restaurants, especially those featuring ethnic foods. Because your mind tends to be active twenty-four hours a day, you need to discover your own way to cut off from pressure, especially if you're frequently faced with nail-biting deadlines.

Charity organizations often contain a good number of Aquarian helpers, for humanitarian causes are always dear to your heart. But remember to be charitable to yourself too, and always allow yourself sufficient time to unwind.

Your Attitude toward Making Money

You are extremely generous and often horrendously extravagant. Your attitude toward money tends to be that if it's there it is meant to be spent, and when it's gone you will start to worry.

This is too frivolous an attitude in today's working world, where long-term job security is rarely a given, with merger mania, downsizing, and bankruptcy. With your penchant for collecting a wide variety of credit cards, plus a failure to keep tabs on your spending, you sometimes invite unnecessary trouble at the end of the month!

Your ruling planet, Uranus, enables you to have hunches and flashes of inspiration that will enhance your business acumen. As one of the most inventive and progressive signs, you are rarely short of clever moneymaking ideas which could perhaps turn you into a millionaire, but you're not terribly good at following through or at making decisive long-term business plans. Your basic attitude tends to be that money is important mainly because it can bring you the freedom to do what you want.

A sign of great integrity, you would rarely refuse or forget to pay back money owed, but you are often not practical enough in creating sufficient income to cover all your needs. Some of you tend to think the world owes you a living, and even become slightly arrogant in your demands for a higher salary.

Organization, strategy, and development are all areas in which the Air signs are supposed to excel. This means that you should possess the power within you to make as much money as you need. You are a sign of reasoning and intellectualism, so that a sensible attitude toward making money is certainly within the realm of possibility.

As a Fixed sign you can be as stubborn as any Taurean, but although you like to think you're *always* right, try to be more willing to listen to constructive advice regarding your moneymaking attitude!

Defy convention in other ways if you must, but make sure you safe-guard your future by putting away sufficient money!

How to Improve Your Work Relationships

Playing up the unpredictable and unconventional side of your personality is rarely the best way to get ahead in today's business climate. Sometimes "doing it your way" isn't the answer!

Since it is always important to cultivate the ability to get on well with your coworkers, the following guide will show you the best way to relate to all the signs, whether they are those of your boss, your peer, or an employee:

Aquarius with Aries Boss: An Aries boss won't lay down hard-and-fast rules on how you should carry out your work—just as long as it's ready on time, or before! Try not to make mistakes because Aries has a short fuse.

Aquarius with Aries Colleague: An unpredictable Aquarius with an impulsive Aries will produce no shortage of stimulating conversations. Your innovative ideas might turn you both into superpowers of the workplace!

Aquarius with Aries Employee: Try to behave more like a boss than this employee's best friend even if you enjoy taking him under your wing. Aries is usually more ambitious than you, so watch out he doesn't try to take over your job!

Aquarius with Taurus Boss: Taurus is determined to do things in the right way, and to do them well even if it does mean going over old ground. Taking shortcuts to save time will definitely not go down well with this boss.

Aquarius with Taurus Colleague: This colleague's slow-moving ways are sure to infuriate you at times. But you have a lot to learn from the realistic and down-to-earth approach of the Bull, especially where money is involved.

Aquarius with Taurus Employee: With this loyal and dependable employee, you will never have to worry about leaving any work unfinished. The Bull can show you how to be a genius and how to keep your feet on the ground too.

Aquarius with Gemini Boss: You won't have time to get bored with this live-wire boss. Work will rarely seem like routine, but you'd better make sure you can keep up with the hectic work schedule required.

Aquarius with Gemini Colleague: You will share lots of stimulating conversations both in and out of work. But you need to stop talking long enough to deal with the tasks at hand.

Aquarius with Gemini Employee: Never behave too unpredictably if you want this employee to stick to the tried-and-true rules of the workplace. Always listen to Gemini's ideas as they can be as innovative as yours!

Aquarius with Cancer Boss: Cancer is sensitive and moody, but often highly ambitious. Watch out your outspoken attitude doesn't create unnecessary waves, because this is a boss who will also be sympathetic and considerate of *your* needs.

Aquarius with Cancer Colleague: You're the intellectual type, while Cancer is ruled by feelings and instincts. You will make an excellent working duo if you're prepared to understand each other's virtues and failings!

Aquarius with Cancer Employee: Since this employee will usually be immensely faithful and supportive, try not to be too erratic and outspoken when things need to be done. Cancer gets upset very easily.

Aquarius with Leo Boss: Not the easiest of combinations since Leo loves to dictate orders and you dislike to be ordered around. But you can learn plenty from your opposite sign of the Zodiac, so be more accommodating in your ways!

Aquarius with Leo Colleague: Mutual attraction or mutual antipathy—depending on whether you're prepared to pool your creativity or argue over your differences. The former way will produce the best results!

Aquarius with Leo Employee: Watch out you're not too unpredictable or undisciplined in your methods, or this employee could be working behind the scenes to take over your position. Leo is always convinced she should be boss.

Aquarius with Virgo Boss: Never forget that Virgo is the most critical and fastidious of all the signs. Sloppy and careless work could soon have you looking for a new job. Try to conform to Virgo's discipline—if you can!

Aquarius with Virgo Colleague: Virgo's realistic appraisal of some of your more way-out and futuristic schemes might infuriate you, but deep down you appreciate the fact that a pragmatic approach can be a blessing in disguise.

Aquarius with Virgo Employee: Be thankful that you will never have to worry about any work being left undone. Virgo's fussy ways may sometimes get on your nerves, but this employee should be very dedicated to detail.

Aquarius with Libra Boss: You will learn a great deal about tact and diplomacy, and will be on the same wavelength on many issues. Don't spoil things by failing to carry your workload when you have such a fair-minded boss!

Aquarius with Libra Colleague: Creatively, this is a brilliant duo. But do get those ideas off the ground, rather than talking them over for hours and hours. Both of you can be time wasters!

Aquarius with Libra Employee: Libra may be happy to fit in with your somewhat flexible way of working, but don't allow this employee to become too laid-back or you may end up with cause for complaint.

Aquarius with Scorpio Boss: Scorpio can be a hard taskmaster and fairly ruthless, so you'd be wise to make very few mistakes in your work. You may be forgiven for one or two errors, but they're unlikely to be forgotten—ever!

Aquarius with Scorpio Colleague: Both of you are very demanding in your own ways. You're convinced that you're a genius, and Scorpio is determined to be unbeatable. On opposing teams it could be a bitter fight to the end!

Aquarius with Scorpio Employee: Regardless of whether Scorpio is employee or boss, this sign doesn't suffer fools gladly. Never allow your working relationship to become too friendly or flexible, especially when you're under pressure.

Aquarius with Sagittarius Boss: Don't be fooled into thinking that because Sagittarius is an easygoing sign you won't have to work hard. With a Sagittarius boss, you must knuckle down and ensure that *everything* is done well.

Aquarius with Sagittarius Colleague: Watch out this relationship isn't all coffee breaks and long discussions about your respective social lives! Both of you are independent freethinkers; together you could make a brilliant team.

Aquarius with Sagittarius Employee: This employee's positive and optimistic personality can make work a pleasure. But don't let yourself get into the position where Sagittarius tells *you* what to do and how to do it.

Aquarius with Capricorn Boss: Your unorthodox approach to life and work is unlikely to go down well with this workaholic boss. Capricorns think the traditional way of doing things is best—and that's the way they want it!

Aquarius with Capricorn Colleague: Considering yourself as a whiz kid is all very well, but don't sit around taking credit for your innovative ideas while you expect your Capricorn colleague to do all the work.

Aquarius with Capricorn Employee: You're an unpredictable and often eccentric boss, and this employee is a stickler for routine and hard work carried out in a traditional way. Perhaps you should simply count your blessings.

Aquarius with Aquarius Boss: If you accept that your boss is even more of a genius than you are, things will be fine. If not, you may find it hard to be an employee for your fellow sign, and may hope to be transferred!

Aquarius with Aquarius Colleague: Since you could mirror each other's thoughts and ideals, this relationship should work out well. In reality you might drive each other crazy because of a double dose of unpredictability.

Aquarius with Aquarius Employee: Try to remember how you felt when you were an employee rather than a boss. You don't have to become best friends, but you can empathize with the plus and the minus points of an Aquarian employee.

Aquarius with Pisces Boss: A Pisces boss is sentimental, sympathetic, and sometimes forgetful, but often very shrewd. Don't try to get away with too much unconventional behavior. Pisceans don't like firing people, but they will if pressed.

Aquarius with Pisces Colleague: Your visionary ideals combined with this colleague's dreams of greater success could bring you both success. But you might need some advice from someone with his feet placed more firmly on the ground.

Aquarius with Pisces Employee: Because Pisces is so very sensitive, do try hard not to upset such a kind and loyal employee. Pisces might seem rather vague but would never let you down intentionally.

Getting Longevity out of Your Career

Be honest, Aquarius. Since you are such a freedom-loving sign, getting longevity out of your career may not appear to be the most important issue in your life. However, since you can be extraordinarily perverse over most issues, you might easily change your mind about this tomorrow.

I am sure you are aware that in the modern job market very few people can take job security for granted. Even an unpredictable Aquarian like you will probably not appreciate losing a job that might be highly motivating and sufficiently well paid to allow you to feel inwardly free.

Always remember to analyze your long-term ambitions, because if you *are* happy and contented in your current employment, you will not want to risk losing it by not measuring up in your own behavior or working techniques.

Make sure you always look at the total picture, which means accepting the long-term consequences of your actions and not simply the possible short-term gains. There are few people who can match your flair for inventiveness and originality of thought and action, but anyone who is too eccentric or outrageous is likely to experience chilly vibes from the people at the top.

There continues to be a great deal of downsizing, not only in corporations but in schools and all kinds of businesses, which means that the remaining workers are forced to work even longer hours and under more pressure than ever. If this situation happens to you, you might well decide that you are sufficiently talented to find other avenues for your work. But before you quit your job, keep in mind that it is a tough world out there, and that unless you are independently wealthy (and would appreciate having lots of free time), it might be difficult to survive.

The great thing about being born under the sign of Aquarius is you are rarely a defeatist. Anything that is new and untried is perfect for you. If you lose your job through no fault of your own, always focus on your ability to be an inspirational and highly creative individual. Continue to keep up with the latest technology (which is usually highly pleasurable for someone with your scientific mind), and utilize your networking skills as much as possible. Never be too laid-back or diffident about sending out an up-to-date résumé to companies that could be interested in your particular abilities.

With your strategic vision and your ability to adapt to changing trends in working methods, the workplace will always find a place for you, regardless of your age!

AQUARIUS CAREER STRATEGIES—A CHECKLIST FOR EVERY AGE

- Never allow your ability to be a versatile and innovative high-flier prevent you from being a good team player too.
- Always try to channel your original thoughts into realistic and decisive actions.
- Never portray yourself as such a rebel (with *or* without a cause) that other people think of you as unreliable and irresponsible.
- Remember that in the corporate world it is often necessary to conform and compromise more than you might like. Nevertheless, your career *is* in your hands, and the choice is yours.
- Never become so changeable in your thoughts and actions that only a saint could put up with you!
- Don't allow your frequently cool and unemotional detachment to be misconstrued as disinterest in your work.
- If routine and regimentation are truly the worst of all possible concepts, perhaps you need to analyze your long-term aims a little more.

PISCES IN THE WORKPLACE

February 19 ☆ *March 20*

If you were born between February 19 and March 20, you were born under the sign of Pisces, twelfth sign of the Zodiac. You are a Feminine, Mutable, Negative, Water sign. Your planetary symbol is the Fish—two fishes swimming in opposite directions, upstream and down.

Neptune, planet of inspiration and imagination, is your ruler, and you are one of the most creative signs of the Zodiac. Neptune is also associated with intuition, dreams, artistic sensitivity, and romanticism, but its negative side can also make you confused, gullible, and vacillating—none of which will benefit you in today's competitive workplace!

Always believe in the magic of your inspirational dreams, but resolve to work harder to ensure that they turn into realities. Being born under your sign certainly has not held back either Rupert Murdoch or David Geffen. It does not have to hold you back either.

Always prove that you can be incisive, creative, energetic, confident, articulate, and credible. All too often you confuse yourself unnecessarily, when it would be so simple to listen and act upon your uncannily accurate sixth sense.

Regardless of where you work, you have something to learn from Virgo, your opposite sign in the Zodiac. Virgo, the critic, analyst, and "sign of service," can teach you a great deal. You can learn something from every sign, which is why you might try to play a different sign once in a while.

Take a workday in the Pisces life. You've just heard of a new position within your company that sounds perfect for your particular talents and abilities. You know that the names under consideration don't include yours, and that one of the candidates is a good friend of yours.

Playing Aries: You go into battle at once, finding out how to get yourself on the applicant list in the shortest possible time. You know that being too soft and sentimental today is a no-no, and that blowing your own trumpet is essential.

Playing Taurus: Before rushing into making any decisions, you find out *exactly* what the opening entails. Then you research the backgrounds of the other contestants so that you can judge whether you stand a chance of beating them.

Playing Gemini: You devise a couple of brilliant ideas to ensure you are definitely in the right place at the right time. You may even talk one of your superiors into singing your praises so highly that your name is soon added to the list!

Playing Cancer: With a double dose of sensitivity, you may hate to compete against friends, or perhaps you'll sulk because you didn't even get the chance! But your instincts do inspire you to consider the long-term possibilities and put yourself forward.

Playing Leo: The very *idea* of not being considered is a major affront to your pride. You probably pretend outwardly you're not interested anyway, or else make some very high-profile attempts to show your talents!

Playing Virgo: You analyze the pros and cons of every tactic before making the slightest move. You overcome feelings of guilt about the other contestants by finding some faults in their work. Then you make *your* pitch.

Playing Libra: Should I, shouldn't I? It may not be easy for you to make a fast decision as to what to do. But you do find a way to suggest diplomatically that perhaps you've been overlooked by mistake.

Playing Scorpio: Let's hope you won't waste time plotting revenge on those who failed to include you. Knowing you have the power to overcome most obstacles, I'm sure you not only manage to get your name on the list of candidates but also end up with the job!

Playing Sagittarius: As a self-confident and optimistic Sagittarian, you state your case loudly and make sure your name is added to the list! Sagittarius is ruled by the lucky planet, Jupiter, which brings good fortune your way, while Neptune's influence adds sensitivity to your choice of words.

Playing Capricorn: Capricorn's concern for long-term material security makes it inevitable that you'll promote yourself fully in every way. You devise a highly practical strategy that ensures you can't possibly be overlooked!

Playing Aquarius: Since Aquarius is the most original and inventive sign of all, you have a touch of genius to add to your creative talents. You soon overcome your shyness in putting yourself forward.

Playing Yourself: You might be too inclined to hide your talents, feeling you'd hate to upset your friend's chances of promotion. On the other hand, your brilliant intuition could inspire you to shoot for the moon instead!

The Positive and Negative Qualities of a Pisces at Work

Anyone who has ever dared to think that Pisceans are wishy-washy characters drifting along on the tide only needs to think of Elizabeth Taylor, Sharon Stone, Ivana Trump, Cindy Crawford, or Bruce Willis, all of whom have made us very aware of *their* personalities.

However, you are too easily inclined to undervalue yourself and your talents. Sometimes you get lost in your daydreams or refuse to act on your intuition.

Pisces is the most unworldly and sensitive of all the signs, but some of you can also be brilliant actors and sometimes quite devious in your methods to get to the top. On the other hand, some of you lack sufficient confidence or willpower to exert yourselves and become cynical and bitter if you don't reach your goals.

Although your ruling planet, Neptune, blesses you with creative talents and inspiration, it is also the planet of illusion, and you cannot afford any kind of illusions. There is always someone coming up behind you who may be after your job. In today's tough business climate, it is unwise to drift through life rather as though you were floating in the sea, taken wherever the tides might choose. Always remember that when *you* believe in your talents and abilities, it makes it a whole lot easier to convince other people of your star qualities.

The positive Piscean is sensitive, sentimental, and sympathetic. You always listen to your instincts and develop your creative talents to the fullest. You make sure that you don't live in the realms of fantasy (even if you are in love!) and strive to become as disciplined and organized as any other sign. You channel your talents into the areas most suitable for you, and refuse to be emotionally destroyed by any turndowns or turnoffs along the way.

The negative Piscean is thrown into confusion by the slightest problem. You have a tendency toward impracticality on all levels and possess a streak of self-pity that must be avoided at all costs. Renowned for viewing the world through rose-tinted glasses, you forget that clear vision is essential in today's competitive workplace.

The wise Pisces will find a balance between the gentle existence you crave inwardly and the harsh realities of the outside world. You will become an expert at navigating the ups and downs of your career and be determined to swim to the top rather than to drift helplessly. You will become strongly self-disciplined, capable of motivating and leading yourself *and* your team onward and upward. You will rarely complain that the pace is too fast for you or the pressure too great. Cast away your rose-tinted glasses, and you will approach each and every day with clarity and motivation.

Careers for Pisces

Piscean careers include all the caring professions, such as medicine (as doctors, nurses, or podiatrists), alternative medicine (especially as aromatherapists and reflexologists), social work, teaching, and community work (especially helping housebound and elderly people). Edgar Cayce, the marvelous psychic healer, was born under your sign. Your creativity leads you into all forms of the arts, and a high number of Pisceans become wonderful painters, musicians, composers, actors, dancers, photographers, writers, movie directors, and set and costume designers.

Famous Pisceans include Florence Nightingale, Albert Einstein, Ralph Nader, Joanne Woodward, Holly Hunter, Karen Carpenter, Ursula Andress, Glenn Close, Raul Julia, Tony Randall, Rudolf Nureyev, Bernardo Bertolucci, Harry Belafonte, Nina Simone, Quincy Jones, Kiri Te Kanawa, John Steinbeck, Tom Wolfe, Shaquille O'Neal, and Bobby Fischer.

Your Attitude toward Work

Naturally, your rising sign, together with all the other factors of your personal horoscope will also influence your attitude toward work.

I have often noticed that many of you tend to undervalue your talents. It is almost as though you feel *self-confidence* is a dirty word! I get so tired of hearing you say "I'm not sure if I can do it," when it is apparent to everyone else that you *can!*

There is also a rather touching humility about you, combined with an almost childlike delight and surprise when your ideals turn into achievements. The realization of your chosen goals is a wonderful feeling, so perhaps you should also admit that it is sometimes your own insecurity or lack of willpower that prevents you from being successful all the time. Sometimes you come across as much too shy and timid—even when you're not! Portraying yourself as a sweet and lovable Pisces may be fine in a romance, but in the fast-paced environment of today's corporate workplace, the people at the top are more interested to know that you can be a hard-hitting professional. You must display entrepreneurial skills, a high level of business acumen, and the ability to work under tight deadlines individually or as part of a team.

Your inherent sixth sense is a marvelous bonus because it enables you to have a strategic business vision of the future *and* to be commercially astute—when you come down out of the clouds! It also makes you clever at knowing what makes people tick. Most of you have learned over the years that your gut reaction is usually the one to go with, and that problems arise when you don't.

Because you are such a caring person, you genuinely try to communicate in the best possible way with everyone in the workplace. Sometimes you are so busy caring about everyone else and making *their* lives a little easier that you neglect your own professional responsibilities, thus making your own life more difficult. Sadly, today's working world has very little time for an overdose of compassion. Always focus your energy on the right targets if you want to move your career forward.

Your attitude toward work must include the determination to make the most of your particular creative talents and abilities, and to incorporate sufficient structure and organization in your working life. Although you are a Mutable Water sign, you don't have to let yourself flow without direction through the workplace! Inconstancy of thought and action will rarely take you any place worthwhile.

Today's corporate workplace has little time for dreamers who are not prepared to fulfill the potential of their dreams within a certain time frame. Piscean Michelangelo would have had a hard time trying to finish his paintings on the Sistine Chapel if he'd had to cope with today's frenetic schedules.

Your ability to empathize with other people means that you often enjoy sharing an office. Since you are so sensitive to atmosphere, it is important for you to have office mates with whom you get along well. There is nothing to stop you from working on your own, other than your tendency to lose yourself in daydreams rather than getting on with your tasks—all too easy to do if no one is looking over your shoulder.

TIPS FOR A HEALTHY WORK ATTITUDE

- Believe wholeheartedly in both your work and your brilliant instincts, and let yourself be inspired to achieve your very best.
- Always focus on your talents and follow through on projects, sticking with them till you achieve your goals.
- Never allow sentimentality to get in the way of tough career decisions—not if you want to get to the top!

Aiming for Promotion

Never be too shy about coming forward! You're too inclined to hide in the shadows, even generously allowing a colleague to take credit for some of your ideas. In Hollywood an actor is only as good as his or her last movie; if it bombs, the actor often loses star status—until staging a brilliant comeback in another film. The corporate workplace isn't like the movies; you rarely get a second chance to prove yourself.

When you are aiming for promotion, define your goals and project yourself in a self-confident way. *Timidity* has no place in the vocabulary of an ambitious worker. Always demonstrate that you have the vision and ability to generate ideas and see them through to fulfillment. A high level of business savvy, combined with motivational and interpersonal strengths, must be continually proven.

Never allow your insecurities to show outwardly—even if you're quaking inside when you discuss a possible promotion with your boss. Remember that your body language is all-important. Your insecurity can be revealed through your gestures and your facial expressions. Your eyes are often one of your best features, but don't forget that the eyes are also the mirrors of the soul and *yours* will invariably reflect what you are feeling inside.

Maintain the right balance between overselling yourself (which you will rarely do!) and giving yourself too low a profile (which so many of you do). Getting ahead in today's workplace means getting out there and proving that you have the required skills and appetite for your desired role.

Your Piscean intuition is a great bonus. It frequently enables you to recognize exactly the right place at the right time. Networking is also important, for it will help you to keep ahead of the game. However, if you're aiming for a promotion that is also highly desired by many of your coworkers, don't be so sympathetic to *their* dreams that you give away your own tips on how to succeed!

Your ability to be a motivational team leader as well as a loyal team member is highly important. In many instances, before you can achieve recognition for your own work, the success of your particular team must be demonstrated.

You are rarely renowned for being one of the most technical or scientific of signs, although Piscean Alexander Graham Bell did invent the telephone. Today it is almost impossible to become a leading light at work without having a reasonable working knowledge of information technology systems. When you want to advance your career, you must also advance your understanding and keep up-to-date with *everything* in your field, because you can be sure that your competitors will be doing so.

- Vow to master the intricacies of the information highway, even if some of them have eluded you till now!
- Forget about the fear of failing. You have everything you need to take you to the top.
- Think big, focus on your unique talents, and start to develop a more competitive streak!

How to Cope with Being Passed Over for Promotion

I would like to print a notice saying "Turndowns must not be construed as Turnoffs" for you to put in front of you at work! Unfortunately, in today's workplace, mental toughness and a killer instinct will be more useful than sensitivity and compassion. Never allow the fact that you're a Pisces to prevent you from aiming for lofty goals. Resolve to adjust your business attitude if necessary. Be honest with yourself, and if you feel you have put insufficient effort into achieving a promotion, don't let this happen again.

Combine your Piscean instincts with the power of positive thinking, and you will soon overcome the dejection at being turned down. You're not the only sign likely to face being passed over for promotion once in a while!

Ambition—or the Lack of It

Sometimes you appear to be unambitious, when this is not the true picture. Unfortunately, your methods of achieving greater success do not always serve you well. You tend to escape the commitment of high-profile self-promotion, not always because you are shy, but sometimes because you figure that it's a waste of your talents. Spiritually you try to convince yourself that if it's *meant* to be it will happen, but in today's workplace anyone who is truly ambitious must be able to prove it in a material way.

It's marvelous to be born under such a caring and sensitive sign as Pisces, but it will be even more marvelous if you apply your sensitivity positively and constructively. Endeavor to concentrate on becoming a victor rather than a victim in the corporate world. Don't drown yourself in a sea of emotions when you know you are worthy of a higher profile. Do you think Pisces Cindy Crawford would have become such a high-profile supermodel if she had not been prepared to use shrewd business acumen alongside her unique beauty?

I don't wish to imply that there is something wrong with you if you're not ambitious. Given the scaled-down workforce and the lack of opportunities for advancement at many companies today, it is probably best that some people are perfectly happy with the status quo. However, there is a marked difference between being unambitious and being lazy! The trouble with many of you is merely that you are too lazy to discipline yourself sufficiently to attain your goals.

When you are ambitious, your sixth sense will be an immense benefit in enabling you to know when and where to make your moves.

Ambition—and Your Love Life

My many years as a professional astrologer have convinced me that no one is as romantic and dreamy-eyed as you. I'm also convinced that most of you would always let your love life take precedence over your ambitions. It's when these become muddled up together that problems can arise.

Emotionally, you are perhaps more undisciplined in your love life than you are in anything else, which does not bode well for the structured life you're expected to lead in the workplace. Although I've rarely met a Piscean who has left a high-profile job because of love, I've met a few who have let good career opportunities slip by because they were romantically involved at the time—and they were the people who had said they were ambitious!

A Piscean friend told me that she likes to look at the world through her rose-tinted glasses because everything looks more positive that way. However, unless you're totally confident of your ability to differentiate between true love and a romantic illusion it's best to leave them off when you have work to do.

Anyone who is involved emotionally with you must be able to persuade you to concentrate on your work *during* the workday—

although if your romantic partner happens to be another Pisces this could be asking for trouble.

I'm sure you can easily visualize just how to balance your ambitions and your love life without the slightest problem. If you are a typical Pisces, the problem is turning your visions into reality.

TIPS FOR COMBINING WORK AND LOVE

- Never make commitments lightly. They're made to be kept both at work and in your love life.
- Try to balance your mystical otherworldliness with a strong dose of levelheadedness.
- Get your perspectives right, and never allow your work to suffer even if you are head over heels in love with a somewhat jealous lover.
- Never drive your more ambitious workmates crazy by telling them all about your latest love affair, and expecting them to have time to listen!

Romance in the Workplace

Unless you are a Piscean with such outstanding business acumen that a little gentle flirtation is unlikely to deflect your attention from your duties, let your sixth sense help you walk away from trouble.

Pisces is very much a "feeling" sign, and when you're stirred up by strong feelings your whole equilibrium can be thrown out of whack. If you could turn your adolescent dreams into realities, one of them would probably include a fairy-tale romance in which you would live happily ever after with the perfect partner. You can fall headlong into love as easily as Aries, but while Ariens thrive on challenges and the excitement of extricating themselves from dangerous situations, you tend to end up totally confused, unsure where to turn for help. Today's workplace is definitely *not* the place to look for understanding or help in your emotional life. Everyone is too busy looking out for themselves in these times of short-term contracts and layoffs.

Sometimes you leave yourself open to difficult situations, failing to spot the office Casanova or femme fatale until that individual has made a pass. You're rarely the sort of person to have an affair with someone purely to help you climb the ladder of success. But sexual attractions can take place all too easily when you are working in close proximity with someone who appeals to your romantic dreams. You often find it difficult enough to concentrate on the pressures of your workday, so it would be disastrous to add to these by becoming involved with a coworker.

Your sensitivity would make it extremely difficult for you to cope with being involved with a married colleague, especially with one who appeared to have no intention of leaving his or her partner. Because you tend to wear your heart on your sleeve, it would also become clear to your coworkers that *something* was going on.

A final note on sexual harassment: Never be too timid to speak up if you feel that someone is sexually harassing you. Your compassion for other people would also inspire you to speak up loudly if one of your workmates ever confided to you that someone was harassing him or her.

You and Your Stress Factor

Stress can affect everyone at any time and at any age. In fact feeling "stressed out" seems to be an everyday occurrence for an increasing number of people.

As a sensitive and gentle soul, you find it difficult to cope if you're under too much stress. It is always important for you to get sufficient sleep, because you seem to suffer from tiredness more than most of the other signs. Another unfortunate Pisces tendency is that when you feel stressed out you are apt to drink too much alcohol and can become addicted all too easily. Your ruling planet, Neptune, which endows you with your intuition, your imagination and your illusions, also rules alcohol and other drugs. I don't wish to imply that every Piscean will turn to the bottle under stress, but I've known more than a few who have succumbed to the temptation to drink heavily and needed help to overcome the habit.

Astrologically, Pisces rules the feet and toes. If your feet feel uncomfortable, it doesn't help the rest of your body, especially when you're under stress, so always try to wear comfortable shoes in the workplace. And remember those sneakers when it's time to take the subway or stand in line for the bus!

Because you are so emotional, your stress factor is increased if you are unhappy in love. Sometimes you become too dependent on a lover, so that if things go wrong it is hard to pick up the pieces and get on with your life. You may start to become addicted not only to drink but also to food—neither of which will help your stress.

Within your personality there is often a recurrent desire and need to escape from reality. If the pressures of your workday become intolerable, it is better by far to lose yourself for a few hours by watching a good movie, seeing some of your favorite actors at the theater, or getting together with some uplifting friends who can make you laugh.

Your gift for empathizing with others serves to make you the most giving of all the signs. Under stress you seem to find it almost impossible to be sufficiently aware of how to give to *yourself*. Sometimes you put even more pressure on yourself by refusing to admit that you *are* under stress. This is when you may start to retreat into your own fantasy world rather than deal with real life.

Everyone has a favorite technique for reducing stress. As a Pisces, you may be drawn to yoga and meditation, and you usually feel wonderful after a good aromatherapy massage. In an earlier book, *Star Signs,* I devised a meditation to help you get in touch with the inner you and find both emotional and spiritual strength.

It is important to make sure that you have a life outside work because this will also help to keep your stress factor low. Most artistic pursuits appeal to you, whether they be poetry, music, acting, or the ballet, and many of you enjoy helping with charity or social work. As a Water sign, and appropriate to your symbol of the Fish, the water is both important and relaxing for you. Water sports, swimming, or simply sitting by the water letting it trickle over your feet—all these things will help you turn off the pressures of the workplace and find the right balance between your mind, your body, and your soul.

Your Attitude toward Making Money

Because you are so unworldly, your attitude toward making money is not always brilliant. I have already mentioned many successful Pisceans, but many of you would rather leave moneymaking to someone else. This attitude is fine if you're financially independent or with a partner who is ready, willing, and able to fulfill all your material needs, but if you're out there in the jungle fending for yourself it's definitely not!

Always remember the three Ds—downsizing, debts, and depression. The first of these can lead all too easily to the other two, creating big problems for you. No one can count on long-term job security when mergers, bankruptcies, and forced early retirements continue to take place on a regular basis.

Because you often veer toward the creative in your choice of work, you are concerned more with the satisfaction gained from your efforts than with the material rewards. Since sticking to a budget is rarely easy for you, this can lead to problems at the end of the month. Idealistic and imaginative, there is no reason that you should be unable to make money. Learn to become more disciplined, and resolve to keep your Pisces feet more firmly on the ground.

You're someone who would give your last dollar to someone worse off than yourself. Unfortunately, your sensitivity and compassion mean that you can be gullible too. Your intuition seems to take a backseat when someone is sobbing on your shoulder with a hard-luck story. This may be very noble if you want to play the martyr, but hardly wise if your checking account is low. You're so emotional that you can easily dissolve in tears if money problems get out of hand, but it is unwise to show any signs of weakness in the workplace.

If *your* attitude toward money is unrealistic, make a sound financial plan, perhaps with the help of a good financial adviser, so that you avoid unnecessary problems for you or your loved ones when you retire.

Remember the chart in the introduction that ranked more than three hundred of the five hundred richest people by star signs? Well, Pisces came in third. You possess the qualities that can make *you* a rich Pisces too.

How to Improve Your Work Relationships

Although you're sometimes an enigma, even to yourself, your instincts usually guide you toward getting along well with other people. But sometimes you are too selfless for your own good—and it *is* a tough world at work these days.

The following guide will show you the best way to relate to all the signs, whether they are those of your boss, your peer, or an employee:

Pisces with Aries Boss: Since practicality is rarely your forte, you'd better try coming to grips with it fast. An Aries boss has little patience with anyone who is too sensitive when under pressure.

Pisces with Aries Colleague: This colleague wants quick results from everyone and everything, so never be too laid-back or dreamy-eyed. You must both take extra care if financial issues come under discussion.

Pisces with Aries Employee: If you're too vague or uncertain when you're telling this employee what to do, he could decide he would make a better boss. Watch out—Aries can be very ambitious and bossy.

Pisces with Taurus Boss: A Taurus boss is patient, persevering, and practical. Come down from cloud nine and show you can be as savvy, sensible, and serious about working hard as any other sign!

Pisces with Taurus Colleague: Your creative ideas combined with the famous Taurean common sense make for a winning duo. If the Bull doesn't instantly agree with your visions, it's better to have their feasibility confirmed before going ahead.

Pisces with Taurus Employee: Never take advantage of Taurus's loyalty and dependability by being too flaky in your work habits. This efficient employee would never let you down—unless you don't prove that you can be a boss!

Pisces with Gemini Boss: Don't ever let your emotional life intrude when you're at work. Gemini will expect you to concentrate on a zillion things at the same time, but your working hours will not be dull.

Pisces with Gemini Colleague: This live-wire colleague will inspire you to get your act together and be more creative than ever. Stimulating conversations could lead to some great projects—if both pairs of feet are on the ground.

Pisces with Gemini Employee: This friendly and well-meaning employee will be able to fill you in on everything in your workplace, but you'd better be firm about getting your work completed on time.

Pisces with Cancer Boss: Don't think you can get away with inefficient work with this soft and sensitive Water-ruled boss. Canceri-

ans are sticklers for hard work and get very moody if it's not done
well.

Pisces with Cancer Colleague: Please don't spend your days discussing your respective love lives and trying to give each other advice.
Today's competitive workplace requires dedication to duty—at all
times.

Pisces with Cancer Employee: Don't give in to the temptation to be
too soft and tender, or your work won't be ready on time. Cancer
will be highly dependable and efficient. You must be too!

Pisces with Leo Boss: This boss will be courteous and kind provided
you work well and praise her once in a while for being brilliant!
But remember that several dictators were born under this sign.

Pisces with Leo Colleague: This forceful Fire sign needs someone to
boost his ego once in a while, and in return he will happily boost
yours. Both of you are creative thinkers; make sure you're both
practical too.

Pisces with Leo Employee: Become more forceful if you want this
bossy sign to take orders from you. Few Lions are terribly good at
being employees. They aim for the limelight and want to be in charge.

Pisces with Virgo Boss: Sorry, Pisces. You cannot afford to make the
slightest mistake when working for your opposite sign. Virgo is the
nitpicker of the Zodiac and will criticize every wrong move you
make!

Pisces with Virgo Colleague: You may not appreciate Virgo's analytical reasoning when you think you've come up with a brilliant business plan. But listen carefully, for the advice will be constructive.

Pisces with Virgo Employee: Don't give this critical employee any
opportunity to find fault with *your* working methods. Be thankful
that your opposite sign believes strongly in fulfilling her duty and
would never let you down.

Pisces with Libra Boss: You couldn't wish for a more understanding
and less demanding boss. But don't escape into realms of fantasy,
forgetting to complete your work on time. Libra won't be fooled by
lame excuses.

Pisces with Libra Colleague: The workplace isn't a social club—
something you both may have to keep reminding yourselves! The
ability to exchange creative ideas is great, but you need to follow
through on them too.

Pisces with Libra Employee: Giving order isn't your forte, but if you're the boss you have no way out! Remember that Librans like to be treated with nonstop charm and diplomacy, just the way they try to treat everyone else.

Pisces with Scorpio Boss: You're both Water signs, but the similarity stops there! Scorpio is a definite power player and won't put up with any signs of weakness from an employee. Maximum efficiency will be required.

Pisces with Scorpio Colleague: Resolve you won't be pushed into the background by this ambitious and sometimes manipulative sign. Never show signs of emotional weakness; Scorpio aims for the jugular, especially if you're on opposing teams!

Pisces with Scorpio Employee: Watch out for the burning intensity of this employee. He could be secretly plotting to overthrow you. Most Scorpios are highly ambitious and feel that the top is where they belong.

Pisces with Sagittarius Boss: Be careful if you have to point out any mistakes made by this boss. The Archer is convinced she is always right! But you will enjoy working for such a positive and optimistic sign.

Pisces with Sagittarius Colleague: There is plenty of camaraderie with this free-and-easy colleague, and Sagittarius inspires you to greater creative heights. Don't spend too much time admiring each other's talents!

Pisces with Sagittarius Employee: Never be too much of a dreamer, or you could miss the fact that this employee likes to take risks and shortcuts. Remember that your position is under jeopardy if things suddenly go wrong.

Pisces with Capricorn Boss: Capricorn is a workaholic traditionalist and also a stickler for work carried out superefficiently. Never lose files or gab on the phone about your love life during working hours!

Pisces with Capricorn Colleague: Your instincts should tell you that this hardworking colleague can inspire you to work even harder too! Capricorn's pragmatism combined with your inspiration makes this a good duo.

Pisces with Capricorn Employee: Remember that the Mountain Goat is an ambitious and dedicated workaholic, so that staying late will rarely be a problem. But if you're too lackadaisical in your working methods, Capricorn may try to take over your job.

Pisces with Aquarius Boss: Aquarius could be like no other boss— friendly one day and coldly uncommunicative the next. Brilliant futuristic ideas are his forte. Your task is to help see those ideas through.

Pisces with Aquarius Colleague: Creatively you could be on the same wavelength, but don't ever bore Aquarius with stories about your latest love affair. Keep your ultrasensitivity out of the office with this colleague.

Pisces with Aquarius Employee: You need to make it clear that you are truly the boss. Aquarius may not be a brilliant timekeeper but is often brilliant at backing up your strategies with original and worthwhile ideas.

Pisces with Pisces Boss: Don't take any risks! Not every Pisces drifts along with no direction, and one who gets to the top will not put up with sloppy working habits from an employee—especially another Pisces!

Pisces with Pisces Colleague: If both of you resolve to come down to earth and turn your creative ideas into realistic projects, you will make a great working duo. If you're on opposing teams, you'll be well aware of each other's faults!

Pisces with Pisces Employee: Resolve to be more shrewd than sensitive for you cannot afford to have an employee taking advantage of you. You know that Pisceans sometimes have a devious streak, especially when trying to get ahead.

Getting Longevity out of Your Career

Getting longevity from a career is rarely easy for anyone these days, and if you are an especially sensitive Piscean you may feel that the corporate workplace is too cruel and competitive for you.

Unfortunately, work security is no longer certain at any age, and keeping a job does not necessarily mean keeping it until you retire. These days, hanging on to a job even for the next few *months* can become a priority to many people.

It would be unfair to suggest that lots of Pisceans live in their very own fantasy worlds, drifting aimlessly and wallowing in sentiment.

However, many of you *will* probably admit that you are not always as motivated as you should be. The consequence of a careless action is no longer likely to be a mild reprimand with a warning to be more careful next time. It is far more likely to be a grim reminder that the people at the top have no time to be sensitive to other people's short-comings, for their own jobs may also be at stake.

Unless you are of independent means and have no financial worries for the future, it is important to put away once more those famous Pisces rose-tinted glasses and to make sure you have a realistic and constructive long-term working plan.

You are not renowned for being one of the most scientific or technical of signs, but I'm sure you don't need me to tell you that you must know how to get around on the information highway. Keep up with the advances in technology, even if this requires taking some classes. Make sure you can always adapt to the fast-changing needs of your particular field.

Focus on your ability to be one of the most creative signs in the Zodiac. Throw any left-over vestiges of timidity out the window, and try to be more gung ho in your work life. Today's workplace requires dynamic, proactive personalities who possess sufficient stature and charisma to build rapport at all levels. Use your sixth sense to ferret out what is expected of you, and rise to the challenges that come your way.

Remember to network constantly so that you know everything that is going on from other people in your particular workplace, and remember to keep your résumé up-to-date. One positive feature of the work scene today is that people are changing their jobs *and* their careers more frequently, and employers often want to hire someone with a wide range of experiences.

Listen to your hunches and come down out of the clouds. Your longevity in the workplace can last as long as you want it to last—regardless of your age.

PISCES CAREER STRATEGIES—A CHECKLIST FOR EVERY AGE

- Never lose yourself in your own little dream world if you want to be a high-flier in the workplace.

- Be dynamic in your approach and prove that you possess the personal qualities and drive to rise to challenges.
- Combine your powerful sixth sense with the determination to exploit your creative talents in the best possible way.
- Believe wholeheartedly in your ability to become a major success first—then you can convince everyone else!
- Always make sure you keep the events in your romantic life separate from your working life.
- Become more financially responsible, even if it means hiring a good financial manager!
- Learn to appreciate the benefits of greater structure and discipline in your working life—and outside it too.